Middle East Oil Money and its Future Expenditure

Nicholas Fallon

Graham & Trotman Ltd
United Kingdom

Published in U.S.A. and Canada by
Crane, Russak & Company Inc.

First published in 1975 by
Graham & Trotman Ltd
20 Fouberts Place, Regent Street, London W1V 1HH, UK
Telephone: 01-439 4001

Printed and bound in Great Britain by
Redwood Burn Limited, Trowbridge & Esher

Contents

		Page
Chapter 1	Background to the 1973/4 Oil Crisis	1
Chapter 2	Two Decades of Energy Industry Development	9
Chapter 3	Oil Prices	19
Chapter 4	Oil Revenues to 1985	33
Chapter 5	Expenditure of the Revenues	49
Chapter 6	Banking	67
Chapter 7	Major Development & Expenditure Sectors	99
Chapter 8	The Oil Producers Development Plans	127
Chapter 9	Aid	181
Chapter 10	The Challenge to Countries & Companies	193
Appendix A	Currencies and the SDR	209
Appendix B	Fiscal Years	213
Appendix C	Index of Banks and other Financial Institutions	215
	Select Bibliography	227
	Index	229

Illustrations

Tables No		Page
2 – 1	Energy Comsumption	12
2 – 2	Middle East Oil Exports in the World	17
4 – 1	Oil Consumption 1974	35
4 – 2	OECD Projected Oil Requirements	39
4 – 3	Future Middle East Oil Supply	42
4 – 4	Index of Prices	43
4 – 5	Government Oil Revenues to 1974	45
5 – 1	Summary of Government Expenditure Plans	50
5 – 2	Middle East Countries' Imports	53
5 – 3	OECD Exporters to Middle East	54
5 – 4	Classification of Exports to Middle East	55
5 – 5	Estimated Deployment of Oil Producers' Surplus 1974	57
5 – 6	Official Reserves of Middle East Oil Producers	58
5 – 7	Producers' Needs to Export	61
7 – 1	Middle East Refineries and Export Capacity	101
7 – 2	Middle East Fertilizer Plants	110
7 – 3	Middle East Shipping at end 1974	112
7 – 4	Cargo Ports in Middle East Oil Producing Countries	118
9 – 1	Aid in 1974	183
9 – 2	Aid Funds	185
9 – 3	IMF Oil Facility 1974–75	189
9 – 4	IMF Oil Facility – 1975 Increments	190

Figures		Page
3 – A	Oil Prices 1960–73	24
3 – B	Oil Prices 1973–75	28
5 – A.B	Variations in Required Export Rates	62
A	Currency Comparison Example OECD Exports to the Middle East.	212
Diagrams		
7 – A	The Petroleum Gases	106
Maps	Middle East Business Maps 1 to 4	242

Preface

The oil producing countries have been fond of quoting 'the doctrine of changing circumstances'; in an ever-changing world they themselves have done much to ensure that recent changes are rapid. To attempt to pin down their circumstances for description in a book, and to suggest possible developments, is to attempt to describe a chameleon whose appearance may alter while the words are being written. It is necessary both to examine its basic shape and past colourations and to consider the environments in which it may find itself in the future.

Similarly a description of the economies of the oil producing countries requires attention to history, and their possible future developments need to be placed against a world-wide background. The first part of this book therefore examines fundamentals of the oil situation before going on to forecasts of the revenues and wealth of the producing countries, with emphasis on the interdependence of producers and consumers. The banks and other financial institutions which are in a position to assist the plans of the Middle East governments and individuals are described, followed by general problems of development. More detail is then given for each country; information available up to the middle of 1975 has generally been used here, as in other sections. A chapter on aid and a general summary conclude the book.

An explanation of some of the terms which are used may be in order, starting with 'Middle East'. The Arabs are strongly conscious of being one people, but only some of the states are significant in oil matters, while Iran cannot be ignored. In oil technology and economics the Gulf and North Africa are two completely different provinces. The countries to be covered are not precisely those described by either term, Arab or Gulf states, and so Middle East has been used to mean the region which includes all the states around the

Gulf and extends westward to Libya but excludes Algeria. This is not a mere matter of prejudice, although Algeria astride the Greenwich meridian is as much Middle West as Middle East, nor is it because the countries of the Maghrib have long historical connections with southern Europe much closer than those further east. It is because Libya is expected to resemble the Arab countries of the Gulf in having a surplus of oil revenues over its own requirements, while Algeria together with the non-Arab OPEC countries will undoubtedly have full employment for all its revenues. A further consideration is that the Arab countries between Libya and the Gulf are likely to be the main beneficiaries of the aid which the surplus states will be able to grant.

Even the Bank of England now uses 'billion' to mean a thousand million; the English purists have lost although logic was on their side, and the French have won no converts to their invention 'milliard'.

The traditional oil measure of the barrel is no more illogical than many other old measures. It is sometimes not appreciated that it is precisely defined, unlike for example barrels of wine which vary from district to district. In the matter of crude oil prices the barrel still rules, but in many other aspects of the industry such as energy, shipping and refining weight is of more fundamental importance than volume, and the metric ton is the unit used here except for questions of price. Crude oils differ in their specific gravity, but a measure frequently seen, barrels per day, may be approximately converted to tons per year by multiplying by fifty.

There is a distinction well appreciated between the oil producing states which already or soon can make use of all their revenues and those which surely will continue to accumulate balances. Some of the terms which have been used to express briefly the antithesis might be thought to have slightly derogatory implications; it is hoped that the words 'populous' and 'surplus' will be acceptable.

I am grateful to the editor of *The Banker* for permission to include the lists at the end of chapter six. Everyone concerned about oil affairs and the Middle East is indebted to the editors of periodicals and individual journalists who provide plentiful and reliable information. After many years in the Middle East and the oil business it is impossible to acknowledge individually all those from whom I have learned. They include however the authors of the works in the select bibliography, from most of whom I have also benefited in meetings and discussions. For assistance while writing this book I would like to thank particularly S. Baker, G.A. Calver, C. Digby Firth, Miss J.M. Mucklow, J.A. Nasmyth, C. Pain, D.E. Parker and H.M. Thomason, but the entire responsibility for the contents is mine.

CHAPTER 1

Background to the 1973/74 Oil Crisis

When the Egyptian troops advanced across the Canal in October 1973, they were the spearhead for a force far greater than any of them can have imagined. Their aim was merely to free the enemy-occupied parts of the land of Egypt. Behind them however the bottle was unstoppered and there began to emerge a jinni of such tremendous size and hideousness that the whole world was in fear. Its name was Oil-Starvation and, although the holders of the bottle replaced the cork before too much of the jinni was visible, and those threatened have managed to lop off a few limbs, its presence still hovers. Efforts to exploit, to restrain or to direct its powers over the coming decade will do much to shape the world for the next generation.

The moment of the venture was propitious. For two or three years the major industrial powers had been growing more conscious that resources which had been taken for granted in the supply of their expanding economies were not as inexhaustible as had been assumed in the heady days of the sixties. Controversies had developed between the pessimists who, drawing their simple exponential curves, had proved to their own satisfaction that many of the world's minerals would be exhausted within one lifetime; and the optimists who considered that the ingenuity of man would always produce timely substitutes. On top of the worry about the distant future there was the simple economic fact that a sharp world-wide boom had been raising the demand for and the prices of raw materials of all kinds to record levels. That autumn the effect of the growing demand for minerals had been reinforced by the need to rebuild reserves of cereals, severely depleted owing to the drought which had affected many parts of the world in 1971/72, and there was hardly a sign of the incipient recession.

The debates between the experts had at least taught the public that future supplies of energy would not be automatic, and in April 1973 a paper by James Akins of the US State Department, 'This time the wolf is here', had aroused particularly widespread interest. The future however still seemed a long way off. Development of nuclear power had consistently lagged behind schedule but it would surely improve soon. The cost of deep-mined coal might be putting it rapidly into the luxury class, but in the US and elsewhere in the world there were large deposits easy to get by surface working. While in the US a new customer was beginning to find difficulty in obtaining a supply of natural gas, the industry in Europe was developing at a great pace. To the US oil rationing was unknown, and to Europe a dim memory.

The memory of the ordinary European would not probably have been good enough to tell him that the pre-tax price of gasoline – petrol in UK – had been no more at the start of 1971 than in 1955. Several increases in taxes had obscured the fact from him, and in comparison the small rises over the next two years seemed negligible. He was probably also ignorant that in Europe gasoline accounts for less than a fifth of oil consumption – in UK the Central Electricity Generating Board takes more than all motorists. Except for road use, taxes on oil products are small, if any, and large users had been more conscious of changes in real prices. With the discounts on quantity which they were able to win from the oil companies, fuel had been costing them some two dollars a ton less than the crude oil from which it was made, and as real crude prices fell during the sixties so did the price of fuel oil. The rises of real crude prices early in 1971 and 1972, accompanied by the reduction or elimination of discounts, had meant that for a big consumer the price of a new contract in 1972 might be almost double that two years earlier.

Meanwhile in the Middle East the oil revenues of the producing countries of the Gulf had tripled from 1960 to 1970 and doubled again by 1972, to $ 8750 million, while those of Libya had grown from nothing to $ 1600 million. For reasons to be explained in the next chapter their unit revenues had been protected from the fall in real prices, and, although in 1970 their terms of trade, comparing revenue with the cost of manufactured goods they needed to import, had deteriorated by six per cent since 1959, by mid-1973 they had improved to a 65 per cent advantage. A general increase in revenue had been agreed at Tehran in February 1971, and another at Geneva in January 1972 to compensate for the fall in the value of the dollar on terms which produced further increases with the second devaluation of the dollar in February 1973 and its subsequent weakening.

The economic boom in all the industrialised countries had increased the demand for oil; at the same time a temporary shortage of tankers in the spot market had rapidly increased charter rates and with them spot prices of oil products in consumer markets. The attention of the OPEC countries had turned from the price of their imports to the increasing costs of competing energy, particularly coal and nuclear electricity. At a meeting in Vienna with the oil companies in September they had argued that the increase in market prices of oil should be reflected by an increase in 'posted prices', the reference values by which their revenues were calculated, but the amounts they suggested were much greater than the companies were prepared to consider. A second meeting after the October war had broken out was short and fruitless.

Two of the developments which were to alarm the world now followed; the third came two months later. Kuwait summoned a meeting on October 16 of the six Gulf producing states, but this time the companies were not invited to attend. Instead, the countries agreed on a unilateral declaration of new posted prices far higher than any which had been previously under discussion, and nearly doubling their revenue. It would seem that the meeting was somewhat emotional and the communique issued at the end of it was far from clear; over the next few days ministers who had been present added their own glosses. To the outside world however the effects of it were overshadowed by the decisions of another meeting the next day.

This session was attended by the ten members of the organisation of Arab petroleum exporting countries (OAPEC). In 1967 an attempt to use restriction of oil supplies as a weapon in the war against Israel had proved something of a fiasco, but now they were determined to make it tell. They agreed to limit further oil production, to induce all consuming states to add to the pressure on Israel. The immediate reduction decreed was ten per cent of the September production figures with a threat of a further five per cent each month until the war situation was resolved. Within a short period these decisions had been elaborated and to achieve the intended October reduction the cut for the remainder of the month would be 25 per cent. Some of the small producers whose needs for revenue were pressing were excused from joining in the cutbacks and Iraq insisted on taking its own line. A ban was decreed on all oil shipments to the United States of America which was held primarily responsible for the Israeli occupation of Arab territory. The Netherlands, whose government was considered not to have uttered a sufficiently strong condemnation of Israel, was added to the US on the embargo list and so was Denmark at a later date. A division was made of the rest of the world into 'friendly states' which included France, UK, Muslim countries and most of Africa, and neutrals of which the most important was Japan, to the surprise of its government which considered that its support for the Arab cause had been warm. For practical purposes the friendly states were assured that their essential needs would be covered, leaving the neutrals apparently to share the full effect of the cutbacks in so far as they were not covered by the elimination of shipments to the US and Netherlands. One consequence which did not appear to have been thought of when the decision to embargo the Netherlands was taken was the position of Germany, which normally imports a considerable proportion of its supplies of crude oil through Rotterdam. After some vacillation the Arabs decided that no exception would be made and the ban on transit shipments through Rotterdam would stand.

The price increase decided by the producers was drastic but at that moment the oil consumers were more concerned to maintain oil supplies than to worry about the price, and their lack of reaction may have helped to produce the next stage. While concerted action at this time by the governments of the consuming countries might have been of some effect, the need for decision came at a time when they were in some disarray. The US in particular felt that its efforts to bring a halt to the fighting in its own way were not receiving the support they deserved from European governments, while the latter had expressed resentment at being expected to go along with decisions on which consultation had been perfunctory. There was no unity among the European governments themselves, which had for years been finding that a common energy policy was one of the most intractable problems of the EEC. France and the UK sent ministers to the Arab countries to make representations to ensure their own supplies of oil while others held back, especially the Dutch who refused to bow to pressure.

Although it was not apparent to some governments at the time, the oil companies had been busy reorganising their supply channels. Oil from the non-Arab producers was coming forward in increased quantities but there was still a need for reductions to be allocated, and in default of any agreement between governments the companies were left with the task. The complaints heard then and later from the government of almost every country, developed or less-developed, that it had been unfairly treated may suggest that rough justice was done. Within each country however, while attempting to satisfy the demands of their regular customers, the importing companies saw no reason to be generous to various small traders who had shown no loyalty in the past. In Europe the latter were not slow in complaining to their national authorities, French, German and the EEC Commission, and in doing so helped to create an exaggerated impression of the shortage.

In the US there are many small companies in the oil business and some took action on their own account. Uncertain where they would be able to find supplies in the normal open market, companies which had never been seen outside their own state now appeared in the ministries of the OPEC countries, offering completely unrealistic prices. In addition to these representatives with their limited knowledge of world oil trade, general dealers from every part of the world – including for instance a machinery salesman from Dacca, a clothing importer from Lagos, and a real estate broker from Toronto – flocked to the scene with offers to buy or sell oil at any sort of price.

All these demands, and the seeming irrelevance of any prices previously quoted in the world oil trade, were clearly noted by the producers. The Arabs had continued the cutback of their rate of production by 25 per cent but as actual hostilities had ceased they made no further cut in December. When OPEC met in Tehran on December 22 it felt assured of the power of its command of oil supplies. The posted price of Saudi Arabian Light, now officially termed the 'marker' crude, was raised from \$ 5.04 to \$ 11.65 per barrel, with increases in proportion for other crude oils. Further requirements, at first imprecisely formulated, were to have the effect of increasing real prices by rather more than the public statements implied, but their quadrupling in less than three months was enough to contemplate for the moment.

This time, without the course of the Arab-Israeli war to distract attention, a realisation of what the rise in prices would mean struck the world with full force. First calculations showed that sums of thousands of millions of dollars would start to accrue in the reserves of the producers and in the trade deficits of the consuming countries. Nevertheless some remained more concerned with assuring supplies than with paying for them, and delegations from the French and British governments visited the Middle East to make further arrangements, which only helped to strengthen the producers' resolution.

In physical terms the worst of the difficulties were over by the end of the year. The cutback had achieved its aim in adding to the pressure which brought about a cease-fire on terms reasonably favourable to the Arabs, and it was becoming clear that to prolong the shortages more than a month after the fighting had ceased would be likely to lose friends. Although it had at first been stated that the cutbacks would be maintained until all Arab claims had been satisfied, production was partly restored in January and was soon equal to demand. It was not however until March that the embargo on the US was lifted by all the Arab countries except Libya.

In the spring of 1974 governments and financial experts throughout the world were contemplating figures that frankly appalled them. Assessments differed in detail but overall there was little disagreement with the World Bank figures which gained general currency. It was thought that the oil revenues of the OPEC countries in 1974 would amount to 87 billion dollars, of which 56 would be for the Gulf countries. The Bank estimated that five billion dollars might be lent to it, and that the countries would spend 25 and add 57 billion dollars to their reserves. After the October 1973 price increases it had been calculated that the additional cost to the industrialised countries of their oil imports would be some 15 billion dollars. Although trade balances would deteriorate there were prospects of increasing exports and attracting investment which should make the deficits manageable. The redoubling of prices raising the total cost of oil for the OECD countries to an estimated 72 billion dollars posed problems of a different order and the industrialised countries would not be able to resolve them by their own action.

The reserves of the OPEC countries as shown by the World Bank stood at 26 billion dollars at the end of 1973 and were expected to rise by 57 billion in 1974. The World Bank forecast that the surplus might reach a total of 650 billion dollars by 1980 and 1200 billion by 1985. In comparison with the total world reserves of 184 billion dollars at the end of 1973, such potential figures for the reserves of the OPEC countries were worrying in their implications for the world's financial system.

In October each country had been so preoccupied with its own difficulties that another problem received no public attention. Only a few men of wide experience realised that, while the industrialised countries might be able to meet the additional cost of oil, the less-developed countries would be quite unable to cope without a large increase in assistance. After the first shock of the December rises a general recognition of the difficulties of the less-developed countries began to spread. It was estimated that the rise in cost of the oil imports they needed, from five to fifteen billion dollars, would exceed the total of Official Development Aid they had received in 1973, and severely affect their prospects of growth. The blow came when many of the poorest countries were already suffering from drought, while two of the biggest, India and Brazil, each faced extra costs of nearly a billion dollars. Dr. Witteveen, Managing Director of the International Monetary Fund, quickly set out proposals for assistance, but it took time for him to gather support.

A year later, in the spring of 1975, many of the problems had taken on a quite different aspect. Some of them had been illusory, and it is now difficult to understand how they came to be debated so seriously. 'Recycling' became a vogue word, but many who used it thought the question was whether the producers would place their earnings with the western financial system, overlooking the fact that they could do little else. The more responsible of the OPEC countries were justifiably annoyed at the suggestion that they would indulge in large-scale currency speculation; their past record was excellent, and even had they been tempted it could be seen that their rapidly increasing balances would soon be of such a size that they would be to a large extent locked in.

The rapid growth of their imports in general might not have been foreseen; the rapid growth of their armaments orders was easily predictable. Even experts forgot that official reserves are merely cash and short-term money; governments can hold many other forms of investments, just as individuals may, which are not reckoned as official reserves. Kuwait had been building up its funds for twenty years and other governments with surpluses were doing the same.

The basic economic factors of supply and demand, prices and sales, were sometimes overlooked; changes of a different order of magnitude from those on which much theory is based called for simple, not sophisticated, analysis. Misunderstanding of the basic factors of the oil industry was also seen, and it may be helpful to commence with a short review of some of the fundamentals.

CHAPTER 2

Two Decades of Energy Industry Development

Before attempting to look into the future trends of oil production and prices it is necessary to look back to the past. There is no intention of presenting here a general history of events, which has been excellently done by several writers whose works are referred to in the bibliography. Rather it is a selection of items which in retrospect can be distinguished from the many other events of the time for their enduring influence.

For the world oil industry the end of the fifties was a seminal period. It marked the end of the reconstruction following World War II and developments flowing directly from it, and the establishment of a new life-style for all concerned with energy. Although there were changes in the sixties and rather more in the early seventies the basic pattern persisted until October 1973. Moreover many of the men in the governments and the industry now directing affairs and making the decisions which will affect the future obtained their experience and formed their attitudes entirely in the conditions of the sixties. Some of the developments in the period came naturally, others were the results of artificial constraints, but they were all part of the scene long enough for their origins to be forgotten in many quarters and the distinction between real and contrived to become blurred.

Tankers

First, and universally recognised, was the remarkable growth in the size of tankers carrying crude oil, and with it the reduction in freight costs. Increases in the capacity of tankers were obtained with much smaller proportionate increases in steel for the hull, in fuel consumption and in other cost elements, while the introduction of modern control systems led to a reduction in manning scales. Behind it all lay the success of the engineering firms in steadily developing more efficient and powerful engines, with each new series bringing a jump in the size of tanker practicable.

In 1956 the first 50,000 ton tanker (all tanker tonnages are deadweight tons) was only recently afloat, a 'supertanker' meant 32,000, and the bulk of the oil fleet forced by the Suez closure to plod around the Cape of Good Hope were of the war-time T2 standard 16,000 tons. For the latter the cost of the round trip – to the owner, not the spot market freight rate – rose from eight to twelve dollars per ton of oil carried, while an additional 50 per cent on voyage time meant that 50 per cent more ships would have been needed to carry the same quantities. They were not there.

The shortage of transport was alleviated within two years of the crisis by new-buildings up to the limits of the dimensions acceptable for Suez Canal transit, which by 1964 implied up to 60,000 tons. The economic cost of transporting a ton of oil from the Gulf to Europe via Suez in such ships was little more than four dollars and even round the Cape only about five and a half. The growth in size continued without break and by mid-1967 there were already twenty Very Large Crude Carriers, as they came to be called, of the 200,000 ton class, and their costs were under three dollars a ton. When the Canal was again blocked already 18 per cent of the oil from the Gulf to Europe was normally on the Cape route. The re-opening of the Canal in 1975 finds some two-thirds of the tankers in service still small enough for transit, but they provide only one quarter of the capacity of the world fleet.

In 1956 almost all tankers could double as crude or product carriers. The new classes of ships had not the facilities for diversified cargoes, and their load was larger than any product terminal could accept. The distinction, now virtually complete, between crude and product carriers stems from this date. Although it was in shipping that the economy of size had its most effective impact on costs, throughout the sixties the companies were seeking similarly to economise on all other aspects of their operations, until it appears that by the mid-seventies there is little more to be gained in this way.

Coal

It is strange to realise than it is less than twenty years since coal was the main source of energy for Europe, supplying over 70 per cent of total energy needs, and although the use of oil had doubled in six years it was still comparatively expensive and regarded as a supplier of speciality products. In 1956, in the shadow of the first Suez crisis, a group of experts – the Hartley Commission – appointed by OEEC, the forerunner of the present OECD, reported on Europe's growing needs of energy and suggested that hard coal production, 478 million tons a year at that time, would require an additional 230 million tons by 1975, while at the same time they expected oil imports to rise from 53 million to 220 million tons. The Suez crisis then broke but hardly had a start been made on the planned increase in coal facilities when it became clear that the oil shortage in Europe had not been a matter of availability but of transport. Also within a short period the new generation of tankers with their much lower costs brought the price of oil to Europe tumbling. Consequently it was reported in 1959 to OEEC by its formally constituted advisory commission under Professor Robinson that expansion of oil imports should meet growing energy requirements, and that the policy for coal production in the future would depend on whether or not it could manage to remain competitive.

Quickly it was apparent that it would not: oil prices continued to move downwards and coal costs upwards. In UK and Germany the governments took the view that the rundown of coal capacity should be a gradual process and applied protective duties of £2 per ton in UK and DM 10 per ton in Germany on fuel oil to ease the impact on the miners. In France and Belgium on the other hand the attention of the governments was concentrated on resolving the special problems of the mining communities and rundown in production was rapid. In Japan also the government saw to it that the decline of coal was gentle and production would in any case have been totally inadequate to meet the needs of that very rapidly expanding economy, so oil was the only possibility. With a clear economic advantage, and under constant pressure from the producing countries to increase exports, the companies were able to establish oil as the basic fuel. The table shows that in the next ten years oil provided over 90 per cent of the increase in energy demand in Western Europe and Japan.

USSR

A third event of the late fifties was the re-emergence of the USSR as an oil exporter, after a gap of twenty years. The largest deal, with

Table 2.1
ENERGY CONSUMPTION
in million tons oil equivalent

		US & Canada	Western Europe	Japan	Rest of non-Communist world
1960					
	Oil	446	187	29	166
	Coal	253	360	42	100
	Gas	332	11	1	19
	Hydro	64	57	15	17
	Total	**1095**	**615**	**87**	**302**
1965					
	Oil	544	343	77	223
	Coal	299	344	43	127
	Gas	438	19	2	33
	Hydro	78	74	18	28
	Nuclear	1	7	–	–
	Total	**1361**	**787**	**140**	**411**
1970					
	Oil	768	626	199	345
	Coal	349	296	61	148
	Gas	569	67	3	48
	Hydro	95	82	20	46
	Nuclear	7	13	1	–
	Total	**1788**	**1084**	**284**	**587**
1974					
	Oil	873	699	261	440
	Coal	347	262	59	175
	Gas	625	146	5	94
	Hydro	136	100	19	55
	Nuclear	34	19	4	1
	Total	**2015**	**1226**	**348**	**765**

Notes
Hydro-electric and nuclear on equivalent oil input basis
Hydro including geothermal etc.
Coal including equivalent other solid fuels

permanent effects, was with Italy under which the state company ENI was supplied with oil at $ 1.12 per barrel – the posted price of Arabian Light was then $ 2.08 – against shipments of large-diameter steel pipe. Barter deals are seldom what they appear; the Russians were trying to buy pipe from other European countries and wanted to set a low price while Signor Enrico Mattei was determined to force the major oil companies to lower their prices, and had already shown his mastery of the interlocking holdings and impenetrable accounts of the Italian state companies. The USSR continued although not so spectacularly to sell cheaply to the west (and expensively to their Comecon partners) in order to gain precious foreign exchange, and together with a growing band of independent marketers brought about a fundamental change. Hitherto there had essentially been a single energy market. The high-cost US domestic oil producers and coal interests everywhere set their selling prices, and low-cost producers, in the developing Middle East fields in particular, were able to meet the prices and after deducting all expenses downstream from the point of loading still show a f.o.b. price many times the cost of production. Under the 50–50 profit-sharing agreements made in 1950 the whole of this economic 'rent' was divided between the companies and the producing government. With the establishment of effective competition to be met by the seven major oil companies, international oil prices ceased to have any relationship to other energy. The benefit went to every consumer of oil, who from this time started to obtain a share in the economic rent from low-cost production.*

US

In the US the position was rather different from that of other industrialised countries. Coal could still be mined very economically and in absolute terms production has continued to expand. OIl there had already taken the leading place in energy production partly because of the importance of the transport sector. However the main factor controlling the rate of growth of both these sources of energy was the availability of natural gas at a very low price. In most oilfields gas contained with the oil comes to the surface automatically with production, and commercial sales of natural gas

Footnote: Dr. Frankel (1971) gave an elegant explanation of what had been happening.

initially developed merely to provide a small bonus to the production of oil, even if the price of the gas yielded a very moderate rate of return. Exploration for oil had discovered various fields containing only gas and as the market grew these too were brought into production. Just as the oil companies were beginning to realise that they were supplying competitors with a source of energy at prices considerably undercutting oil, the Federal Power Commission stepped in and by virtue of its powers to regulate inter-state commerce insisted on the reduction of the already low prices of gas to mere utility rates. The various attempts to find satisfactory formulae which could be applied to achieve this end and the companies' legal efforts to curb the authority rumbled on throughout the sixties but the artificial cheapness of natural gas ensured that any energy user would endeavour by hook or by crook to obtain a supply before considering any other source of energy. Indeed the point was reached when the companies together with the state governments would offer considerable inducements to industries to set up in those states where the internal price of gas was not subject to federal legislation, and the benefits of the margin between its federal price and the cost of competing oil could be shared by all three parties.

Another action by the US government in 1959 had unforeseen consequences. At the start of the fifties the US was still a net exporter of oil and the rapid change in the situation had caused difficulties. Although the companies with low-cost overseas production had themselves moved gingerly in increasing their imports, traders were finding it possible to obtain an increasing flow of cheap supplies and the hundreds of small and medium oil companies felt their interests threatened. Though vociferously proclaiming at every convention their belief in the US virtues of competition and freedom from regulation they also clamoured for the foreign competition to be hamstrung by strict legislation. They mobilised support; in the US, contrary to most other countries, the individual landholder still retains the sub-surface rights and the hundreds of thousands of royalty owners were made aware of the danger to their incomes. There were too many voters for a government to ignore and President Eisenhower signed a decree limiting imports, except on the West Coast, to their level at that time of 12.2 per cent of requirements. Subsequent developments in the

US need not be discussed here, but there were effects overseas. Some of the smaller companies had ventured into exploration abroad confident that their domestic markets would provide a profitable offtake for any discovery. Now they would have to develop not only production but also markets abroad. A few of them did strike oil, especially in Libya, and their efforts to break into the market caused a second wave of world price reductions in the mid-sixties more severe than the fall at the end of the fifties.

Venezuela

Venezuela had been the first country to develop oil production primarily for export, but in 1958 a conscious decision was taken to prolong the profitable life of its oilfields. Though production was not formally limited, taxes and levies were set, and have continued to be adjusted, so as to retain its attraction to the North American markets, aided by its proximity, while surrendering the fast-growing European market to the Middle East producers. At the same time all existing exploration rights were cancelled; the wisdom of that move is debatable since later efforts by the national company, alone or with partners, to resume work have met with little success. Since the foundation of OPEC Venezuela has consistently advocated in it the policy of restricting production in order to raise prices.

OPEC

Last but not least came the foundation of the Organisation of Petroleum Exporting Countries in November 1960. The five original members, Iran, Iraq, Kuwait, Saudi Arabia and Venezuela, were soon joined by Indonesia, Libya and Qatar; Abu Dhabi and Algeria were added in the late sixties, and since then Nigeria and Ecuador, with Gabon as an associate.

Prices for oil had risen steeply at the time of the Suez crisis, but had fallen back steadily with the restoration of normal conditions and the impact of growing competition. Companies had reduced posted prices to correspond early in 1958 and 1959, and a third round started in August 1960. The producing countries met and then formed OPEC with the announced aims of stabilising international crude oil prices and specifically of restoring posted prices to their pre-1960 level. They met with no success in these two aims but did with a third. In meetings with the companies the governments stressed the importance of stability of revenues for the purpose of planning their developments. Tacitly the companies conceded the point and by the end of September 1960 the latest reductions had been partially annulled and there was no further move.

From then on posted prices ceased to be prices in any real sense and became mere reference values for calculating payments to the governments. In establishing this principle it is arguable that the producing countries achieved the greatest success in the first ten years of OPEC's existence before it was formally constituted. When international markets refused to be stabilised and consumers drew a larger share of the economic rent inherent in the real price of oil, they took it from the companies' share leaving the share of the producing countries untouched. The extremely low real cost of their product had enabled the governments to obtain an insulation from economic forces impossible for any other primary producer. The lack of contact with reality did however engender a certain blindness even at times affecting the most perspicacious.

Developments after 1960

On the supply side the sixties saw the emergence of Africa as a producer, with Algeria, Libya and later Nigeria. Ignoring this, the Gulf countries individually and through OPEC continually pressed the companies for more rapid increases in production. OPEC itself for two years ran a system of allocating production increases which merely caused bitterness among those who failed to reach their allocation and was laughed at by those who exceeded it. OPEC had more success in its campaign for 'royalty expensing', effectively increasing the government/company profit split to 56/44, though the companies obtained agreement on a schedule for phasing-in the change.

A sign that the interests of producing countries and major companies were not too far apart came when Libya was supported by both OPEC and Esso in its endeavours to revise the concessions of the independent companies on to 'OPEC terms'. In 1970 Libya adroitly used the weakness of these companies, which now had markets but no alternative supply, together with one of the periods of shortage of tankers which occurred after Suez was closed. It succeeded in breaking the ten-year standstill on posted prices, a move which was soon followed by the Gulf producers at Tehran in

Table 2.2
ME OIL EXPORTS IN THE WORLD

	1960	1965	1970	1972	1974
			Million Tons		
Exports from Middle East	234	383	641	842	993
Exports from North Africa	9	83	225	167	125
	243	466	866	1009	1118
As a percentage of world inter-area trade (excluding Canada-US)					
Middle East exports	53.3	52.0	52.0	58.1	61.9
North Africa exports	2.1	11.3	18.2	11.5	7.8
	55.4	63.3	70.2	69.6	69.7
As a percentage of world consumption (excluding USSR etc)					
Middle East exports	25.4	29.3	33.1	38.6	42.4
North Africa exports	1.0	6.3	11.6	7.6	5.3
	26.4	35.6	44.7	46.2	47.7

February 1971. After then, further increases to match the subsequent dollar devaluations were a foregone conclusion. Finally at the end of 1972 agreement was reached on an initial 25 per cent participation of the producers in the shareholdings and management of the operating companies.

All this time the consuming countries had stayed passive, except for a brief flurry of concern in 1967. In Europe there had been only a few who questioned the growing dependence on imported oil, and the fact that apart from its premium use it had taken over the supply of general energy requirements to a point where any appreciable reduction would affect whole economies. As the competitive advantage of oil widened, and the nuclear programmes which had been expected to develop an alternative for balancing supply requirements continued to drop behind schedule and increase in cost, governments took little apparent note of the dangers inherent in the position. To any one country it appeared that a serious effort to develop sources of energy more expensive than oil would have rendered its costs distinctly uncompetitive with its neighbours. Europe as a whole feared the competition of Japan, which in default of any other sources of energy was completely committed to oil and obtained it at a low cost.

By the beginning of the seventies the depletion by US of its hydrocarbon resources began to receive general attention. For natural gas in particular the lack of new production to be devoted to inter-state commerce was hitting the states which were big consumers, while the statistics showed that overall consumption had overtaken the rate of new discoveries and reserves were falling. Simultaneously the reserves of oil within the 48 states were static and the only relief apparent – the Alaskan oilfields – had been delayed since their discovery in 1969 by the various legal objections taken on environmental grounds. The rapid growth of oil imports was the general expectation and plans to import large quantities of natural gas in liquefied form had been formulated. Only the cost in terms of foreign exchange and not the availability of the foreign sources was a matter of concern.

In the US and to a lesser extent in other countries the formation of practical energy policies became confused by two groups which attained widespread influence. Conservationists busily extrapolated current growth of use of the earth's natural resources at exponential rates and foretold a complete collapse in the next century unless use was strictly curtailed. Environmentalists pointed to various extreme examples of pollution, called for action to prevent it whatever the cost in additional resources, and failed to distinguish the degrees of action necessary in the vastly greater areas where pollution was small. Each group could quote respectable scientific work partly supporting its case, but most of the matter with which legislators and the public have been bombarded shows more skill in publicity than in science. Although the actions called for by the two groups are diametrically opposed, there has been general confusion between the two and many have shown their hearts are bigger than their heads by support of both causes.

CHAPTER 3

Oil Prices

To the man in the street the price of oil means simply the price at the pump of the gasoline (petrol in UK) which he puts in his car, and he remains largely ignorant that this is only a fraction of the total of oil sales. As a householder he may have oil-fired central heating and here his concern is the price of domestic heating oil. Businessmen are aware of other prices, of road diesel fuel and of furnace oil for factories, but in all these cases the price of oil as it is understood by the ordinary man is the price of an oil product. Prices of crude oil, with all their complexity and variety in actual practice, are seldom understood by those outside the industry, although there are a few expert journalists who attempt to spread their knowledge. In most public mention of the price of oil, in ordinary newspaper articles or broadcasting, in international conferences, by statesmen and by academics, what is referred to as the price of oil is not truly a price: it is the 'posted price' which for many years has simply been a reference value. Even some who know better occasionally allow themselves to be influenced by the misused word. Although the posted price system is on the way out there are still relics of the misconceptions it has caused and a little explanation may be necessary.

In 1950 when the first 50–50 profit sharing agreements between the oil companies and the producing countries were settled, there was a serious difficulty in deciding on what basis these profits should be assessed. The basing-point system for crude oil prices which had prevailed before and during the Second World War was already under strong attack and obviously untenable, even before it was demolished completely by the report to the US Senate on the alleged 'International Petroleum Cartel'. The producing companies in the Middle East were largely consortia of the major oil companies which were competing in selling their products to consumers, and for commercial reasons each major company was extremely reluctant to enable its competitors to find out the prices at which it was selling crude. A method of setting a sales value for the calculation of profits which did not involve revealing individual sales was sought. For many years in the US there had been a system whereby refiners and pipeline companies 'posted' a price at which they would be willing to buy from any of the thousands of independent producers who function in the industry there. The system was transposed, and it was agreed that each partner in the producing companies of the Middle East would post a price at which it was prepared to sell to any buyer. As in the US this did not mean necessarily that transactions took place at the posted price, but rather that it was a reference value to which all transactions could be related. Again, as in the US, when the cumulative effect of actual deals became strong posted prices were changed from time to time in sympathy with long-term market values. A similar system of prices for oil products posted by the seller became common for export refineries, notably in the Caribbean.

The system of posted prices for export crude oil lasted with reasonable efficiency for ten years. However the Suez crisis of 1956/7 pushed them up to levels which could not be sustained in the long run in a competitive market and they began to fall again. The third such reduction in August 1960 was the occasion for the foundation of OPEC, as has been mentioned. Posted prices for crude oil exports became frozen for the next ten years regardless of market conditions and technical requirements, and the producing countries' unit revenues remained protected.

One difficulty caused by the system of posted prices frozen at the 1960 level appears not to have been foreseen by the companies. It was the posting of appropriate prices for new crude oil production, which indeed may have seemed quite simple to them. They were accustomed to estimating the comparative value of a particular crude for refining purposes, and discounting the long-term freight costs, and posted their prices accordingly. To the governments however, especially those seeing production for the first time and with even less knowledge of consumer requirements than the old established producers possessed, the calculations of the companies were never acceptable, and although unable to produce arguments of substance the governments nurtured a constant grievance. It came to a head after the closure of the Suez Canal in 1967 when, however reasonable the calculations earlier, Mediterranean crude oils now had an enhanced freight advantage which could not be reflected if posted prices were to remain immutable. The companies were conscious that a single change would open the whole of Pandora's box, as was proved later, while product prices failed to rise in line with increased freight costs. The dissatisfaction of the short-haul producers gathered force and boiled over in Libya in 1970.

The complexity of posting an acceptable price for crude at the start of the fifties should not be under-estimated, although once one had been determined prices for the rest relative to it could be arrived at by technical and transport considerations. Consumers require a variety of oil products in all sorts of quantities and have their own ideas of what they are willing to pay. The cost of crude oil production to the companies is also determinate. In between there is only one real margin which arises from the whole stream of transport, refining and distribution; at that time almost all international operations were in the hands of integrated companies and the decision which proportion of the profit to ascribe to which stage of the operation was necessarily somewhat arbitrary. For reasons of American legislation it suited the American companies to put as much of the profit as possible against the producing operation and to pay revenues to the producing governments ostensibly in the form of income tax, and it was Aramco in Saudi Arabia which first devised the system. In the fifties independent refiners and distributors started to appear in Europe but they were still dependent on supply from the major companies. They did however begin to provide an independent indication of appropriate price and profit levels, and posted prices were affected. The arrival of Russian crude oil presented a fresh problem which put the companies in some difficulty, as now the governments in consuming countries could begin to make their own judgments on the level of oil import prices. The companies did not exactly help themselves by speaking with two tongues. To the producing countries they stressed the importance of the competition and the necessity of lowering posted prices to meet it, while to the consuming countries they explained that such relatively small quantities at what might be termed distress prices were no indication of true values.

The major oil companies had another reason for not wishing to see Middle East prices slide too far and for dissociating price from the actual costs of production, and that was their regard for their numerous other interests throughout the world. It would have been possible for instance for Venezuelan production to have been completely replaced by the Middle East in a comparatively short period, at lower delivered prices throughout the world, but that would have been unwelcome for the companies most of which had important interests there. Even more significantly the US has thousands of small high-cost producers and hundreds of thousands of royalty owners and their political influence had to be respected.

In an analysis of the oil market at the start of the sixties it was estimated that around eighty per cent of Europe's crude oil was still moving under inter-affiliate arrangements or on other long-term contracts. Most of the remainder was still being imported under short-term contracts but annually buyers were sought for some seven per cent of imports, either by renewal of short-term contracts or in spot sales. Competition for crude oil sales therefore was concentrated on this seven per cent and, unwilling as the companies were to admit it, it was already a large enough fraction to constitute a true market. As Russia was followed by the independent companies and then by the producers' national companies in selling crude oil, while the share of the majors was shrinking, arms-length prices for crude became commoner. It was however the market for oil products which showed the greater development and now influences the price of crude.

The consumer does not buy crude oil but a particular product from it, and except under a monopoly the law of supply and demand is of greater effect than some people in oil companies as well as in governments have been willing to admit. It is true that the market involved is marginal in the sense that the quantities in which it deals are small compared with those handled on a regular long-term basis, but they are not inconsiderable in themselves and are the pacemakers for all prices. Work by Professor Deam and his colleagues has shown that market price movements in one quarter of the year are reflected in the next quarter by a move in contract prices about halfway towards market values. The major market is Germany, where the number of independent refiners and marketers and the quantities required, allied to the government's policy of non-interference in the market, result in competitive and flexible pricing. The other large free market is the East Coast of the US, with prices based on New

York harbour, and although there are buyers in plenty from other nations they do not match the weight of the two large markets. Similarly products may be on offer from any part of the world, but the large Italian export-oriented refineries are predominant in supply. Brokers and traders in New York, London, Hamburg, Rotterdam and Milan are all in constant awareness of trading levels, and prices in one area cannot get seriously out of line with those in another. The market works back to crude oil prices, in that the ultimate level of prices which a refiner can obtain for the range of products he can make from a particular crude sets an upper limit to the price he can afford to pay for it. In times of shortage the prices for products in the market can rise very rapidly with repercussions on the crude prices. In normal times the seasonal changes, with gasoline in summer demand and heating oil in winter, form the basis of market movements, but the surplus of crude production normally available has been a factor tending to depress prices.

Even within Europe the various countries have different demand patterns for oil products; different crude oils vary in their suitability for meeting the demand pattern. The value of a particular crude to a French refinery is distinctly different from its value to an Italian one and markedly more so between US and Japan. In consequence no unique value can be given to the precise advantage of one crude over another at the point of production. When the companies posted prices they took into account the relative values of the crude oils in furnishing products for their markets generally, as well as their relative position in terms of transport costs. The changes in posted prices that took place between 1970 and 1973 still had regard to the reality of demand. The product emerging from a refinery is made to definite specification and the price to the consumer cannot vary according to the origin of the crude. Some of the decisions on prices taken by individual governments in October 1973 and later have been taken more on supposition than on knowledge of what refineries are prepared to pay in the form of differential between different crudes.

It may not be unfair to suggest that some of the OPEC staff work shows the result of academic training too far removed from reality. In theory it may well seem plausible that if the price of A is doubled so should that of B and the differential between them, unless it is thoroughly understood that percentages are merely a derivative from

OIL PRICES 1960 - 1973

Figure 3a

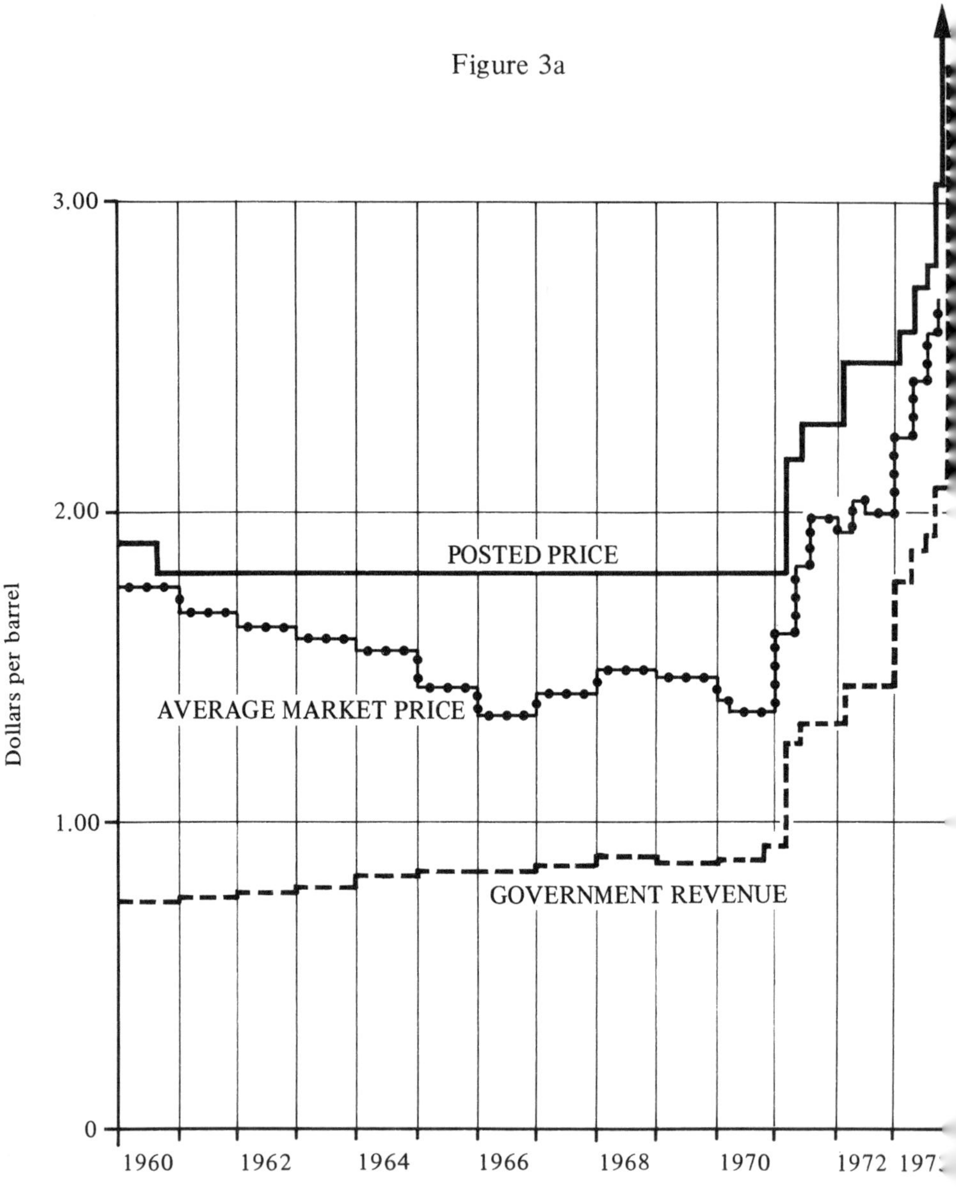

Posted Price and Government Revenue
for Arabian Light Average Market Price
calculated from German Import statistics

real figures. When prices were doubled in October 1973 the first published proposals for further increases were expressed in terms of various percentages; if one of those responsible had paused to translate them into real terms he would have seen them irreconcilable. In December habits of thinking in percentages instead of money were again apparent.

The long-term implications of the take-over by the OPEC countries of control of oil production need to be better understood by consuming countries. It has already been pointed out that the producers had since 1960 been shielded by the companies from fluctuations of the market, but so had the consumers because a large proportion of their imports came through the major companies accustomed to taking a long view and slow to adjusting prices in circumstances which they expected to be temporary. The apparent stability which both producers and consumers enjoyed was given to them by the companies. In reality there were long periods of downward pressure on prices, with surplus capacity at each stage in the chain between producer and consumer, interrupted by brief periods when one link had not been developed fast enough or was subjected to unforeseen strains. The hidden instability will now become more apparent and there will develop a danger, from the consumers' point of view, that the periods of inadequate facilities will become longer and may result in actual shortages, because the incentives to invest have been reduced.

The Chase Manhattan Bank makes an annual study of capital investments by the industry, and the total for 1973 was 31.7 billion dollars, of which 13.3 was in US and Canada. In the rest of the world, 5.1 went into exploration and production facilities, 6.5 to tankers and 6.8 billion dollars into further downstream investments. The companies will now have to be much more selective in their investments, partly because they are no longer assured of oil to supply world-wide developments and partly because the share of the profits on production now left to them by OPEC is in itself inadequate for investment on such a scale and also reduces their ability to borrow. Figures from Shell suggest that approximately two-thirds of the industry's investment has gone into expansion and one-third into replacement of existing facilities, and even if the need for the former is now somewhat reduced the latter remains. The effects will not be felt at once, probably not till after 1980, but then the results of inadequate investment are likely to be painful unless governments can show as much foresight as companies have done.

When the OPEC countries decided to set posted prices unilaterally with no consultation with the companies they were, almost certainly unwittingly, preparing further complications. Accompanying the December decision which more than doubled posted prices again there was an explicit statement that a government take of seven dollars a barrel on the marker crude – Arabian Light – was economically justified and the posted price had been set accordingly. With all the complexities of costs of competing energy in various parts of the world no such figure can be more than a very rough estimate, and though definitely higher than general estimates of 5 – 6 dollars it was not too unreasonable. In the somewhat heady atmosphere of the time however it appears to have been genuinely overlooked, at least by the speaker, that his figure applied only to equity oil, the proportion of the crude which the companies were enabled to lift as their share of production, and did not reckon the additional advantage which the government was to obtain on its 25 per cent participation share which the companies were also mostly obliged to lift. They of course could not sell the oil at two separate prices and had to reckon on the average cost. Agreements previously reached on the additional buy-back payments the companies were to make for lifting the governments' share had been declared unsatisfactory, but no alternative had been fixed, with the result that for some months the companies had to take this oil and include it in their sales to consumers without knowing the cost. The position was further complicated when the Kuwait Assembly rejected the 25 per cent terms and insisted that 60 per cent participation should be obtained, a move that was clearly likely to be followed elsewhere, while at the same time a formula for buy-back price and third-party sales at 93 per cent of posted prices became the general demand.

The consequence of the quadrupling of posted prices was that the cost of the companies' equity oil differed so much from the amounts demanded on a straight sales basis that there was no possibility for independents to bridge the gap. In 1973, with the posted price of under three dollars and the cost to the companies of their equity crude around two dollars, sales by both governments and companies to independents at around two-and-a-half dollars were possible, with the flexibility of the independents' operations still enabling them to compete in the consumer markets. In March 1974 however, with the posted price of 11.65 dollars and companies still unsure of the average cost of their oil, but invoicing to purchasers at some three dollars lower, there was nowhere for the independents to obtain oil at a competitive price. A number of very high-priced sales which the governments thought they had made at the end of 1973 had failed to materialise, and now they found sales of their own oil to outsiders becoming negligible. With the weakening of demand becoming apparent, it seemed that the stage was set for a reduction in sales prices in line with the declared objective of a seven dollar government take.

What actually happened was somewhat of a surprise. First in Qatar, then in Kuwait followed by other countries, the companies agreed on the 93 per cent buy-back formula, which together with the sixty per cent participation change raised the producing governments' take and the prices to consumers by more than two dollars a barrel. Even so the disparity between the average price of crude to the companies and the decreed selling price was still too great to admit competition. Realistic discussions of ways in which the whole of the posted price and tax system could be revised to take care of the new levels of prices might have been useful. They would seem to have been inhibited on the governments' side by single-minded preoccupation with the companies' equity costs compared with the decreed levels, ignoring both participation costs and all the evidence from the markets of real price levels, and on the companies' side by what appears to have been a determination to hold on to any advantage that possession of equity oil gave them however reduced and whatever the consequences to consumers.

As the year went by and markets weakened further it was not surprising to see governments trying to close the gap, so that their national oil companies could find buyers, not by reducing selling prices but by making successive advances in the levels of royalty and of taxation on equity crude. By the end of the year the cost to consumers, which had aroused loud protests when increased at the start of the year, had quietly been raised by a further forty per cent without the majority appearing to be aware of it.

Posted prices had been constant for most of the year but were reduced at the end when the final larger increases in company costs were imposed. It is a measure of how little these purely reference

OIL PRICES 1973 - 1975

Figure 3b

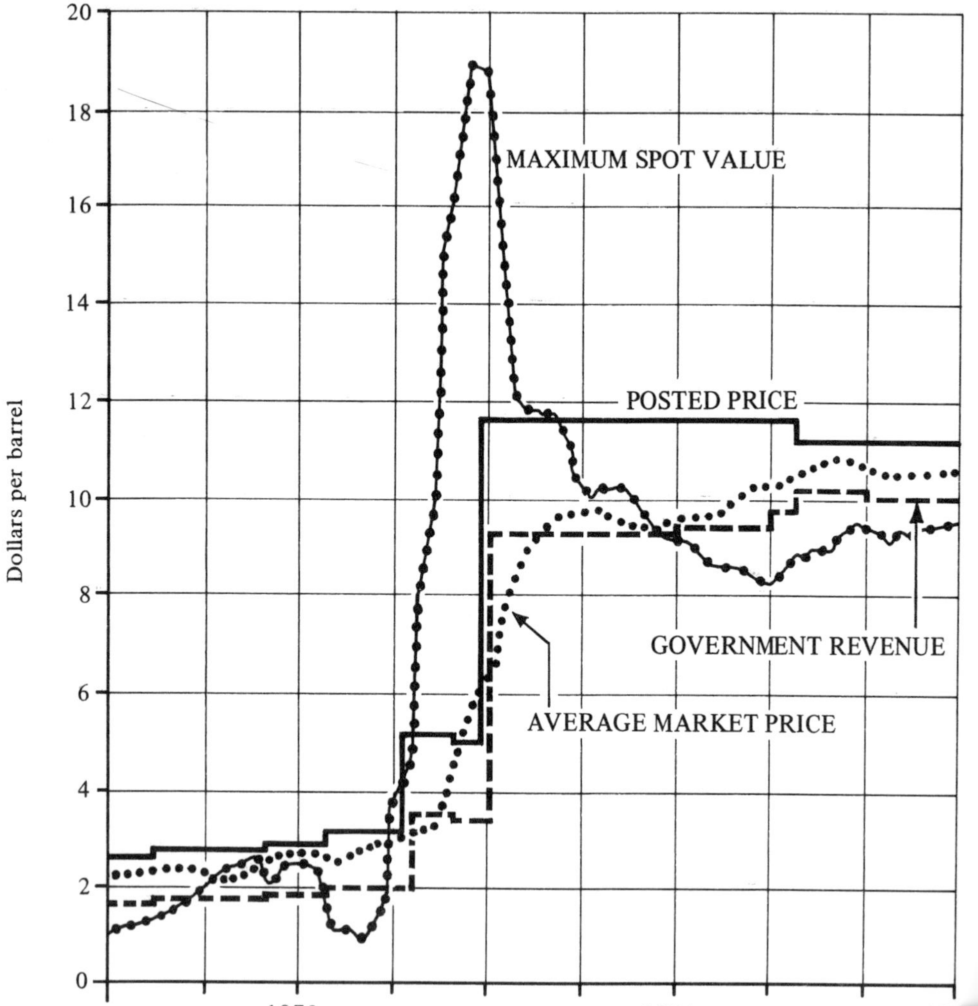

Maximum spot value : Source : Europ-Oil Prices

values are understood that the move could still be announced by the producers and accepted in the west as a price reduction. At the end of the year demands for 100 per cent ownership had been conceded in principle throughout the Gulf, and with its implementation the relevance of posted prices as tax reference values should theoretically be ending, although the fine print of agreements still to be reached may leave them some residual significance, and the retention of the term alongside a different 'government selling price' is still confusing.

The complete divorce between posted prices and real prices which has prevailed since 1960 has applied only to crude postings. In the other two fields in which it was earlier noted that posted prices are normally quoted, the US domestic market and products from major export refineries, the system has continued to function in the commercially useful manner, and movements of posted prices have responded to the medium-term prospects.

What will happen if the governments manage 100 per cent of sales of crude is not yet clear (while this is being written it appears that some are having second thoughts on the matter). It certainly seems to suggest that it may be significantly different from conditions when the companies operated the system freely. Posted prices may make infrequent moves; and when they do it will be for political effect rather than commercial significance. Meanwhile, the state organisations will be employing the various methods by which the companies used to compete for sales beneath the blanket of a fixed posted price: discounts for quantity and regularity of offtake, extended credit terms, subsidised freights and even at times plain barter.

Some of the methods are already in use, while reality has been dawning. Most of the excessive rises in the prices of African and Abu Dhabi crudes have had to be withdrawn and other inducements offered on the side. Credit terms have been extended beyond three months, and Libya has been using some unusual practices in attempts to restore its sales. Algeria and Iraq, both needing all the revenue they can get, have found that an extra ten cents discount can be enough to clinch a doubtful sale.

While in such ways OPEC countries may try to adjust or improve their share of the market against each other it would probably be a mistake for consumers to expect more than marginal reductions of real prices from them. Saudi Arabia holds the key and the price it sets will cover all other transactions. Its place as balancing force in the world's energy demand picture is unassailable in the medium term. The dominance of oil in meeting the world energy needs is not going to be quickly reversed, and as oil demand has grown and the limitations of other producers become more apparent the pre-eminent position of Saudi Arabia has become clear. There have been times when other producing states held a similar position, notably Kuwait in the early sixties, much as there have been attempts to promote other sources of energy to take over the balancing functions. Cheaply-mined US coal, tar sands, shale and natural gas have all been candidates, while nuclear energy has all along held potential which has proved difficult to put into practice. The price of oil is now well in excess of the cost of competitive energy, and all consuming countries have been planning diversification of energy sources and development of indigenous supply.

Natural gas is an attractive fuel, and the amount discovered to date is equivalent to two-thirds of the world's reserves of oil. Besides the established processes for liquefying it and transporting it in that state, the alternative methanol process, which itself costs more but offers considerable transport savings, has been receiving attention. From the consumers' view however it may well be that, since most of the very large investment required would have to be in some of the countries which are now supplying oil, the question of security of supply will be considered an obstacle, while producers may decide not to develop major gasfields in rivalry to their own oil. The tar sands processes have proved disappointingly costly, and reports at one time current of a breakthrough in the cost of obtaining oil from shale do not seem to have been borne out by an actual project.

It would certainly appear at present that the major role in meeting growing energy requirements will be taken over by nuclear power. Plans already in hand throughout the world, even allowing for the long lead times of nuclear plant construction, seem likely to quadruple availability by 1980 and to be considerably accelerated thereafter. In most industrialised countries the largest share in new energy investment is already scheduled for the nuclear industry. As regards oil the considerable surplus capacity which is now apparent in all sectors of the industry has reduced the attraction and urgency of further investments, although with the normal lead time for major projects there will be further growth in capacity resulting from earlier investment decisions. If it be assumed that the cyclical behaviour of the world's economy may produce a strong upturn in 1976/77, it will be before the nuclear industry has gone far enough to develop its potential, but the reserve capacity of the oil industry will be capable of meeting the demands. Whether that might mark the last surge in demand for oil or whether there are further waves to come is something that at the moment can only be speculation.

In due course the development of other energy supplies will reach a point when the oil producers will have to bring their prices into line or lose their markets. The time may come at the start of the eighties, if early warnings are heeded, or in the later part of the decade if they wait until they have no alternative. Meanwhile so long as the cartel holds together the producers are in control of prices.

It is ironical that the only country to benefit by the rise in oil prices, apart from the producers, has been the US. Until 1973 its oil was always more expensive than supplies to its industrialised competitors, although cheaper natural gas and coal provided compensation. Now, with the price of domestic oil held at 5.25 dollars, its average oil cost is a little over nine dollars a barrel compared with twelve in Europe. At the time of writing the OPEC countries are considering the quotation of oil prices in SDR (see Appendix A) instead of dollars, and a further rise in price; their presentation of their moves will probably again need interpretation. The other producers however have been learning that they cannot maintain prices out of line with those of Saudi Arabia; the actions Saudi Arabia decides to take, after listening to all the conflicting advice offered, will determine oil prices during the next five years and probably longer.

Footnote:
As this book was going to press, the results of the OPEC meeting in Vienna on September 27 were announced. The government selling price of the marker crude was raised by ten per cent from \$ 10.46 to \$ 11.51, but there was no reference to posted prices. The question of OPEC-set differentials for other crude oils was left in abeyance. With the dollar still strengthening, there was no further mention of quoting prices in SDR. The influential position of Saudi Arabia was clear.

CHAPTER 4

Oil Revenues to 1985

There are various forecasts current of the future growth of revenues of the OPEC countries as a whole, although forecasts for each of them separately are less common. In the overall picture there come questions of supply both of non-OPEC production and of competing energy sources, and for these it is reasonable to say that any development large enough to affect the overall supply position by 1980 is already known with a fair degree of accuracy, although the position by 1985 is considerably less definite. The principal problem for the forecaster is the size of consumption. It must not be forgotten that the producers' revenues depend ultimately on those who consume oil products, and reactions of the consumer to price changes by alterations in demand and by conservation measures are rather more difficult to predict.

Before the October 1973 price rises projections of future demands had been made by various authorities, which will be referred to in more detail later. Since the beginning of the decade there had been a growing concern, not least in the US, whether the large projected figures would indeed prove practicable with the oil reserves which were already known and with the current rate of discovery. The conservationists were taken seriously and, without acceptance of the extreme views of some of them, the concern they were expressing was shared by a number of those directly involved in the supply of energy, and of oil in particular. The actions that would need to be taken to retard the increasing demand for oil and enlarge the supply of other forms of energy required very definite action by governments and heavy financial investments, and although there was some uneasiness about the situation there was no sense of urgency or determination to deal with it. One reason for the indecision may have been a certain lack of confidence in the forecasts, even by the government departments themselves.

Before the October 1973 price rises projections of future demands had been made by various authorities, which will be referred to in more detail later. Since the beginning of the decade there had been a growing concern, not least in the US, whether the large projected figures would indeed prove practicable with the oil reserves which were already known and with the current rate of discovery. The conservationists were taken seriously and, without acceptance of the extreme views of some of them, the concern they were expressing was shared by a number of those directly involved in the supply of energy, and of oil in particular. The actions that would need to be taken to retard the increasing demand for oil and enlarge the supply of other forms of energy required very definite action by governments and heavy financial investments, and although there was some uneasiness about the situation there was no sense of urgency or determination to deal with it. One reason for the indecision may have been a certain lack of confidence in the forecasts, even by the government departments themselves.

It is one of the problems of forecasting the demand for energy that human nature has shown itself unpredictable. In general the methods of forecasting used by the governments, companies and individuals for the last fifteen years had fallen into a routine pattern. Estimates of the growth of GNP were made, worldwide, for a country or on a sector basis, from which the growth of the corresponding energy demand was deduced by the means of elasticity coefficients, which themselves had become somewhat standardised. Allowances were then made for the availability and expected increase in all forms of energy, such as coal production, natural gas supply and primary electricity, with the remainder to meet demand ascribed to oil. Then, allowing for any indigenous oil production, it was regularly assumed that imported oil would be available in such quantities as would be required to make good the deficiency in the energy balance. Underlying all the calculations, however much attention was seemingly paid to individual problems, there was always a bias towards the expectation of a constant rate of growth. Forecasts are necessary, because the lead time for developing any major energy project is long and the impact of such a project can be considerable – it is a convenient abstraction to consider the development of energy resources as a continual growth, but it does not correspond with reality. The forecaster who has practical responsibilities needs to be aware of what plans are to be made on the basis of his forecasts, to be flexible and quick to revise his figures with each change in the situation, and to ensure that before plans made on the basis of earlier forecasts are finalised a review of the latest position is made.

The standard forecasting approach had not proved a very reliable guide to changes from one year to the next, and only moderately successful in the longer term. Refinements had been added and alternatives sought, both academically and within the energy organisations, but little real progress was being made. The abrupt changes in the energy picture that took place in 1974 will certainly provide considerably more material to work on, and has made existing procedures even more suspect.

Table 4.1
OIL CONSUMPTION 1974
Million Tons

	1972	1973	1974	Percent 72/73	Change 73/74	1974 if growth had been at 1968/73 average	1974 below average growth level by percentage
US/Canada	855	902	874	+ 5.4	– 3.1	947	– 7.8
Western Europe	701	749	699	+ 6.7	– 6.6	782	– 10.6
including							
UK	110	113	106	+ 2.6	– 6.7	119	– 10.8
Germany	141	150	134	+ 6.2	– 10.2	161	– 16.5
France	114	127	120	+ 10.2	– 5.7	142	– 15.5
Italy	98	104	101	+ 6.4	– 2.7	112	– 10.2
Japan	234	268	261	+ 14.0	– 2.7	293	– 10.9
Rest of World *	394	423	440	+ 7.3	+ 4.1	455	– 3.3
Total *	**2184**	**2342**	**2274**	**+ 6.8**	**– 2.9**	**2477**	**– 8.2**

* Non-Communist

Source: **BP Statistical Review**

In general assessments of the fall in demand in 1974 three main reasons have been given. The first is the world economic recession, the second is the particularly mild winter of 1974-5, and the third is the reaction by consumers to the price increases. It is certainly not possible to assess the relative importance of each of the three reasons with any precision, but there are some approximate indications. The important figures for this purpose are those in the last column of the table which show the amount by which actual consumption in 1974 fell below what it would it would have been if the average growth rate in the last five years had continued.

In previous recessions consumption figures have not fallen markedly below predictions. It has been rather during the subsequent recoveries that they have shown unexpected growth. Evidence suggests that a reduction in the average growth rate of oil demand might amount to some two per cent, and even with the more severe recession of 1974 the effect was probably not more than three per cent. The mild winter is more difficult because it is only with particular products, especially heating oil, that the effect is felt and, although it can be very marked over the season, in the full year and with all other products in the total consumption figures the effects of a severe or mild winter are definitely attenuated. In 1974-75 the particularly anomalous warm weather fell at the start of 1975, so not affecting the 1974 figures, and it is thought that at most a two per cent fall can be ascribed to the weather. Something over three per cent would then remain as the result of real economies made by consumers, although in turn this contains an involuntary element by reason of the spot shortages that developed in certain parts of the US at the beginning of the year, and by the effects in UK of the three-day working week at the same time.

The evidence for the correlation between growth in energy demand and growth in GNP, which had already been coming into question, now clearly needs further consideration, as perhaps does the evidence for other economic assumptions on which the events of 1974 have thrown doubts. Although the figures for consumption above are only those for oil, provisional energy demand totals show a fall of 2.2 per cent in US and five per cent in Germany. While in US, UK and Japan GNP measured in real terms fell in 1974, in Germany, France and Italy GNP rose, yet in these countries the drop in oil demand was particularly severe. The other feature of interest brought out by the table is that while the industrialised countries were strongly reducing demand the figure for the rest of the world shows a much smaller change from the forecast one. The overall figure hides certain differences, since part of the growth is accounted for by growth in consumption in the Middle East itself, and in Latin America and Australasia demand continued to grow at only a slightly slower pace. The less developed countries of Asia and Africa show a fall in demand not unexpected among those least able to bear the increase in prices, but even so the fall was not comparable with those in the industrialised countries. It may be thought that for countries at this stage of development the use of energy, at least that recorded in statistics, covers only essentials and consequently little reduction is possible.

The figures for consumption for the European countries surely show that a start has been made on energy-saving measures. In the OECD review of energy prospects it was suggested that 5 to 10 per cent reduction in energy demand, compared with previous forecasts, could be achieved in the fairly short term and 15 to 20 per cent by 1985, although it was emphasised that only some of the potential reductions were likely to be achieved. Not all experts are in agreement, taking the OECD figures to be on the high side, but there is general acceptance of 5 per cent as the possible saving in the short term, although the longer-term estimates show more variety. The proposed economies may come either by more efficient use of energy to do the same amount of work or by a reduction in the use of energy at some sacrifice. For instance the OECD forecast puts the reduction in domestic heating requirements which might be achieved by better insulation around 25 per cent, an economy by efficiency, but also estimates at 25 per cent the saving that could be achieved by a reduction of the maintained temperature from 24° C to 20° C, an economy by sacrifice of comfort. The strain may be less than expected; one of the retail groups in UK, already renowned for its efficiency, found that it was able in 1974 to cut its energy consumption by 15 per cent by almost imperceptible means.

Before the crisis broke the actual forecasts being made of future requirements were considerably higher than many people thought desirable, even if they would be practicable. With additions for the non-OECD countries, the OECD base case (the forecast it was making based on the figures up to 1972, see below) implied a total oil requirement in the non-communist world of perhaps 3400 million tons in 1980 and 4300 million tons in 1985. There were other estimates current for the world, regional organisations and individual countries which could be summed in various ways to give totals between 3100 and 3600 million tons in 1980; a few forecasts for 1985 suggested that the OECD base case might be an underestimate. The increase in prices has rendered all such calculations obsolete.

The comprehensive forecasts which are currently the ones normally quoted are those from the OECD publication *Energy Prospects to 1985.* There are considerable difficulties in any comprehensive work on energy since each type is normally measured in its own units. Although a thermal equivalent base is generally taken, there is no general agreement on the equivalents to be used and each authority which publishes statistics and forecasts has a different interpretation both of units and of the items which are to be reckoned in consumption. No figures published by two different bodies can strictly be compared without adjustments which take their particular definitions into account. There is no need here to expand on the subject, save to note that the definition of a ton of oil equivalent used in OECD publications is the statistically convenient one of 10^7 kilocalories, which does not however correspond with crude oils that are in the actual production. As the subject of this chapter is the oil which may actually be exported by OPEC countries, the generally published figures of the OECD have been adjusted in the table below by a factor of 1.04 in order they may be more readily comparable. The OECD had prior to October 1973 been preparing a set of energy forecasts, which it now terms 'the base case', and after the rise in prices proceeded to evaluate alternatives which the publication refers to as the 'six dollar case' and the 'nine dollar case' in terms of 1972 dollars, which in terms of 1974 dollars become \$ 7.20 and \$ 10.80 cases. The various assumptions and predictions for other forms of energy do not need to be considered here except that it is to be remembered that the figures for oil are in all cases residuals deduced from the predictions for the other forms.

The OECD study is now generally quoted; it gives the total OECD requirements in 1980 as 2350 million tons in the \$ 7.20 case and 2090 in the \$ 10.80 one. Other estimates which have recently been made for the developed countries are a little higher, 2250 – 2500. The needs of the rest of the non-communist world may be

Table 4.2
OECD PROJECTED OIL REQUIREMENTS

		TOTAL ENERGY MILLION TONS OECD OIL EQUIVALENT	OIL REQUIREMENTS MILLION TONS OIL TOTAL	IMPORTS
US / CANADA				
1972		1924	874	233
1980	Base Case	2593	1197	533
	$ 7.20 Case	2467	1047	320
	$ 10.80 Case	2376	925	127
1985	Base Case	3174	1393	753
	$ 7.20 Case	2939	1077	290
	$ 10.80 Case	2771	935	–80
OECD EUROPE				
1972		1158	703	690
1980	Base Case	1730	1097	912
	$ 7.20 Case	1632	865	654
	$ 10.80 Case	1562	751	524
1985	Base Case	2245	1386	1144
	$ 7.20 Case	2121	1078	804
	$ 10.80 Case	2023	930	641
JAPAN				
1972		318	236	238
1980	Base Case	636	460	458
	$ 7.20 Case	577	394	392
	$ 10.80 Case	554	370	367
1985	Base Case	854	598	596
	$ 7.20 Case	758	491	486
	$ 10.80 Case	708	438	431

Note: The Base Case refers to conditions prior to October 1973; $ 7.20 Case and $ 10.80 Case – 1974 dollar terms – are prices for the marker crude, Arabian Light, f.o.b. Gulf.

Source: OECD Energy Prospects to 1985

460 – 540 million tons in 1980, and the total may be in the range 2700 – 2950 million tons.

On the supply side it is again felt to be beyond the scope of this book to examine non-oil forecasts in any detail. There is however an interest in assessing the extent to which non-OPEC oil production will contribute. Generally in this book the role of the communist world has been ignored, because it is too speculative. The very debatable assumptions made here are that USSR will continue to export about 50 million tons a year to the non-communist world, for the sake of the foreign exchange it can earn thereby, that it will endeavour to raise its production so that its exports to its Comecon partners continue to be the major share of their needs, in order to retain a degree of control over their economies, and that the remaining net requirements of these countries will expand at a fairly slow rate with comparatively small influence on the exports of OPEC countries.

The biggest surprise recently on the international oil scene has been the emergence of China as an exporter of oil. In 1973 it exported less than one million tons, in 1974 four million tons, almost all to Japan, and that rate is to be doubled in 1975. The further increases to be expected have not been spelled out with precision, but figures have been mentioned as high as 100 million tons by 1980, Such a rate of growth would parallel that achieved by Libya in the sixties and whether it is possible with Chinese resources is a question which cannot be answered in the outside world. A more conservative figure of 60 million tons has been adopted here and even that would represent a considerably achievement.

The North Sea has been the subject of a great number of articles and forecasts, but these have largely been based on scientific and economic grounds. In both Britain and Norway the politicians have now taken over as the determinants of possible growth, which reduces forecasting to mere guesswork. In the British sector each official forecast as it is published has to record further delays in the programme, due partly to technical difficulties and partly to the recurrent labour trouble in the onshore suppliers. Undoubtedly all the fields for which production equipment has been ordered will come on stream, but the development of others which have been counted on in forecasts has been put at risk by a combination of rapidly escalating costs and government demands. For the time being the prospects for further descoveries have been dimmed by an administration which appears unable to comprehend the risks of exploration and to learn from the lack of gas discoveries after 1967 – it is a coincidence that discovery of new mineral resources has recently been jeopardised by the policies of a number of governments. In Norway also developments in progress will come to fruition but here it is the government's fear of imported inflation and not its distrust of enterprise that is likely to keep further progress at a minimal level.

The Petroleum Economist in February 1975 recorded other interesting discoveries. Malaysia now produces five million tons but offshore finds could make 25-35 possible. There is a small discovery in Zaire, and one in the Greek Aegean is expected to be producing three million tons in 1977. New production in Mexico will enable it to export again after nearly forty years, with perhaps nine million tons in 1975. Offshore discoveries in Brazil will, according to officials, raise production from ten to fifty million tons by the end of the decade.

With the various alternatives already discussed, which are by no means exhaustive of the possibilities, the assembly of figures which can show the amount of OPEC production potentially required necessitates some selection. The figures below are suggested as a range within which the actual outcome may appear, discarding the more extreme possibilities arising from the combination of forecasts. The 1985 figures are merely tentative; nobody acquainted with the history of energy will expect anything else. The 1980 figures are the general focus of interest at present, but before that 1977 may be an important year and forecasts are included. It was suggested in the chapter on prices that a world recovery in 1976-77 is likely, before any of the new alternatives are able to make an effective contribution, and then the fuel saving measures that have shown themselves practicable under recession will be under severe test. The figures for potential production by the OPEC producers outside the Middle East assume that the need to maintain revenues by a high level of production will be paramount for them, and that the amount of exports required from the Middle East will be governed accordingly.

To translate the forecasts of exports into forecasts of revenue, an assumption has to be made on the future of prices. The current

Table 4.3
FUTURE ME OIL SUPPLY

	Million tons			
	1974	1977	1980	1985
Non-communist world oil consumption	2274	2480 – 2650	2700 – 2950	3050 – 3500
Supply				
US/Canada	593	640 – 660	720 – 800	800 – 900
Other non-OPEC production	224	330 – 360	510 – 540	750
Net imports from communist states	52	70	110	110
OPEC production outside Middle East	389	430	450	470
	1258	1470 – 1520	1890 – 2000	2180 ?
Required of ME-OPEC producers	1016	960 – 1180	700 – 1060	1100 ?
Add for unrecorded stock changes and military use	+108	+ 30	+ 30	+ 30
ME-OPEC production	1124			
Subtract for producers' internal demand	– 31	– 40	– 60	– 110
ME-OPEC exports	1093	950 – 1170	670 – 1030	1020 ?

government export price of $ 10.46 for Arabian Light is already close to the higher level assumed by the OECD forecasts and if OPEC makes further increases this autumn, such as are being considered, it will probably exceed even that level. The OPEC countries have made various proposals about indexing oil prices, starting in 1973 with references to the cost of other energy, changing with the boom in prices for the primary producers to an index related to the prices of other raw materials and, when those started to fall, changing again to the index for manufactured goods which has been rising sharply, partly as a result of the increase in the price of oil and other raw materials.

Similarly the adoption of SDR instead of dollars as the accounting unit in which the price of oil would be expressed seemed just a possibility at the start of 1975, was strongly supported by statements from several OPEC countries in the spring, but by June had lost favour as the dollar has recovered on the exchanges. the competent statisticians of OPEC can be relied on to produce figures to seem to justify in public any price move the ministers may decide.

The OPEC countries depend on the industrialised ones not only as customers for most of the oil they export but also as suppliers of the goods and services they need. It would not be in their interest to induce such a recession as to imperil their supplies and they are conscious that the increase in oil prices was a factor in the deepest depression in the world's economy since the war. Whatever may be said in public, they are aware of some figures such as the following.

Table 4.4

INDEX OF PRICES

Year	Index of world manufactured goods export prices	Index of government oil revenue per barrel
	Base 1959 = 100	
1960	102	99
1965	107	110
1970	123	116
1971	129	166
1972	140	190
1973	164	508
1974	208	1224

Source: Financial Times October 1974
1974 estimates updated

There would appear to be a definite division both within OPEC and within some of the countries on the future of prices, although it should not be exaggerated. In the short run the world has no alternative to OPEC oil, and one side wishes to adopt the standard cartel approach of restricting production to push prices up further. The other side sees that to accelerate inflation in the industrialised countries is to reduce the real value of oil revenues – it is estimated that the present level of prices has an inflationary effect of between 1.5 and 4 per cent varying with a country's dependence on oil imports. One side aims for the maximum present revenues, the other is conscious of the present lower level of demand and the long-term effect of hastening the development of substitutes for oil. What compromise may be reached is not clear, but it seems probable that for the next two years oil prices may be increased by rather more than would be necessary to maintain their value in real terms. After 1977 other factors will come into play.

The total of OPEC oil revenues as a result of the 1974 price increases is well known but the figures for individual countries may not be. In the table the values for earlier years are taken from publications by *Pirinc* and the quantities exported in 1973 and 1974 from *The Petroleum Economist.*

The revenues given are those due in respect of the oil exported, whereas revenues reported by governments are those received within the accounting period. Sometimes there have been differences which are to be explained by the settlement of large retrospective claims which the governments have made, with interest. Always there are leads and lags because payment dates differ between countries and differ for royalty, for tax and for direct purchases. The Bank of England and the US Treasury both estimate the outstandings for the OPEC countries at the end of 1974 at $ 15 or 16 billion – at the end of 1973 they may have been $ 4 billion – and the Bank has put their actual receipts at $ 94.5 billion. In the two years there was a number of changes in the value of the government revenues per barrel and the figures above are averages generally of values calculated by the *Middle East Economic Survey.* The total revenues agree well with calculations by *Rassegna Petrolifera,* though not with those in other journals, and they in turn make a total close to that of the Bank of England.

In the past the figures of revenues given by government and

Table 4.5
GOVERNMENT OIL REVENUES TO 1974
Estimates on Basis of oil exported

		1960	1965	1970	1973	1974
SAUDI ARABIA						
Exports	(million barrels)	474	787	1359	2850	3060
Revenue	(million dollars)	355	655	1200	5600	28900
"	($ per barrel)	0. 75	0. 83	0. 88	1. 96	9. 45
IRAN						
Exports	(million barrels)	356	644	1332	2037	2072
Revenue	(million dollars)	285	522	1093	4200	20100
"	($ per barrel)	0. 80	0. 81	0. 82	2. 07	9. 69
KUWAIT						
Exports	(million barrels)	608	851	1082	1078	905
Revenue	(million dollars)	465	671	895	2100	8500
"	($ per barrel)	0. 76	0. 79	0. 83	1. 97	9. 43
IRAQ						
Exports	(million barrels)	339	459	545	705	670
Revenue	(million dollars)	266	375	521	1600	7100
"	($ per barrel)	0. 79	0. 82	0. 96	2. 27	10. 60
QATAR						
Exports	(million barrels)	63	83	133	208	189
Revenue	(million dollars)	54	68	122	460	1900
"	($ per barrel)	0. 86	0. 82	0. 92	2. 21	9. 94
ABU DHABI						
Exports	(million barrels)	–	102	254	475	518
Revenue	(million dollars)	–	33	233	1100	5300
"	($ per barrel)	–	0. 32	0. 92	2. 36	10. 21
OTHER GULF						
Exports	(million barrels)	16	20	180	212	226
Revenue	(million dollars)	13	16	150	400	2100
"	($ per barrel)	0. 79	0. 81	0. 84	1. 88	9. 29
LIBYA						
Exports	(million barrels)	–	443	1188	794	547
Revenue	(million dollars)	–	371	1295	2400	7000
"	($ per barrel)	–	0. 84	1. 09	3. 02	12. 80
TOTAL MIDDLE EAST						
Exports	(million barrels)	1856	3389	6072	8359	8187
Revenue	(million dollars)	1439	2713	5509	17860	80900
"	($ per barrel)	0. 78	0. 80	0. 91	2. 14	9. 88

Sources: see text

industry sources could usually be reconciled. Revenue figures which some of the governments have announced for 1974 are however so far below estimates as to defy the normal financial explanations. The editor of *The Petroleum Economist* in a footnote to the article cited above remarked on 'the current difficulty in arriving at reasonably accurate figures not only for revenues but also for oil production and exports. In the past, when operations were largely in the hands of the oil companies, it was possible to obtain from them precise figures, but now the exporting countries have taken over most of the responsibility this is no longer so'. Even when the revenues paid by the companies were almost the total received by the governments there were sometimes discrepancies between the precise figures and those announced by the governments which could not be accounted for by retrospective or delayed amounts. As the governments increase direct sales the facts about their revenues may become further obscured.

When announced government revenues have in the past been less than the known figures after adjustment for leads and lags, four possible explanations have been found. There may be confusion between calendar and fiscal year (see Appendix B), usually a simple mistake by spokesman or reporter but on occasion deliberately indulged in for public relations purposes; in due course appearance of the full official record clarifies these cases. Sometimes money from oil revenues appears to be paid out the moment it is received, so never figuring in the balances; probably payments on arms account are the reason. A third possibility is that in barter transactions the monetary value is omitted from oil revenues. A fourth practice was rare but is becoming commoner; payments to the national oil company for direct purchases are entered in the accounts of that organisation and not reckoned as part of the government's revenues. Unless the accounts of the NOC show the receipts clearly and are published at the same time as the government revenues it is not easy to arrive at an accurate assessment of the revenues, while there are indications that in some cases part of the revenues is credited to accounts about which nothing is published. So it may happen that statements about the government oil revenues may be technically correct but the sum reported is very different from the country's total oil receipts.

The amounts referred to here as the government oil revenues mean as in the past the total of a country's profits from the export of oil. On its direct sales each country is now having to bear its proportion of the costs of operation, and its receipts from the companies are at present reduced until purchase of its participation share is completed, but both deductions are small compared with the profits.

At the average level of government revenue per barrel which is received on exports in 1975 the exports forecast in Table 4.3 would earn for the Middle East producers total revenues of 71-88 billion dollars in 1977 and 50-77 in 1980, compared with 80.9 in 1974. The World Bank has estimated that to keep its value in real terms the government selling price of $ 10.46 per barrel may need to rise to $ 14.25 by 1980. If in fact corresponding rises take place the total government revenues would be 79-98 in 1977 and 68-105 billion dollars in 1980 in cash terms. The question of how such revenues may be divided among the individual producers is considered after their requirements have been described.

CHAPTER 5

Expenditure of the Revenues

The great increase in the oil earnings took place so rapidly and unexpectedly that although government budgets and development plans have expanded to correspond they are still in a state of flux with important changes every few months. Certainly there has been a great relaxation of any sort of restraint on government expenditure, exemplified by the growth in the rate of imports almost monthly throughout 1974. The increase in expenditure has been reflected in the rapid growth of consumer demand, which has caused difficulties for the governments endeavouring to check the rate of inflation. The ordinary or current budgets of the governments, while including consumable materials and external services, are largely made up of expenditure on personnel in the form of wages, salaries, and social benefits, resulting in increased spending power of the ordinary individual. Nevertheless although the import statistics suggest that goods for personal consumption have been increasing rapidly they do not form the major portion of the total requirements.

Among the ordinary budget headings there is one in which material purchases are far from negligible. Each of the countries has defence as the principal item in its expenditure allocations, and while the governments are mindful that a satisfactory level of salaries for defence personnel is an important factor contributing to the stability of the state, the military appetite for new equipment is insatiable. Detailed information of purchases of arms is seldom available, both as regards the quantities of supplies and as regards the terms of payment offered. Although major orders for equipment placed in the western countries receive attention, it is less easy to account for the many minor items and the spares which military equipment requires in quantity. The figures in governments' accounts relating to arms purchases are not detailed, and at least in some cases refer to the amounts required for annual instalments on the various contracts rather than the total of purchases during the year. Hence to forecast the sums that will appear under this heading in forthcoming years is not a thing that can be done with any accuracy.

The development plans of the governments, which largely account for the import of capital goods, will be examined in more detail in later chapters. The outline figures only are considered here although they need to be read with caution. Governments seem to have little difficulty in spending up to the allocations in the ordinary budget, but so far as development is concerned the published figures are more often aspirations than expectations. Browning thought

'A man's reach should exceed his grasp
Or what's a heaven for'

and makers of development plans take the same attitude. To the extent that the executors of the plans are stimulated thereby the practice has its uses, but it makes difficult a realistic assessment of performance.

Table 5.1
SUMMARY OF GOVERNMENT EXPENDITURE PLANS

$ billion (1974 dollars)

	Planned Government Expenditure					Current Development Plan Average Annual Rate of Expenditure
	Year	Current*	including Defence	Capital	Total	
Iran	75/76	20.2	7.7	6.3	26.5	11.1
Iraq (at annual rate)	75	3.7	(1.3)	4.4	8.1	3.4
Kuwait	74/75	0.9	0.1	0.6	1.5	
Saudi Arabia	74/75	5.5	2.8	7.4	12.9	28.8
Qatar	75/76	0.6	—	0.5	1.1	
Abu Dhabi	75	2.3	(0.2)	0.9	3.2	
Oman	74	0.3	0.1	0.3	0.7	
Libya	74	2.5	0.4	2.5	5.0	2.8

* Current includes Aid but excludes semi-governmental budgets

() Estimates

In most of the Middle East capital expenditure on any large scale remains a matter for governments. In Iraq this is a consequence of the Ba'ath party rule but even in Saudi Arabia, where it is official government policy to encourage private enterprise to the maximum, the state must undertake the major projects. Development of infrastructure is a primary requirement everywhere, and necessarily falls within the government sector. Transport and communications are often unable to handle the materials for many other developments scheduled, and ports, roads, railways perhaps, telecommunications and air services must all rank high in the priory list. The construction sector needs to produce the offices from which the vastly expanded activities of the state can be controlled, the schools in which the next generation of nationals may be trained to enable them to take a greater part in the running of their country, and above all the housing to replace the tents and reed-mat huts. Power and water supplies are required in rapidly increasing quantities as the standard of living improves; and in the Gulf states in particular water is of an importance that it is difficult for westerners to grasp. The imports that these programmes require have formed a large part of the countries' totals so far and will in the near future expand considerably faster than personal requirements.

At the same time there are limits to the rate at which expansion can be expected, both physical and human limits. The financial limits have disappeared, but on the physical side the transport and port facilities in particular are likely to force governments to choose between priorities in the other sectors.

The human limitations come into the account because it is difficult to increase suddenly the range of activities which can be controlled with any success by management, whether it be management by a government department or in private enterprise. At too rapid a rate of build-up there comes a point when control is clearly lost and a period of retrenchment is necessary in order to gather up the reins again. Recent histories of the states which have gained sudden wealth afford several examples of the process.

There is some difficulty in ascertaining actual government expenditure by the Middle East states because the figures, if published at all, appear very late and do not receive the publicity given to budgets. From the evidence available it is not easy to see consistent relationships between budgetary provisions and amounts finally reported. No attempt therefore has been made to assess possible variations in the expenditure plans in the above table, and for projected budget requirements in 1977 and 1980 a growth rate of twenty per cent has been assumed.

In the above summary the amounts which the governments are providing for aid in their budgets have been included under current account, but provisions merely for investment of surpluses have been excluded. Most governments also publish supplementary budgets for semi-governmental organisations, which may be revenue-earning, such as electricity authorities, or largely maintained, such as universities. Generally it would seem that net figures are recorded among the ordinary budget items, and inclusion of the gross figures as part of the total government requirements would be misleading.

The oil revenues have two functions in the economies of the producer countries. They provide the bulk of the revenues required to cover government expenditure and they also furnish the foreign exchange required for the imports of goods and services. The forecasts that were made of the producers' surpluses in 1974 proved to have been overstated by not allowing sufficiently for the rate of increase in imports which in spite of handicaps they managed to achieve.

The increase of 75 per cent overall which the table shows was more than twice the expected figure, and even Kuwait in its already advanced stage of development increased imports by nearly 50 per cent. Some of the increase is due to inflation, as the UN price index for exports from the industrialised countries (1970 = 100) rose from 136 in 1973 to 169 in 1974. The reaction of the countries to their increased spending power soon manifested itself and, although the first quarter of the year did not show a large increase on preceding quarters, from the second quarter onwards the acceleration was marked. Iran and Iraq particularly felt a freedom from previous financial constraints, but the increases in the other countries were unexpectedly large.

It is of interest to compare these figures with those reported by the main industrialised countries.

The statistics show that in general the exports from these trading partners have more than doubled, suggesting that a large part of the increased import demand was for the more sophisticated goods. Although food prices continued to rise throughout 1974 those of

Table 5.2
ME COUNTRIES IMPORTS

$ Millions

Years		Iran	Iraq	Kuwait	Saudi Arabia	Qatar	UAE	Libya	Total
1972		2410	713	797	1136	138	496	1038	6728
1973		3370	899	1042	1993	195	825	1723	10047
1974		5974	(1900)	1529	3473	271	(1392)	3140	(17679)
Quarters *									
1973	I	824	224	235	385	40	157	346	2211
	II	731	202	258	476	47	210	419	2343
	III	866	236	248	478	53	196	465	2542
	IV	950	238	305	580	54	263	494	2884
1974	I	1057	253	278	612	48	286	497	3031
	II	1272	428	387	850	72	400	825	4234
	III	1557	495	375	951	72		909	
	IV	2088		492	1060	79		913	

Source: International Financial Statistics: total imports c.i.f.

* Quarterly provisional figures may not agree with annual totals; for 1974 estimates are shown in brackets.

other raw materials declined steeply after the first quarter, to the benefit of those producers which also have manufacturing industries.

It is possible to read too much into detailed statistics of foreign trade. A large proportion of the imports into the Middle East comprises goods destined for capital projects, and the arrival of a shipment of particular value can often have considerably effect on percentage comparisons either between suppliers or month by month, unless the circumstances are recognised. There are nevertheless interesting points in the table such as the close relation between Italy and Libya, while distance makes Japan a less important trading partner for Libya than for the Gulf states. It is also apparent that Iraq has been able to make use of the large rise in disposable income by a remarkable increase in its rate of imports from the industrialised countries, which should enable its development to proceed more smoothly than in the past. The classification of trade for the two previous years is available, and the importance of machinery and transport equipment in the requirements of the Middle East countries can hardly be better shown.

Table 5.3

OECD EXPORTERS TO MIDDLE EAST

$ million

Exports f.o.b.

1973 first half
1973 second half
1974 first half
1974 second half

From	Iran	Iraq	Kuwait	Saudi Arabia	Qatar UAE & Bahrain	Libya
US	375	13	59	202	79	60
	397	43	60	240	103	43
	583	73	85	353	160	53
	1152	212	124	482	183	86
UK	181	35	46	68	114	67
	232	31	43	74	115	83
	241	51	49	127	156	65
	388	92	90	156	155	82
FRANCE	94	41	23	23	67	85
	110	43	23	33	53	116
	107	100	29	52	49	169
	150	114	35	69	37	193
GERMANY	278	17	30	53	22	103
	440	25	40	73	26	107
	472	76	72	116	49	180
	669	298	88	172	82	222
ITALY	68	11	15	31	9	182
	109	20	24	47	16	270
	107	37	21	61	22	348
	176	59	44	73	38	506
ALL OECD EUROPE	821	191	154	253	265	541
	1153	206	186	349	266	710
	1210	398	259	515	333	971
	1806	746	354	696	493	1284
JAPAN	203	19	75	186	105	43
	283	31	92	203	113	68
	365	113	115	245	171	106
	649	362	165	432	246	128

Source: OECD Statistics of Foreign Trade: Monthly Bulletin

Table 5.4
CLASSIFICATION OF EXPORTS FROM DEVELOPED COUNTRIES TO THE MIDDLE EAST
$ Million

		EEC	USA	JAPAN	ALL DEVELOPED
All Exports	1972	3970	1660	1030	7690
	1973	5590	2210	1610	10900
SITC Sections O & 1	1972	290	185	16	620
Food, Drink and	%	7. 3	11. 1	1. 6	8. 1
Tobacco	1973	460	345	21	1000
	%	8. 2	15. 6	1. 3	9. 2
Section 7	1972	2010	810	375	3520
Machinery and	%	50. 6	48. 8	36. 4	45. 8
Transport	1973	2670	990	600	4700
Equipment	%	47. 8	44. 8	37. 3	43. 1
Division 67	1972	210	40	210	530
Iron and	%	5. 3	2. 4	20. 4	6. 9
Steel	1973	415	46	395	940
	%	7. 4	2. 1	24. 5	8. 6
Section 6	1972	780	125	380	1550
(exc. Div. 67)	%	19. 6	7. 5	36. 9	20. 2
Manufactured	1973	1105	180	525	2240
Materials	%	19. 8	8. 1	32. 6	20. 6
& Section 8					
Other Manufacture					
Section 5	1972	510	70	20	700
Chemicals inc.	%	12. 8	4. 2	1. 9	9. 1
Pharmaceutical	1973	710	110	25	1020
	%	12. 7	5. 0	1. 6	9. 4

Source: UN Monthly Bulletin of Statistics

The term 'Middle East' in this table excludes Libya and the comparative proximity of Japan to the Gulf is again clearly reflected in its exports of iron and steel and other manufactured materials. On the other hand the consistency of some of the other figures would seem to emphasise the entrenched positions of traditional suppliers.

Only some of the relevant figures for 1974 are currently available, and in spite of the big increase in totals the relative importance of the various classes of export do not appear to have altered significantly. There are always some special features, such as the opening of new colour television services in the Gulf bringing increases in that section of the classification, while food exports from the wheat-growing countries suggest that 1974 was again a year of poor harvests in the Middle East.

While the growth of imports of consumer goods and particularly of consumer durables is likely to be rapid, as there is more general benefit from the increased wealth of the producing states, the principal growth is likely to be seen in capital goods. In Iran and Saudi Arabia, and to a lesser extent in other states, there is positive encouragement by the governments for the development of private enterprise; the merchant tradition remains strong, activities in the services sector are growing fast, but the initiation of manufacturing ventures needs a long-term outlook. In this process it may be that the banks which have specialized in other parts of the world in backing entrepreneurial activity may have an important role to play in fostering developments in the producing countries. The major enterprises which will call for multi-million dollar imports are those of the governments; and among the exporting countries those who take trouble to associate themselves with the plans of the Middle East governments and firmly support their own manufacturers are likely to benefit from the increase in trade.

While at the start of 1974 there was considerable apprehension about the future of the surpluses which the oil producers would accumulate, the problem has so far been more manageable than was expected. In part this stems from the considerable increase in imports – apart from those in the Middle East the other OPEC countries increased their imports from 9.3 billion dollars in 1973 to 14.5 in 1974. At that time also there was considerable discussion about the recycling of the producers' revenues, and a certain amount of confusion about what recycling meant. It should have been apparent at an early stage that some of the worries were unfounded. There was nowhere for the producers to place the larger part of the funds they were accumulating except with the financial institutions of the west and in that sense recycling was automatic. It is now better understood that recycling is a problem to be settled among the consumer countries themselves, arranging that while OPEC countries place their surpluses where they wish the financial arrangements among the recipients provide for funds to go where they are needed. The \$ 25 billion fund originally suggested by Dr. Kissinger and being constituted under the International Energy Agency is a fall-back scheme to achieve redistribution if it proves beyond the capacity of the normal financial processes.

In fact the surpluses of the producers have been of such size that only the New York and London markets could cope with more than a fraction of them, and it can be seen that placements by the producers have made expected use of their facilities while endeavouring to maintain a spread of interests.

Table 5.5

ESTIMATED DEPLOYMENT OF OIL PRODUCERS' SURPLUSES

			$ billions		1974	1975	
	Q.I	Q.II	Q.III	Q.IV	Total	Q.I	Q.II
UK							
Sterling							
Government stocks and bills	0.8	0.8	0.9	1.1	3.6	0.7	– 0.2
Other deposits and investments	–	0.9	1.4	0.1	2.4	0.1	– 0.1
Foreign currency deposits and loans	2.5	5.0	3.7	3.8	15.00	1.7	0.5
US							
Government and agency securities	0.5	1.4	2.3	1.8	6.0	0.9	0.4
Other deposits and investments	0.6	0.9	2.7	0.8	5.0	– 0.2	1.1
OTHER COUNTRIES							
Deposits	1.5	3.5	1.5	2.5	9.0	2.5	2.5
Bilaterial facilities and investments	1.1	2.5	3.0	5.0	11.6	1.8	3.5
INTERNATIONAL ORGANISATIONS	–	0.5	0.8	2.3	3.6	1.2	0.3
TOTAL	7.0	15.5	16.3	17.4	56.2	8.7	8.0
Estimated Producers' Receipts	11.7	24.4	29.3	29.1	94.5	25.8	25.6

Source: Bank of England Quarterly Bulletin

It is emphasised that the producers have displayed a great sense of responsibility in managing the funds they are accumulating and are as conscious as statesmen in the west of the dangers of disturbance to the world's financial system. For some of the producers who foresee the need to use in the near future the reserves they are now accumulating there has naturally been a tendency to hold funds at short notice while of those that will surely remain in surplus Saudi Arabia has only recently begun to think of investment in the longer term. The preceding table may be compared with the figures for official reserves as published by the IMF.

Table 5.6
OFFICIAL RESERVES OF ME OIL PRODUCERS

$ Million

	Iran	Iraq	Kuwait	Saudi Arabia	Libya	Total of five
End 1972	960	782	363	2500	2925	7530
End 1973	1237	1553	501	3877	2127	9295
End March 1974	2160	2238	657	4864	2478	12397
End June 1974	5540	2878	959	7087	2996	19460
End September 1974	6370	2981	1037	11549	3682	25639
End December 1974	8383	3273	1397	14285	3616	30954
End March 1975	8331	2910	1711	19018	2984	34954
End June 1975	9686	(2807 May)	1672	20589	2355	(37109)

Source: International Financial Statistics

The definition of official reserves essentially implies gold and short-term funds and there was originally some misunderstanding of the position. Kuwait in particular keeps only a fraction of its reserves in short-term funds regularly reported, and in contrast with the official figure of $ 657 million at the end of March 1974 other government holdings amounted to $ 3681 million, having risen in twelve months from $ 1454, whereas the official reserve figures for Iran and Iraq do not reflect the amounts of their long-term debts.

As the surpluses continue to accumulate there is the question whether the markets will be able to accommodate them. In this respect the size of the public debt in US and UK is such that the funds could easily be absorbed, while the entry in the above table of foreign currency deposits in the UK is largely accounted for by funds placed in the Eurodollar market, also large and ready to accept increased deposits from the producers. On the other hand the producing governments, like other investors, are displaying anxiety about finding long-term investments which offer a good return combined with limited risk, and at the current rates of inflation are finding it difficult to maintain the value of their savings.

Some of the surplus states have been broadening the field of their investments; the Kuwait Investment Fund and the Abu Dhabi Investment Advisory Committee have been functioning for a number of years and there are now several similar organisations, often more than one to a country. Some of their activities, such as purchases of property both in England and the US, have received public attention, and shareholdings in a number of industrial companies are also coming to light. Much of this investment merely shows the normal growth of a portfolio in the accustomed sense. Kuwait in particular has made it clear that it does not intend to go in for operational control but prefers to keep its investments in any particular company under the ten per cent at which the possibility of control arises, although Daimler-Benz was an exception. In contrast, Iran's purchase of 25 per cent of Krupps, the great German steel firm, definitely envisages a coordination of activities in the two countries.

As a result of these purchases the Germans are taking steps to restrict the possibility of foreigners gaining control of their industries. A similar note can be heard from the United States, where a Kuwaiti investment in a West Coast bank, with an effective say in its management, had to be dropped after action in the courts. It is somewhat ironic to consider the position of the industrialised countries in this respect, since a considerable stimulus to their economic growth, not to mention the complete development of the oil industry in the Middle East, stemmed from their investments in overseas countries. The fact that they are showing themselves resentful when overseas countries wish to return the compliment and invest in them is one of the less pleasant features of the current world monetary system. The xenophobic attitudes are not all one-sided, however, and the first meeting of producers, consumers and third world has done little to mitigate them.

Another important way in which the producers are putting their revenues to work is in the form of aid. There is a certain amount of misunderstanding about developments to date. The description of some of the loans which the countries have offered makes it unclear whether they can really rank as aid, being on what seem to be normal commercial terms. The scope for development loans and investments is vast, but so far only Egypt and to a lesser extent other Muslim countries have been favoured recipients; the oil producing countries appear to mistrust the security of investment in other LDCs. An alternative form of painless aid has been shown in that given by Iraq and Iran to India, furnishing a supply of oil but requiring only a proportion of it to be settled directly, with the rest establishing a credit balance to be paid off by goods over future years.

The accumulation of surplus funds will of itself generate investment income. Already for 1975 it is estimated that interest and dividends may reach $ 7 billion and in two years' time be double that amount. Even if in later years the populous countries will have little surplus and investment earnings, the other producers will continue to accumulate, and the total income to rise though at a slower rate. Of the producers only Iran has significant non-oil exports – $ 635 million in 1973/74 – but when the export-oriented facilities in which the countries are investing come into operation there should be other figures in the accounts. A third element to be reckoned in the predictions of the balance of payments is the outgoings for services. The number of foreigners who will be partaking in the development of the states, either by direct employment or through consultants and contractors, will be large and foreign exchange outgoings will therefore be considerable. Approximately the sum for services to the Middle East producers may be balanced by the investment income and non-oil export earnings until 1980, at least to the degree of accuracy with which it is possible to forecast the much larger sums of oil revenues and import requirements.

The expectation of surplus revenues continuing to accumulate to some at least of the producers has resulted in widely different estimates of the total surplus which will arise. At first, early in 1974, sums between $ 200 and 650 billion by 1980 were suggested. Late in the year forecasts of $ 800, 1200 or even 1600 billion in 1985 appeared, while other experts were predicting that an actual decline in the total surplus would start in 1977 or 1978. In the spring of

1975 sights had been lowered to a 1980 target of between \$ 100 and 460 million, with \$ 200 – 250 most often forecast.

The wide differences in the estimates of the accumulated surplus reflect different views on the use the countries will make of their revenues. The two essential functions of the oil revenues, disregarding contributions from other activities which are generally small, are to cover the governmental expenditure and to cover import needs. The difficulty of estimating the former, and the assumptions

Table 5.7
PRODUCERS' NEEDS TO EXPORT

million tons of oil (b)

	Exports	Forecast Capacity (a)	Exports to cover Government budgets (b) (c)		Exports to cover Import requirements (b) (d)	
	1974	1980	1977	1980	1977	1980
Iran	283	400	510	880	175	340
Iraq	90	200	150	260	55	105
Kuwait	124	165	35	60	45	90
Saudi Arabia	418	660	300	520	100	200
Qatar	25	35	20	35	10	15
UAE	81	145	60	100	40	75
Oman (e)	15	18	15	25	15	25
Libya	72	110	100	175	75	140
TOTAL (e) of ME-OPEC	**1093**	**1715**	**1175**	**2030**	**500**	**965**

Possible Export Demand (Table 4.3) 1977 950 – 1170
1980 670 – 1030

Notes: (a) OECD "Energy Prospects" quoting M.I.T. May 1974
(b) Assuming constant price relationship
(c) Based on explanation in text page 51.
(d) Based on explanation in text page 61.
(e) Oman is omitted from totals.

VARIATIONS IN REQUIRED OIL EXPORT RATES
Example : IRAN, to cover import requirements

A. Different import growths	1974	75	76	77	78-80
Growth rate in Base Case %	76	40	25	25	25
Growth rate in High Case %		50	33	33	25
Growth rate in Low Case %		35	25	15	15

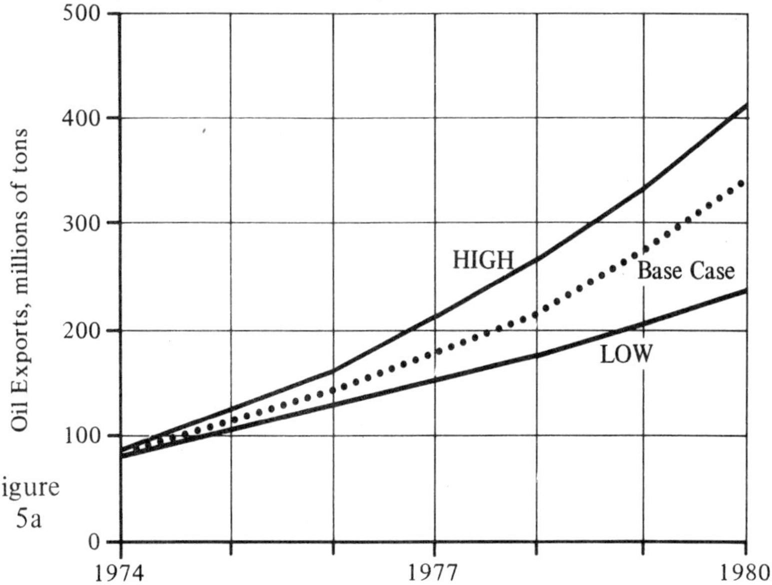

Figure 5a

B. with Differential Inflation

High Case	;	oil price increasing 5% less than import prices
Base Case	;	oil price increasing same rate as import prices
Low Case	;	oil price increasing 5% more than import prices

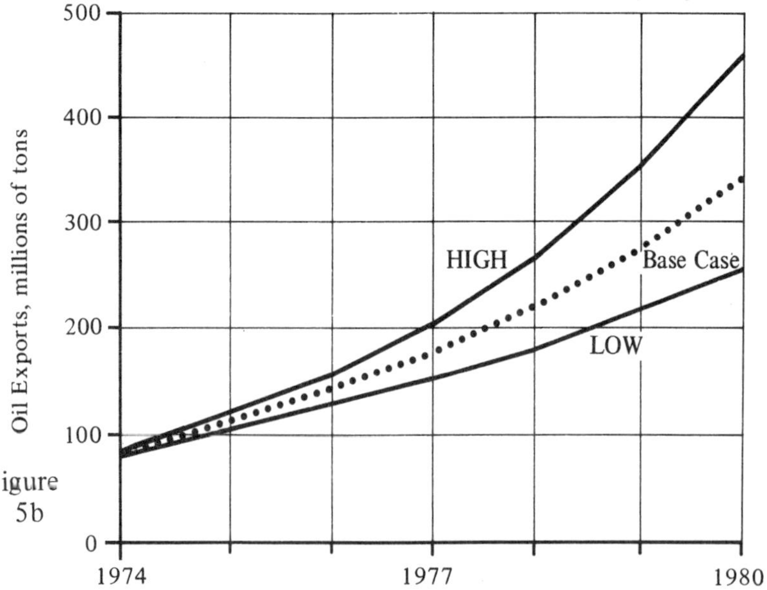

Figure 5b

made here in doing so, were mentioned earlier in the chapter. The imports in 1974 are known, and it is assumed for the calculations here that the 75 per cent rise in 1974 will be followed by 40 per cent in 1975 and 25 per cent thereafter.

The resulting figures are expressed in the table as the quantity of oil which must be exported to cover the financial requirements. The governments' revenues per barrel are those in effect in 1975, and a constant price relationship is implied.

Recently Saudi ministers have been saying that the country's actual needs can be met by exports of 175 million tons. In Libya, where exports in the first half of 1975 have been at an annual rate of less than 50 million tons, the government has stated that it needs the equivalent of 85 million. Iranian statesmen have emphasised that the country will have no surplus by 1977. Figures in the table may be judged in the light of these three statements. In Iran the non-oil items are of appreciable effect, providing the equivalent of some 35 million tons of oil to the revenues and 10 million tons to the exports, while the industries aiming for exports are expected to increase their contribution substantially.

The assumptions which have been made are such that clearly the figures are no more than a guide to expectations. The government revenues per barrel may be increased by more than the increase in domestic or import prices, bringing a reduction in oil export requirements. The budgetary estimates are very tentative and it would not be surprising if actual figures differed by up to forty per cent. On the other hand the rates of growth assumed for imports will probably be regarded as too low, although in a study by the Walter J. Levy consultancy the rate of growth of imports was reckoned at only fifteen per cent.

The critical importance of the table lies in the comparison between the quantities the Middle East oil producers will need to export and the requirements of the consumers. The days are gone when a producing country could contemplate reverting to a subsistence economy; although the country would survive its rulers would not. The estimates here are far from precise but are of the order that the exporters must aim for. The indications for Libya are interesting, as it is generally taken to be among the surplus countries, but it may be noted that other experts put its capacity in 1980 at 150 million tons; actual information is particularly scarce. The other surplus countries show no surprises; Iranian budget expectations are clearly overstated, and the comparatively modest import figures for Iraq may be the result of projecting from too low a base. Some consequences of varying the assumptions may be presented graphically.

Two US banks in the spring of 1975 issued estimates of current accounts and accumulated surpluses up to 1980 for OPEC as a whole. Morgan Guaranty suggested that the overall current account would move into deficit in 1979 with the surpluses reaching a maximum of $ 248 billion, while Irving Trust suggested 1980 and $ 265 billion. For the latter the economists Dr. Arnold Safer and Anne Mills went further, and on the assumption that non-communist world demand in 1977 might be no more than 2375 million tons put forward the alternative possibility that the need of OPEC countries to export would then exceed demand, competition develop and prices fall. Deficits would thus start in 1978, with the peak of the surpluses a little over $ 200 billion, but admittedly real price increases up to 1977 would defer the break.

The calculations here for the Middle East producers do not support the argument for 1977 as the critical year. The budget requirements may not be met but are flexible, and at any reasonable rate of increase import requirements will be covered. Of the other OPEC countries, Nigeria and Indonesia have realistic programmes, Venezuela will still be in surplus and Algeria is experienced in living beyond its means.

Around 1980 however the need to export may well exceed demand. Even allowing for budgetary distortions several governments may be in difficulties with their expenditure, and the cover for projected import requirements may be near the ceiling of consumer demand, and at a faster rate of growth might be above it. With the reserves which they have accumulated the governments will not be under immediate pressure, and the rate of decline in prices assumed in the Irving Trust paper underestimates the effect of time-contract sales in retarding change. Nevertheless, with production potential in the ME-OPEC countries probably double the demand for exports, some producers will surely be tempted to place their own needs above those of their partners. Even if they do not, they will need to be sustained in their resolution by loans from countries remaining in surplus, which in practice means Saudi Arabia, and the overall surplus will cease to accumulate. It is thought that the higher figures which have been suggested for the cumulative surplus are improbable, and the problem of dealing with them in the world's financial system will not arise. There will be enough problems in handling the surpluses forecast here, and the experience of established financial institutions is likely to be in demand.

CHAPTER 6

Banking

An alphabetical list of banks and institutions mentioned in this chapter will be found at the end in Appendix C.

(1) Modern banking in the Gulf has developed more or less contemporaneously with the growth of the oil industry. Some of the first tablets of history however deal largely with trade, showing Sumer – Iraq in contact with Magan – Oman via Dilmun – Bahrain. In each centre the voyager could already call for finance and supplies on an agent of the merchant in his home town, while the principals settled their accounts in correspondence with each other. Such early banking practices extended the possibilities of simple trade, and records in subsequent times show them continuing in use until today.

The growth of the great eastern trading companies of Europe, of Britain, France and Holland, followed a similar style with the agents of the home companies living overseas in 'factories' as they were termed. The nineteenth century saw multilateral trading develop from simple direct deals, and the growth of 'eastern exchange banks' bringing their skills to handle the financial complications. Another important activity of these banks was the establishment of a regular exchange for currency. Hitherto many different forms of local currency were in use, often in limited amounts, and the fluctuating exchange rates gave difficulty to regular traders. By taking the market from a lot of fragmented transactions in the bazaar and establishing a regular basis the exchange banks were able to smooth the flow of trade.

There were still risks to be run, and in the 1890s the eastern banks were in particular difficulties owing to the worldwide fall in the value of silver. The events gave William Jennings Bryan his place in American history and are immortalised for every playgoer in Miss Prism's instruction: 'Omit the chapter on the Fall of the Rupee. It is somewhat too sensational'.

Even now it is not possible to say that banking services in the Gulf are developed to an extent that is adequate for the personal wealth that is available. The habits of trade still dominate the thoughts of those to whom the wealth is accruing in the Gulf, and the quick returns and freedom of action to which they are accustomed do not encourage them to look to longer-term investment. When they do, the traditional choice is to put money into land and property, and the Lebanon in particular has seen a great development as a result of such investment. The idea of developing long-term businesses with initial slow repayment is still somewhat novel and therefore the banking services which should match that process have still to develop.

In parallel with the growth of commercial banking in the Middle East the need of central banking institutions was felt. One of the purposes of the International Monetary Fund on its foundation was to encourage such growth of responsibility in the less developed countries, usually through the preliminary stage of a currency board. Some of the Gulf countries have availed themselves of IMF assistance while others have chosen their own advisers and by now this development is almost complete.

Nevertheless the sheer weight of money is bringing rapid changes, and description of the present situation in the various countries is unavoidably of temporary value. At the time of writing there is a standstill throughout the area on new banks opening, since the UAE, the last oil producing country in which establishment was freely permitted, imposed restrictions in February 1975. Outside the field of retail banking however considerable expansion will be seen. The authorities have been overwhelmed by financial propositions, and are viewing them all with caution, which in some cases is well justified, but when they are convinced of genuine benefits to the state the developments will come.

(2) IRAN

Central Banking

Modern banking in Iran dates from 1889 when Baron de Reuter obtained a concession to establish a state bank for the Persian Empire under the title of Imperial Bank of Persia. While acting as the state bank, it had the exclusive right to issue banknotes as well as to manage the silver currency, and in its first year opened branches in eight principal cities as well as Tehran. It did not originally prosper, with depressed trading conditions and the sharp decline in silver values in the nineties. Conditions improved and the Bank flourished particularly in the 1920s when it had twentysix branches spread throughout the country. Several changes of name took place – it is now BBME – and the Bank had to withdraw between 1952 and 1959 but returned as a minority holder with 51 per cent Iranian interests in the Bank of Iran and the Middle East.

Meanwhile its position as state bank and responsibility for the note issue had been taken over in 1929 by the Bank Melli founded by Iranian national and private interests. The Bank has steadily grown in importance and now has nearly three hundred branches in Iran as well as twentyone overseas, including London, Paris, Frankfurt, Tokyo and New York.

The Bank Melli surrendered its state role however with the formation of the Central Bank of Iran, or Bank Markazi, in 1960, with a subsidiary Credit and Currency Board. Recently the Central Bank has been active in its regulatory function, imposing deposit requirements and lending limits on the commercial banks in the effort to restrain inflation. Permission for new banks to open is granted only if exceptional advantages are offered to Iran, but there is less restriction on representative offices and the banking climate is generally encouraging.

(2b) Commercial Banks

With the exception of the state holding in Bank Melli, commercial banking is in the private sector. A complete official list is not available but would include:

Iranian

Bank Melli Iran
Bank Bazargani Iran
Bank Saderat Iran
Bank Bimeh Iran
Bank Pars
Bank Sepah
Shahryar Bank
Iran Industries Bank

Iranian with Foreign Minority

Bank of Iran and the Middle East (BBME)
Bank of Tehran (Paribas group)
Banque Etebarate Iran (Crédit Lyonnais group)
Iranians' Bank (FNCB)
International Bank of Iran and Japan (Bank of Tokyo)
Irano-British Bank (Chartered Bank)

Mercantile Bank of Iran and Holland
(Algemene Bank Nederland)
Iran Chase International Bank (Chase Manhattan Bank)
Foreign Trade Bank of Iran
(Bank of America; Deutsche Bank; Banca Commerciale Italiana)
Bank Dariush (Continental Illinois NB & TC; Sanwa Bank)

Representative Offices
Commerzbank
Deutsche Bank
Dresdner Bank
Algemene Bank Nederland
Vereinsbank in Hamburg
Crédit Suisse
Bayerische Vereins Bank
Bayerische Hypotheken und Wechsel Bank
Berliner Bank
Osterreichische Landebank
Banque de Bruxelles
International Bank (Washington)
Chase Manhattan Bank
FNCB
Bank of America NT & SA
Barclays Bank
Grindlays Bank
Singer and Friedlander
United Bank (Pakistan)
Habib Bank (Pakistan)
Industrial Bank of Japan
Société Générale

(2c) Government Banks
In addition to the Bank Markazi (present governor Jahangir Amuzegar), the Agricultural Development Bank has long functioned in the customary role of assisting the farming community with low interest loans and under its present director Mehdi Samii its capital has doubled. The Mortgage Bank and the Industrial Bank are other government institutions.

Besides the commercial banks with joint holdings shown above, the government has drawn foreign banking interests into the progress of its Development Plans. At the start of the Second Plan in 1959 the Industrial and Mining Development Bank of Iran was founded and, although the Plan funds are mainly responsible for its financing, private Iranian interests and twentytwo foreign banks are involved and have arranged borrowings on the Eurodollar market.

As the Plans have progressed the IMDBI has tended to concentrate on the largest projects and the Development and Investment Bank of Iran with Gholam Reza Moghaddam as chairman was established to function similarly on a smaller scale. Shareholders include Williams and Glyn's Bank (UK), Dresdner Bank (Germany), Long-Term Credit Bank of Japan (Japan) and First National Bank of Boston and Mellon Bank (US).

In a further move to gain access to funds for development the government established the Iranian Overseas Investment Bank with its own interests represented by the IMDBI and Bank Melli, and partners:

Bank of America NT & SA	Barclays Bank International
Manufacturers Hanover Trust	Midland Bank
Bank of Tokyo	Deutsche Bank
Industrial Bank of Japn	Société Générale.

With the excess of wealth from the higher oil prices the IOIB is functioning more as a vehicle for placing Iran's funds overseas than for seeking new finance.

(2d) Other Institutions

The government has ambitions to make Tehran a major financial centre but is aware that there is a long way to go. At March 20, 1974 there were thirtyfour stocks listed on the local exchange with a total paid up capitalisation of 27,600 million rials ($ 400 million) and turnover in the year was 2734 million rials. Secondary trading in government and municipal bonds has yet to develop, while the rigid control which was maintained until recently on foreign exchange produced an expertise in finding by-ways but no readiness for open dealings. The commercial banking field is already over-cultivated; it is in the provision of more specialized financial services and in the training of Iranians to take a full part in them that newcomers are most likely to be welcome and established banks to be able to expand.

(3) IRAQ

The Central Bank of Iraq was established in 1951 with the responsibility of the currency issue, maintenance of cover and supervision of the commercial banks. The revolution of 1958 and subsequent changes leading to the assumption of power by the Ba'ath Party in 1967 brought real if not formal alteration in its status, but under its present governor Fawzi al Kaissi it retains a position of influence.

The same cannot be said of the commercial banks which, after a period of Iraqisation of the foreign-owned ones, were all nationalised in 1964 and formed temporarily into three groups Gradual redistribution of functions led to the Commercial Bank handling all internal business and the Rafidain Bank the foreign side. The Central Bank however retained control except for routine small transactions. In 1974 the Rafidain Bank took over the Commercial Bank and there are signs that it is gaining a little more freedom.

It has been officially estimated that state organisations now account for ninety per cent of all economic activity in Iraq. The various specialized banks have however shown little growth – they consist of:

Real Estate Bank
Cooperative Agricultural Bank
Industrial Bank

– statistics for the group sometimes include the National Insurance Company. On the other hand the Ministry of Oil has since 1969 shared with the Ministry of Defence a degree of freedom from Central Bank control.

(4a) KUWAIT

Central Banking

The functions of a government bank were originally undertaken by the Imperial Bank of Iran (BBME) with the grant of a thirty-year charter in 1942; no other foreign commercial bank has ever been permitted to operate in Kuwait. At that time the currency in general circulation in the Gulf was the Indian rupee but during the fifties the Indian government found its economic difficulties accentuated by the drainage of foreign currency to the Gulf, not to mention the activities of smugglers. Consequently in 1958 it issued a separate Gulf rupee which could not be used for purchases of foreign currency except officially through Bombay but this in turn was found too restrictive by the Gulf states. Kuwait led the way by the constitution of a currency board and the issue of the Kuwaiti dinar in 1961.

It was not however until 1969 that the Central Bank of Kuwait was formed and took over the Currency Board, with its general objectives defined by the Government as:-

(1) The sole right to issue currency
(2) Maintenance of the stability and convertibility of the currency
(3) Supervision of the banking system
(4) Advising the government on finance
(5) Acting as government banker
(6) Furthering social and economic progress and the growth of national income.

In its control of the commercial banks the Central Bank of Kuwait under its governor Hamza Abbas has taken a very conservative view, restricting interest payments to seven per cent and requiring twentyfive per cent of deposits to be covered by assets with less than thirty days' maturity, as well as by effectively blocking the entry of foreign financial interests.

A consequence of the financial sophistication of Kuwait is that the Central Bank reserves although often described as the official reserves amount to only a fraction of the foreign assets of the state. In its report to March 1974 the Bank stated that the value of its holdings which function as currency and trade reserves was KD 157 million while the government reserve held separately amounted to KD 1089 million ($ 3680 million). Concurrently the commercial banks' holdings were considerably higher than in other oil producing states, amounting at that time to KD 390 million.

(4b) Commercial Banks

There are five commercial banks, all entirely with private Kuwaiti shareholding except for a fiftyone per cent government participation in the Bank of Kuwait and the Middle East which was formed in 1971 on the expiry of the charter of the BBME agreement, with the latter being granted a management contract. The National Bank of Kuwait founded in 1952 is now the largest independent bank in the Arab world and recruits its managers individually, as does the Gulf Bank, while the Commercial Bank of Kuwait has a management contract with Chase Manhattan and the most recently authorised bank, the Alahli of 1968, is similarly associated with Crédit Lyonnais. Internally all the commercial banks have found their progress steady but slow under the restrictions imposed by the Central Bank and with the cautious percolation of the government's wealth to the private sector, and have developed interests overseas.

(4c) Government Banks

The Credit Bank of Kuwait was founded in 1961 to stimulate small-scale private industrial projects. Rather more successful has been the Savings and Credit Bank which set out to attract personal savings and has found itself largely financing property investment. Recent foundations with commercial partnership, the Kuwait Real Estate Bank at the end of 1973 and the Industrial Bank of Kuwait in 1974, have yet to establish their presence.

At the opposite end of the scale of the state's banking is the Kuwait Investment Office, originally the Kuwait Investment Board, which for twenty years has been managing funds held in London. Holdings at first were merely short-term, ready for use in development at home, but a longer view now predominates; and while advice is still taken from international experts the decisions are now made by a Kuwaiti board under the finance minister Abd al Rahman al Atiqi. The Central Bank of Kuwait is believed to be studying the establishment of a Kuwait International Bank to take care of the government's major investments, which would probably be located in London and absorb the Kuwait Investment Office.

The important work of KFAED lending on non-commercial terms is described in the chapter on Aid.

(4d) Other institutions

Three Kuwaiti investment groups have been rapidly increasing in weight on the international stage and are now managing as well as subscribing to major syndicated loans. The Kuwait Foreign Trading Contracting and Investment Company, KFTCIC, is eighty per cent government-owned and nominally concentrates on the Arab world and Africa; the Kuwait Investment Company, KIC, fifty per cent government, has a general brief; the Kuwait International Investment Company, KIIC, is the most recently formed and entirely private. The, two former with four of the commercial banks (not BKME) set up the United Bank of Kuwait in London, and there are Kuwaiti partners in most of the consortium banks mentioned later. The investment companies clearly prefer to work among strong international groupings, but KIC showed its initiative in 1968 in sponsoring an issue for the World Bank denominated in Kuwaiti dinars. It has been responsible for KD loans totalling 130 million to date, and the other two companies have recently also initiated public issue of KD loans.

The authorities have permitted three companies to be formed, with Kuwaiti majorities, for financial advisory services. Robert Fleming, William Kent and Banque Worms share in International Financial Advisers; Arbuthnot Latham, Philadelphia National Bank, Banque de Suez and Taiyo Kobe Bank are behind the Arab Financial Consultants Company; the International Bank (a Washington merchant bank) has joined Shaikh 'Ali Sabah Salem al Sabah and partners in Kuwait Financial Centre. To assist personal investors Kidder Peabody and Merrill Lynch have representatives in Kuwait.

There are dealings in the stocks of a number of local companies but the market has become something of a speculators' playground with minute dividend yields unrelated to any realistic assessment. The government has recently formed the Industrial Bank of Kuwait to foster new ventures until they are ready to go public, and have brought in Phillips & Drew of London to advise on the establishment of a properly regulated stock exchange to bring order to the capital market.

(5a) SAUDI ARABIA

Central Banking

In the days before oil the Pilgrimage was of vital importance to the economy of Arabia. At the same time a variety of silver coinage was in circulation, including the Maria Theresa dollar and Turkish lira as well as the rupee, and the exchange rate against the official riyal as the pilgrims brought money in could fall to two-thirds or even a half of the rate in other seasons. The Saudi Arabian Monetary Agency was established in 1952 to assist the minister of finance in bringing order to the government's receipts and payments, and almost immediately made the first issue of paper money in the form of 'pilgrims' receipts'. The stabilising effect was felt at once, and although the Saudi government had its financial difficulties in the 1950s and the charter of SAMA was amended several times pilgrims' receipts remained current until under new legislation a proper issue of paper money was made at the start of 1960, and a par value for the riyal was notified to the International Monetary Fund.

The states of the Arabian peninsula have been fortunate in attracting a number of outstanding public servants, and the work of Anwar Ali at SAMA was a remarkable achievement even though he had the full support of the late King Faisal. Its powers were further extended in 1966, although its original role of promoting good order in the finances of the Kingdom remains of primary importance. It supervises the operations of the commercial banks, laying down reserve requirements and lequidity ratios, while encouraging the growth of specialized banks. SAMA has also had the task of the investment of the country's reserves; while they were largely confined to short-term assets they were managed with a great sense of responsibility, and now that Saudi Arabia has started to make long-term investments it consults only institutions of the highest repute.

In the early days of Islam both giving and taking of interest were frowned on as usury, and the fundamentalist principles of Wahabism have made it necessary for the Kingdom to move cautiously in adapting its organisation to the modern world. By its very nature SAMA was liable to be a target of attack, and the fact there has been hardly any criticism indicates the good sense and discretion with which it has been managed. Tolerance is growing; the many millions in interest received by the government on its deposits, or demanded from Aramco with each retrospective claim, have not aroused one religious voice in protest.

(5b) Commercial Banks

The Saudi commercial banks are the National Commercial Bank and the Riyad Bank, and both have been encouraged by SAMA to open branches nationwide. For some years no new foreign bank has been permitted to enter and no new branch has been allowed to those already established, which are:

Other Arab
Arab Bank
Banque du Caire
Banque du Liban et d'Outre-Mer

Other Foreign
Algemene Bank Nederland
Bank Melli Iran
Banque de L'Indochine
British Bank of the Middle East
First National City Bank
National Bank of Pakistan

An excess of liquidity had been a problem for the commercial banks with the limited opportunities for the employment of funds in Saudi Arabia. In the last year reported however, to June 1974, the growth of deposits was SR 1200 million to reach a total of SR 4500 million while loans and credits grew by SR 1270, largely to finance increased imports, it is thought, to total SR 3100 million ($ 870 million).

(5c) Government Banks

The first of the Saudi specialist banks was the Agricultural Credit Bank, founded in 1964 to encourage medium-term investment in agriculture. There has lately been a noticeable reduction in the average value of loans together with an increase in their number, which suggest that the smaller farmers have begun to take advantage of their opportunities. In 1973 the Saudi Credit Bank was established with the power to grant interest-free loans to Saudi nationals up to a general limit of SR 7500. There is some doubt at the moment as to its effectiveness in providing loans for development purposes rather than simply personal expenditure. The third of the Saudi specialist banks, established only in 1974, is the Industrial Development Fund to encourage private productive development with a capital of SR 500 million, but to date there is no indication of the type or scale of industry which it is intended to promote.

(5d) Other institutions

As mentioned above, the Saudi government has been discussing long-term investment plans but there is little indication as yet of the form a managing institution would take. It is therefore of interest that approval was given in February 1975 for the National Commercial Bank to set up a joint investment bank with the American underwriting house, First National Bank of Boston, to operate from the Bank's headquarters in Jeddah.

Meanwhile SAMA is believed to maintain a list of about thirty international banks approved for handling its funds, but appears in practice to concentrate on the large US banks, Morgan Guaranty and Chase being particularly mentioned.

(6) QATAR

Qatar was among the states in which the currency was still the Gulf rupee when in 1966 India suspended convertibility. The ruling families of Qatar and Dubai have long been connected and they moved swiftly together to set up a currency board to manage a Qatar Dubai riyal (equivalent to the old rupee: 4.76 per SDR) which the more northern Trucial States also adopted. When the United Arab Emirates came into being in 1971 the QDR became the Qatari riyal under the Qatar Monetary Agency. The QMA has been allotted functions in the supervision of the commercial banks but the role of state bank belongs to the Qatar National Bank founded in 1965.

The latter also functions as a commercial bank and is the only one permitted to open further branches in the peninsula. The foreign commercial banks are:

Chartered Bank	Arab Bank (Jordan)
Grindlays Bank	United Bank (Pakistan)
British Bank of the Middle East	Bank Saderat Iran
First National City Bank	Bank of Oman
Banque de Paris et des Pays Bas	

Between the generous limits of action of the commercial banks and the personal relationships of a small state the need for specialized banks has not been felt.

Qatar has not had a large income by Gulf standards and at one time the personal interests of members of the ruling family were unduly favoured. Even so the reserves were built up with the help of an investment advisory board in London. After the accession of Shaikh Khalifa bin Hamad al-Thani in 1972 development planning took a much more positive turn without being overburdened by administrative bodies, and the same is likely to remain true of investment planning.

There are a few public shareholdings in Qatari companies but they are open only to Qatari nationals and as in Kuwait appear to be traded more for prestige than for investment value.

(7) UNITED ARAB EMIRATES

The UAE have a Babel of banks. The Currency Board was established in 1973 to issue the new common currency, the UAE dirham which replaced the Bahrain dinar used in Abu Dhabi since 1966 and the Qatar-Dubai riyal. The Board is intended to develop into a central bank and meanwhile has limited responsibility for monetary policy, supervision of audits of commercial banks and control of their opening. It was finally driven to stop further authorisations of foreign banks in February 1975 at which point it had approved thirtyeight banks, received applications from twentynine more, and believed around twenty to be in preparation.

The list of commercial banks in February 1975 is:-

Banks in United Arab Emirates
(* = Head Office)

Abu Dhabi
Arab Bank
Banque du Caire
Bank of Credit and Commerce
International
Bank of Oman
Banque du Paris et des Pays Bas
Bank Saderat Iran
British Bank of the Middle East

United Bank

Ras al-Khaimah
Arab Bank
Bank Saderat Iran
British Bank of the Middle East
Grindlays Bank
Habib Bank
United Bank

Chartered Bank
Commercial Bank of Dubai
First National City Bank
Grindlays Bank
Habib Bank
Janta Bank (Bangladesh)
National Bank of Abu Dhabi*
National Bank of Dubai
National Bank for Investment & Development
United Bank

Dubai
Algemene Nederland Bank
Arab African Bank (Cairo)
Arab Bank
Bank of Baroda (India)
Bank Melli Iran
Bank of Oman
Bank Omram of Iran
British Bank of the Middle East
Chartered Bank
Chase Manhattan Overseas Corporation
Commercial Bank of Dubai*
Dubai Bank
First National Bank of Chicago
First National City Bank
Grindlays Bank
Habib Bank
National Bank of Dubai*
United Bank

Fujairah
Bank Saderat Iran
British Bank of the Middle East

Sharjah
Arab Bank
Bank of Credit and Commerce International
Bank Melli Iran
Bank Saderat Iran
Bank of Sharjah*
British Bank of the Middle East
Chartered Bank
Commercial Bank of Dubai
First National City Bank
Habib Bank
United Bank

Umm al-Qaiwain
Bank of Credit and Commerce International
Habib Bank
National Bank of Dubai
United Bank

Ajman
Arab Bank
Bank of Credit and Commerce International
Bank of Oman
Bank Saderat Iran

Unplaced in UAE
Distributors Co-operative Credit Bank

Source: UAE Currency Board.

At the end of June 1974 total assets of the commercial banks were Dh 4963 million ($ 1250 million) with twentythree of the banks each having assets less than Dh 100 million and only five more than Dh 300 million, and the total of bank credits was Dh 2450 million.

Most government banking assistance has been channelled through the ministries but the UAE Development Bank is being set up to provide favourable credit terms for fishermen, farmers and small-scale enterprise. In Dubai Shaikh Rashid bin Sa'id al Maktum has established a property development bank to assist individuals to build their own housing.

Merchant banking is represented in Dubai by Wardleys and by Oryx Investments, a consortium under Arbuthnot Latham with the Chartered Bank and partners from six of the Gulf countries. There are two finance houses, Middle East Finances, a BBME subsidiary, and Gulf Citicorp (FNCB) and four brokers offices, James Capel, Merrill Lynch, W.I. Carr and Sons, and Gillett Brothers. There are only small private holdings in local companies and no demand for a stock exchange.

(8) OMAN

The Oman Currency Board was established in 1970 and became the Central Bank of Oman in April 1975. In addition to the currency issue it has the powers of licensing the commercial banks, laying down their capital and reserve requirements, demanding deposits from them, and inspecting their audits.

The commercial banks which have been authorised are:-

National
Bank of Oman Bahrain and Kuwait
National Bank of Oman

Foreign
Arab African Bank
Arab Bank
Bank of Credit and Commerce International
Bank Melli Iran
British Bank of the Middle East
Chartered Bank
Grindlays Bank
Habib Bank

Oman has large development and military commitments and at present no prospects of surplus income, such as the other Gulf states have, and financial institutions offering to assist its development have been few. The only noteworthy progress to date has been the establishment of the Oman Housing Development Association, a partnership between the government and the BBME, to promote home ownership.

(9) LIBYA

A currency board was established in 1951 in preparation for the creation of Libya as an independent state and was absorbed into the new Central Bank at an early stage. The Bank was cautious in granting permits for commercial banks to open and strict in their control so that it was relatively simple to Libyanise them immediately after the revolution of 1969 and to nationalise them the next year. Their present titles are:-

National Commercial Bank
Gumhouria Bank
Wahda Bank
Umma Bank
Sahara Bank.

In 1971 the Libyan pound was renamed the Libyan dinar. In the same year the Central Bank established a subsidiary, the Libyan Arab Foreign Bank, through which foreign operations could be directed. The division of responsibility appears to be that the Central Bank acts directly in maintaining the bulk of the State's reserves in short-term form while the LAFB is the channel for commercial investments, having under the chairmanship of Abdullah Saudi built up links with foreign banks in consortium operations and underwriting international issues.

(10) BANKS OUTSIDE THE OPEC COUNTRIES

Financial institutions established in the oil producing countries will have an important part to play in the redeployment of the oil revenues, but in other countries there are complementary institutions which will share their work. It is already clear that a large proportion of the surplus revenues of the lightly-populated Gulf countries will be devoted to the development of other Arab countries and of Egypt and Syria in particular. It is therefore worth recording, in addition to those banks in the producing countries, the banks of the countries around the eastern Mediterranean which will also be involved in the search for productive investment by the surplus countries. In addition there is a number of consortium banks established in Europe, as well as the partnerships already mentioned established in the Gulf countries, which will also be playing a part and this chapter concludes with information about them.

(11) EGYPT

For nearly a hundred years banks in Egypt had a status in the world of international finance without rival among the Arab states. The 1952 revolution changed all that in the matter of months, although it was not until 1961 that the banks in Egypt were completely nationalised. The emphasis of the Nasser government on political rather than economic ends and its nationalistic fervour drove all financial initiative from Egypt. Beirut was the beneficiary and with remarkable speed and drive took over the leadership of the Arab financial world. Only very recently in Egypt have there been signs of greater freedom for cooperation with foreign financial institutions, but whether after the lapse of a generation it will be sufficient to restore some of its previous importance to Cairo must be doubtful. On the positive side there is the size of Egypt's population and the need for investment on the largest scale, which would justify a great rise in international banking activity. Against it are the past actions which have reduced Egypt's credit in the world, and the time needed to regain a sound reputation.

The steps taken so far show themselves largely in the permission granted to foreign banks to re-establish themselves in partnership with Egyptian banks but restricted to external transactions only (listed under consortium banks in section 18). Various amalgamations followed the nationalisation of 1961 and the four remaining commercial banks are:

National Bank of Egypt
Bank of Alexandria
Banque Misr
Banque du Caire

Previously the National Bank of Egypt had acted both as state bank and as the bank of currency issue but the Central Bank was then established to take over these functions. With its enormous load of debt the Central Bank has been preoccupied with foreign exchange matters and the operations of the commercial banks tended to be controlled by the ministries whose business they mainly transacted. Again there are signs of more flexibility and both the commercial banks and the Central Bank itself have been concerned in various of the international consortia mentioned later.

Two investment banks have been founded by the Egyptian and other Arab governments in cooperation. The Arab African Bank has been functioning since 1958; Kuwait is the principal partner with Egypt and others are Iraq, Algeria, Jordan and Qatar. The Arab International Bank which, in addition to Egypt, includes Libya, UAE, Oman and Qatar, was set up in 1971. These are permitted to operate only in foreign currency and have little effect on the Egyptian economy. Manufacturers Hanover and Morgan Grenfell also now have offices.

(12) LEBANON

When Cairo chose the nationalistic path in the fifties Beirut gladly took over the lead of Arab internationalism. It was already free of any form of currency control, and its role as a banking centre was enhanced by the law of 1956 enjoining secrecy on all banking operations, on the pattern of similar laws in Switzerland. Indeed progress was too rapid and although the Banque du Liban was formally constituted in 1964 as the Central Bank to take over from the Banque de Syrie et du Liban the authority for the note issue, the Intra Bank crash of 1966 came before it had been able to gain any control over the commercial banks. In the crisis both sides took considerable risks to enable Lebanon to maintain its reputation and in the process gained understanding and appreciation of the other's role which might normally have taken much longer to develop. Nevertheless it took some time for confidence of both international and Lebanese clients to recover, but now, although prejudice in favour of foreign over Lebanese banks has not quite been eradicated, the banking system generally has fully regained its strength.

(12b)

The original government bank with authority for the note issue under the French mandate was the Banque de Syrie et du Liban but after 1948 when Syria separated its economy from that of the Lebanon the Banque acted solely for the Lebanese side; it had always taken part in commercial operations as well as governmental. Now the list of commercial banks, pruned after the Intra Bank affair, reads as follows:

Banque Francaise pour le Moyen-Orient
Banco di Roma
Banque Misr-Liban
Banque Tohme
Arab Bank
Banque Nationale de Paris (Intercontinentale)
British Bank of the Middle East
Société Bancaire du Liban
Rafidain Bank
Banque Libano-Francaise
Banque Libanaise pour le Commerce
Banqu Sabbag
Banque G. Trad – Crédit Lyonnais
Banque du Liban et d'Outre-Mer
Bank Al-Mashrek
Federal Bank of Lebanon
National Commercial Bank (Saudi)
Banque Nationale pour le Developpement Industriel et Touristique
Société Générale Libano-Européenne de Banque
Algemene Bank Nederland
Banque de Crédit Agricole Industriel et Foncier
Banque de la Mediterranée
Chase Manhatten Bank
First National City Bank
Chartered Bank
Bank of Credit and Commere International
Banque Saradar
Banque de Beyrouth et des Pays Arabes
Lebanese Arab Bank
Bank of America (National Trust & Saving Association)
Banque Majdalany
Rif Bank
Bank Handlowy for the Middle East
Bank of Beirut
Toronto Dominion Bank (Middle East)
Prosperity Bank of Lebanon
Chemical Bank (Middle East)
Jammal Investment Bank
Banque J. Lati et Fils
First National Bank of Chicago (Lebanon)
Beirut Riyad Bank
Investment & Finance Bank
Syrian Lebanese Commercial Bank
Banque Pharaon & Chiha
Banque de Crédit National
Banque Mebco
Bank of the Near East
Byblos Bank
Adcom Bank (Advances & Commerce Bank)
Union Bank
Banque de Financement
Royal Bank of Canada (Middle East)
Banque de l'Industrie et du Travail
Jordan National Bank
Banque Libano-Bresilienne
Continental Development Bank
Crédit Libanais
Banque Beyrouth pour le Commerce
Banque Audi
Banque Nasr Libano-Africaine
Bank of Kuwait & the Arab World
Banque Joseph Geagea
Arab Libyan Tunisian Bank
Crédit Suisse (Moyen-Orient)
Banque du Crédit Populaire
Bank Saderat Iran
Société Nouvelle de la Banque de Syrie et du Liban
Moscow Narodny Bank
Banque Libanaise des Emigres
Liberal Bank
Habib Bank (Overseas)
Bank of Nova Scotia
Litex Bank
Trans-Orient Bank
Banque Arabo-Africaine
Banque de la Bekaa
British Bank of the Lebanon
Banque de Crédit Agricole

Banque de l'Essor Economique Libanais	
United Bank of Lebanon & Pakistan	**Source**: Banque du Liban

(12c)
There is at present a ban on the establishment of any further commercial banks until 1979. That has not stopped a number of banks wishing to get into the Middle East scene by having an office in Beirut, and the authorities have cooperated by permitting a simp representative office to be opened. This course has been taken by a number of banks; they are not recorded individually here but this paragraph reference (12c) will be found against their names in the index

(12d)
Support of one of the weaker Lebanese banks has provided an entry to active operations for the Chemical Bank of US, taking over the Rabiya Bank as the Chemical Bank (ME) and for Credit Commercial with the Banque Libanaise des Emigrés, while BBME took over the Trust Bank as a subsidiary renaming it the British Bank of the Lebanon.

Kidder Peabody in 1967 accepted the key role in the long and complicated business of sorting out the affairs of the Intra Bank and reconstituting its parts, and naturally remains strong in Beirut. The London merchant bank of Schroder Wagg has for some time had connections with the Asseily family and has now gone into formal partnership. Other more broadly based groups appear in the list of consortia (section 17).

With the strngth of the private sector the government has provided little in the specialized field except for a share in the Banque de Crédit Agricole Industriel et Foncier. Its recent effort to found a development bank is being watched with interest.

There is a number of companies with shares quoted on the Beirut Stock Exchange, but very few of them are large enough to make trading a regular activity. The sophisticated Lebanese investor, with good communications and a time advantage, deals in Paris, London or New York.

(13) SYRIA

Syria gained independence in 1943 and split economically from the Lebanon in 1948, and the banks there had a somewhat checkered career under frequent changes of government. They were nationalised in 1961 along with those in Egypt when Syria was part of the UAR, briefly were independent again, and were renationalised by the Ba'ath Party in 1963.

Under the socialist regime the banks have been reorganised on functional lines. Apart from the Central Bank there are the Agricultural Bank, the Industrial Bank, the Real Estate Bank, the Popular Credit Bank and the Commercial Bank of Syria. The last is the only one permitted foreign transactions and almost all trade matters fall within its province. It has however no control over the foreign exchange it needs, for which responsibility remains with the Central Bank. With Syria's heavy deficit financing and inadequate cover of import requirements, the country has for a long time had difficulty in meeting its foreign exchange obligations, and delays of six months on debt service and nine or ten months in meeting trade bills have been common, but the situation is improving with the influx of Arab aid funds. The physical potentialities of Syria offer undoubted opportunities for Arab development finance, if the government reinforces its verbal encouragement of investment with appropriate measures.

(14) JORDAN

On the international scene the Arab Bank has played a considerable part. It was founded as long ago as 1930 by Abdul Hamid Shoman but in 1948 the bank was driven from Jerusalem to re-establish itself in Amman. It has always been an outward looking and progressive bank, and in consequence has at times suffered together with British and other foreign banks from nationalisation measures in various Arab states. The bank still has branches throughout the Arab world wherever possible and additionally in London, Frankfurt, Lagos and Zurich. With assets of JD 310 million at the end of 1973 it is one of the largest in the Middle East. It has recently formed a partnership with Morgan Grenfell in London called the Arab and Morgan Grenfell Finance Company, besides participating in various of the consortia banks. No other Jordanian bank has branches abroad, but the Bank of Jordan and the Jordan National Bank are also participants in the UBAF consortium.

(15) BAHRAIN

From the earliest days Bahrain has lived by trade and its merchants have had an international outlook. The Eastern (now Chartered) Bank in the twenties was the first foreign bank to open on the southern side of the Gulf. From the central position of Bahrain its banks were able to play a part in the early oil developments in all the countries around, although Bahrain is not itself a member of OPEC. Its oilfield discovered in 1932 is small and, while the revenues have been sufficient for the steady, planned development of the state, there has been no temptation to extravagance.

In common with the other Gulf states Bahrain was using the Gulf rupee as normal currency. A currency board was established in 1965 and when India suspended convertibility it was prepared for the immediate issue of its own currency, the Bahrain dinar. Abu Dhabi supported the issue from the start until the UAE dirham was introduced in 1973, and at the end of the year the Currency Board was reconstituted as the Bahrain Monetary Agency.

Two commercial banks have been established in the island, the Bank of Bahrain and Kuwait and the National Bank of Bahrain, and other banks with branches are:

Chartered Bank
BBME
Grindlays Bank
FNCB
Bank Melli Iran
Chase Manhattan Bank
United Bank
Habib Bank
Arab Bank
Rafidain Bank
Banque du Caire

Representatives
National Westminster
Union Bank of Switzerland

(16) CONSORTIUM BANKS

Various joint banking ventures have been founded bringing together experience in the Middle Eastern conditions and developed financial skills. Some appear to be constituted with relatively small capitalisation to provide merchant banking and advisory services while others, notably the groups with French leadership, are acting more as deposit-takers and are prominent among subscribers to international issues. The partnerships in Iran have been referred to in parts of that section (2). The full list published by *The Banker* provides a very convenient tabulation of the rest and is reproduced here by permission of the editor.

Joint banking ventures by Middle East and Western banks

The following is a list of consortium banks and banking partnerships bringing together Middle East and Western partners.

EUROPE

Shareholders	**Shareholdings %**
(16a) Banque Franco-Arabe d'Investissements Internationaux (FRAB)	
Est 1969, Paris, capital Fr. Fr. 70m	
Société Générale (France)	25.00
Société Générale de Banque (Belgium)	7.00
Swiss Bank Corporation (Switzerland)	6.00
Banco Urquijo (Spain)	1.00
Industrial Bank of Japan (Japan)	5.00
Amsterdam-Rotterdam Bank (Netherlands)	5.00
National Investment Bank for Industrial Development (Greece)	1.00
Kuwait Group:	26.50
Kuwait Investment Company	
Kuwait Foreign Trading, Contracting and Investment Company	
National Bank of Kuwait	
The Kuwait Insurance Company	
Commercial Bank of Kuwait	
Various companies and private individuals	
Arabian Gulf Group:	3.32
Bank of Bahrain	

Shareholders	**Shareholdings %**
Bank of Oman	
Miscellaneous companies and private individuals	
Libyan Group:	3.50
Sahara Bank	
Libya Insurance Company	
Tunisian Group:	1.68
Banque de Tunisie	
Société Générale d'Investissement	
Saudi Arabian Group	12.00
Algerian Group	1.50
Moroccan Group	1.50

(16b) Union de Banques Arabes et Francaises (UBAF)

Est 1970, Paris, capital Fr. Fr. 110m

Crédit Lyonnais (France)	31.95
Banque Française du Commerce Extérieur	8.00
Arab Bank (Jordan)	6.33
Banque Extérieure d'Algérie (Algeria)	6.33
Commercial Bank of Syria (Syria)	6.33
Libyan Arab Foreign Bank (Libya)	6.33
Rafidain Bank (Iraq)	6.33
Central Bank of Egypt (Egypt)	6.32
Arab African Bank (Arab multinational)	5.82
Banque du Maroc (Morocco)	3.57
Alahli Bank of Kuwait (Kuwait)	1.86
Riyad Bank (Saudi Arabia)	1.78
Bank of Jordan (Jordan)	1.07
Société Tunisienne de Banque (Tunisia)	1.07
National Bank of Abu Dhabi (Abu Dhabi)	0.91
Ministry of Finance and Petroleum (Qatar)	0.91
Sudan Commercial Bank (Sudan)	0.71
Jordan National Bank (Jordan)	0.54
Banque Audi (Lebanon)	0.47
Banque G. Trad (Crédit Lyonnais) (Lebanon)	0.47
Alahli Bank (Dubai)	0.45
Bank of Bahrain and Kuwait (Bahrain)	0.45
National Bank of Yemen (Yemen)	0.45
Yemen Bank for Reconstruction and Development (Yemen)	0.45
Banque Arabe Libyenne Mauritanienne pour le Commerce Extérieur et le Développement (Mauritania)	0.45
Oman Currency Board (Oman)	0.45

Shareholders	**Shareholdings %**
Somali National Bank	
Central Bank of Yemen	
UBAF's Affiliates	
(i) UBAF Ltd	
Est 1972, London, capital $5m	
UBAF (Paris)	50.00
Midland Bank (United Kingdom)	25.00
Libyan Arab Foreign Bank (Libya)	25.00
(ii) Unione di Banche Arabe ed Europee (Italia) SpA (UBAE Roma)	
Est 1972, Rome, capital L5,000m	
UBAF (Paris)	51.00
Banco di Roma (Italy)	9.50
Banco Nazionale del Lavoro (Italy)	9.50
Istituto di Credito per le Imprese di Pubblica Utilita (ICIPU) (Italy)	6.00
Istituto Ligure Interessenze Industriali e Commerciali (Italy)	6.00
Societa Finanziamenti Idrocarburi SOFID (Italy)	6.00
Societa Finanziari Telefonica per Azioni STET	6.00
Societa Italiana per Condotte d'Acqua	6.00
(iii) Union de Banques Arabes et Européenes (UBAE)	
Est 1973, Luxembourg and Frankfurt, capital DM 30m	
UBAF (paris)	33.33
Arab Bank (Jordan))	33.33
Arab Bank Overseas (Switzerland))	
Bayerische Vereinsbank (Germany)	
Commerzbank (Germany))	33.33
Commerzbank International (Luxembourg))	
Westdeutsche Landesbank Girozentrale (Germany))	
(iv) Union de Banques Arabes et Nippon (UBAN-Arab Japanese Finance)	
Est 1974, Hong Kong, capital HK$25m	
UBAF (Paris)	20.00
Alahli Bank of Kuwait (Kuwait)	7.00
Arab African Bank (Arab multinational)	7.00

Shareholders	Shareholdings %
Arab Bank (Jordan)	7.00
Libyan Arab Foreign Bank (Libya)	7.00
Banque Arabe Libyenne Mauritanienne pour le Commerce Extérieur et le Développement (Mauritania)	2.50
Banque Audi (Lebanon)	2.50
National Bank of Abu Dhabi (Abu Dhabi)	2.50
Sudan Commercial Bank (Sudan)	2.50
Yemen Bank for Reconstruction and Development (Yemen)	2.00
Bank of Tokyo (Japan)	8.00
Long-Term Credit Bank of Japan (Japan)	8.00
Mitsui Bank (Japan)	8.00
Nomura Securities (Japan)	8.00
Sanwa Bank (Japan)	8.00

UBAF Financial Services Ltd
Est 1974, London, capital $1m

UBAF (Paris)	35.00
UBAF Ltd (London)	7.50
UBAE (luxembourg)	2.50
UBAE (Italy)	2.50
UBAN (Hong Kong)	2.50
Crédit Lyonnais (France)	10.00
Hambros Bank (United Kingdom)	20.00
Midland and International Banks (United Kingdom)	20.00

(16c) European Arab Holding SA
Est 1972, Luxembourg, capital Lux. Fr. 1,000m

FRAB Bank (*see above*)	10.00
Creditanstalt-Bankverein (Austria)*	5.69
Deutsche Bank (Germany)*	5.69
Amsterdam-Rotterdam Bank (Netherlands)*	5.19
Midland Bank (United Kingdom)*	5.69
Banca Commerciale Italiana (Italy)*	5.69
Société Générale de Banque (Belgium)*	4.99
Abu Dhabi Fund for Arab Economic Development (Abu Dhabi)	4.16
Banque Nationale d'Algérie (Algeria)	4.16
Arab International Bank (Egypt)	4.16
National Bank of Egypt (Egypt)	4.16
National Bank of Kuwait (Kuwait)	4.16
National Commercial Bank (Libya)	4.16

Shareholders	**Shareholdings %**
National Commercial Bank (Saudi Arabia)	4.16
Bank of Sudan (Sudan)	4.16
Central Bank of Syria (Syria)	4.16
Société Générale (France)*	3.20
Credit Suisse (Switzerland)	2.84
Fuji Bank (Japan)	2.84
Industrial Bank of Japan (Japan)	2.34
Banque Marocaine du Commerce Extérieur (Morocco)	2.08
Issue Dept (Oman)	2.08
Banque Libanaise pour le Commerce (Lebanon)	1.06
Banque Misr-Liban (Lebanon)	1.06
Crédit Libanais (Lebanon)	1.06
Société Génŕale Libano-Européene de Banque (Lebanon)	1.06

*Denotes member of EBIC– European Banks International Company

Subsidiaries of European Arab Holding SA

(i) European Arab Bank (Brussels) SA

Brussels, capital BF 500m

As above

(ii) Europaisch-Arabische Bank GmbH

Frankfurt, capital DM 15m

As above

(16d) Compagnie Arabe et Internationale d'Investissement (CAII)

Est 1973, Luxembourg, capital $30m

Kuwait Investment Company (Kuwait)	
Government of Abu Dhabi	*n.a.*
Bank of Kuwait and the Middle East	*n.a.*
Banque du Liban et d'Outre Mer (Lebanon)	*n.a.*
Banque Nationale de Tunisie (Tunisia)	*n.a.*
National Commercial Bank (Saudi Arabia)	*n.a.*
National Investment Company (Libya)	*n.a.*
Banque Centrale Populaire (Morocco)	*n.a.*
Banque Marocaine pour le Commerce et l'Industrie (Morocco)	*n.a.*
Banque Nationale pour le Développement Economique (Morocco)	*n.a.*

Shareholders	**Shareholdings %**
Gulf Bank (Kuwait)	
Bank of Sudan	
Qatar National Bank (Qatar)	*n.a.*
Union Bancaire pour le Commerce et l'Industrie (Tunisia)	*n.a.*
Banque Nationale de Paris (France)	*n.a.*
Banque Nationale de Paris Internationale (France)	*n.a.*
Banco Central (Spain)	*n.a.*
Canadian Imperial Bank of Commerce (Canada)	*n.a.*
Oesterreichische Laenderbank (Austria)	*n.a.*
Union de Banques Suisses (Switzerland)	*n.a.*
Banco do Brasil (Brazil)	*n.a.*
Société Financière Européene	25.00

Subsidiary of CAII
(i) Banque Arabe et Internationale d'Investissement (BAII)
Est 1973, Paris, capital Fr. Fr. 50m
As above

(16e) Iran Overseas Investment Bank
Est 1973, London, capital £5m

Barclays Bank International (United Kingdom)	10.00
Bank Melli Iran (Iran)	10.00
Bank of America (USA)	10.00
Bank of Tokyo (Japan)	10.00
Deutsche Bank (Germany)	10.00
Industrial Bank of Japan (Japan)	10.00
Industrial and Mining Development Bank of Iran	10.00
Manufacturers Hanover Trust (USA)	10.00
Midland Bank (United Kingdom)	10.00
Société Générale (France)	10.00

Arab and Morgan Grenfell Finance Company
Est 1974, London, capital £1m

Morgan Grenfell Holdings (United Kingdom)	50.00
Arab Bank (Jordan)	45.00
Arab Bank Overseas (Switzerland)	5.00

Shareholders	Shareholdings %
Arab International Finance Company (ARINFI)	
Est 1974, incorporated in Switzerland but operating out of Beirut, capital SwFr 14m	
International Marine Banking Co (United Kingdom)	12.50
Marine Midland Bank (USA)	12.50
A.K. Holdings (Luxembourg)	*n.a.*
Kuwait International Investment Co (Kuwait)	*n.a.*
Other Arab investors	*n.a.*
(17) LEBANON	
Banque d'Investissement et de Financement (INFI)	
Est 1974, Beirut, capital Leb £15m	
Banque Audi (Lebanon)	35.00
Caisse Centrale de Banques Populaires (France)	8.00
Hambros Bank (United Kingdom)	8.00
Mitsui Bank (Japan)	8.00
Nomura Securities (Japan)	8.00
Groupe Renault (France)	8.00
Non-institutional Arab shareholders	25.00
Arab Finance Corp.	
Est 1974, Beirut, capital Leb £6m	
Manufacturers Hanover Trust (United States)	18.00
Kuwait Investment Company (Kuwait)	18.00
Investment Promotion Group (Lebanon)	18.00
Banque de l'Union Européene (France)	18.00
Bank of Tokyo (Japan)	10.00
Beirut-Riyad Bank (Lebanon)	9.00
Crédit Libanais (Lebanon) and its Brussels subsidiary Banque Européene pour le Moyen-Orient	9.00
J. Henry Schroder & Co	
Est 1974, Beirut	
J. Henry Schroder Wagg (United Kingdom)	*n.a.*
Asseily family (Lebanon)	*n.a.*

Shareholders	**Shareholdings %**
Société Financière pour le Moyen-Orient (SOFIMO)	
Est 1975, Beirut, capital Leb £6m	
Société Générale (France)	42.50
Kuwait International Investment Company (Kuwait)	*n.a.*
Société Générale Libano-Européene de Banque (Lebanon)	*n.a.*
FRAB Bank (France)	*n.a.*
Almana Trading Co (Qatar)	*n.a.*
Other Arab investors	*n.a.*

(18) EGYPT

Cairo Barclays International Bank	
Est 1974, Cairo, capital US$ 10m	
Barclays Bank International (United Kingdom)	50.00
Banque du Caire (Egypt)	50.00
Chase National Bank of Egypt	
Est 1975, Cairo	
Chase Manhattan Bank (USA)	49.00
National Bank of Egypt (Egypt)	51.00
Misr International Bank	
Est 1975, Cairo, capital US$ 2.5m	
Bank Misr (Egypt)	20.00
Commercial and industrial companies in which Bank Misr has a participation	10.00
Public subscription by Egyptian nationals	21.00
Banco di Roma (Italy)	19.00*
UBAF Ltd (United Kingdom)	10.00

*of which 9.00% to be made available within one year to international banks approved by the founding members.

Egyptian American Bank	
Est 1975, Cairo, capital $30m	
Bank of Alexandria (Egypt)	51.00
American Express (USA)	49.00

(19) DUBAI

National Bank of Dubai

Est 1963, Dubai, capital QDR18.3m

Shareholders	Shareholdings %
National Bank of Kuwait (Kuwait)	30.00
Grindlays Bank (United Kingdom)	10.00
Bank of America (USA)	4.00
Local Dubai merchants	56.00
Commercial Bank of Dubai	
Est 1969, Dubai, capital D 20m	
Commerzbank (Germany)	*n.a.*
Chase Manhattan Bank (USA)	*n.a.*
Commercial Bank of Kuwait (Kuwait)	*n.a.*
Dubai Bank Ltd	
Est 1970, Dubai, capital D 11.5m	
Hambros Bank (United Kingdom)	10.00
Wells Fargo (USA)	10.00
Banque de l'Union Européene (France)	5.00
Local investors	75.00
Oryx Investments Ltd	
Est 1974, Dubai, capital US$ 1.25m	
Arbuthnot Latham (United Kingdom)	20.00
Standard and Chartered Banking Group (United Kingdom)	20.00
(from Abu Dhabi, Bahrain, Dubai, Kuwait, Qatar and Saudi Arabia)	60.00
(20) KUWAIT	
International Financial Advisers	
Est 1974, Kuwait, capital KD 500,000	
Robert Fleming & Co (United Kingdom)	15.00
William Kent & Co (United States)	15.00
Banque Worms (France)	15.00
Private Kuwaiti individuals	55.00
Arab Financial Consultants Company	
Est 1974, Kuwait, Capital KD500,000	
Kuwaiti interests	51.00
Other Arab investors	25.00
Arbuthnot Latham (United Kingdom)	6.00

Shareholders	Shareholdings %
Taiyo Kobe Bank (Japan)	6.00
Philadelphia National Bank (USA)	6.00
Banque de Suez et Union des Mines (France)	6.00

CHAPTER 7

Major Development & Expenditure Sectors

The oil producing countries have always had an advantage over other less-developed countries in having an important natural resource to develop which has had an assured market in the outside world. In consequence they have also not suffered the second general shortage of other LDCs which is adequate finance for development, although it has not always been seen that way because much of the income resulting from oil has been employed to cover day to day needs for which other governments have to provide by taxes on their own inhabitants. The shortage that the oil producers do share with other less-developed countries is the shortage of human resources of trained and skilled administrators, technicians and handymen. Although for a whole generation the inhabitants of the oil producing countries have had the benefits of education and training, and the progress of many of their citizens to the top and their performance in senior responsible positions have been remarkable, there is still a great shortage of men with the talent and training appropriate for jobs below the top. It applies less to the oil business, where the training has been extremely thorough, than to other fields of activity, and the result is that although great strides have been made in infrastructural development there is still a long way to go to meet the full needs of the countries.

In common with other less-developed countries the oil producers have from an early stage had their eyes set on general development, although their approach has varied. In some countries the early ways of thought have persisted and developments took place as the situation demanded, largely as a result of individual initiatives. Other countries have preferred to rely on a formal development plan. The development plans in themselves have tended to be of the type which professional planners refer to as aspirations rather than plans, consisting of a long list of the targets the government would like to see achieved. With some there has been a theoretical assessment of the likelihood of fulfilment, of the inter-actions of the targets on each other, or of the availability of resources, but a sense of the practical has been lacking. With the far greater financial resources now available a new series of such plans is coming out, but again with seemingly some lack of regard for the other resources that in reality may not be available.

After the effective nationalisation of the oil industries in the Gulf countries, first attention in the development plans is being paid to oil-related projects. Kuwait indeed has gone on record as saying it intends to invest in no major developments except in this field, while in both Saudi Arabia and Iraq such developments have been given priority over all others. Naturally with such large resources available many of the projects being discussed are on a very large scale, while there is also a number of smaller ones, and are likely to have an impact on the economics of the industries elsewhere in the world.

Export Refineries

There are several projects mooted, though few have yet gone beyond that stage, for refineries for export. The oil producing countries have in the last twenty years seen the shift from refining on the spot and export of products to exporting crude with the refining operations carried out in the consuming countries. They feel that the opportunities now open to them will make it more profitable to insist on future refining developments being carried out in their own countries rather than continue as simply exporters of crude. The economic questions are debatable. The producing countries may have gained a false impression from what was happening when the integrated companies handled the vast bulk of international oil from wellhead to consumer, and do not appreciate fully the various factors involved.

Refining in the oil producing countries would start with the advantage that fuel is available at cost, which is virtually negligible. This begs a question which will be reverted to later, whether using their fuel resources for manufacture within their own states at a true cost of a few cents a barrel is really the economical way of using that fuel. The input to the manufacturing plant is cheap, but conversely the profits that would be obtained from export of the fuel consumed are being lost, so that although an operation may look well on paper more careful consideration of the economics may produce a different conclusion. The second advantage which the producing countries possess for the establishment of new refineries is that they can be set up in barren areas in which pollution will cause few of the problems that have recently been obstructing the development of refineries in heavily-populated countries.

Table 7.1
ME REFINERIES AND EXPORT CAPACITY

	Site	Capacity mta (D = domestic use)	Status*	Associate
IRAN	(3 domestic)	(8.7)	E	
	(3 domestic)	(16.3)	U P	
	Abadan	21.5 (inc. 3.8D)	E	Consortium
	Bushehr	12.5	P ?	Deminex
	?	12.5	P ?	Shell Oil group
	?	12.5	P ?	Japanese group
IRAQ	(6 domestic)	(4.9)	E	
	(2 domestic)	(14)	U ?	
	Basrah	3.5	E	Czech
	Basrah	10	P	
	Umm Qasr	10	P	
KUWAIT	Ahmadi	15 (inc. 4D)	E	KOC
	Shuaiba	6.8	E	
		+ 2.2	U	
	3 partitioned zone	10.5 (not fully utilised)	E	Aminoil, Getty, AOC
SAUDI ARABIA	(2 domestic)	(3)	E	
	Ras Tanura	20.7 (inc. 1.5D)	E	Aramco
	Jubail	12.5	P	Mitsubishi
	Jubail ?	12.5	P	Shell
	Yanbu	12.5	P	Mobil
BAHRAIN	Awali	12.5	E	Bapco
QATAR	(domestic)	(0.3	E	
		+ 0.7)	P	
	Umm Said	10	P	
ABU DHABI	(domestic)	(0.75)	U	
	?	15	P	

* E = Existing
U = Underway
P = Planned

Table 7.1 contd......

SOUTH YEMEN	Aden	8	E	BP
GULF REGION				
Existing total Export Capacity (excluding all domestic use)		88.2		
Possible total including all plans		210		
LIBYA	5 domestic	(0.9)	E	
	Zawia	3 (inc. 0.7D)	E	
		+ 3	U	
	Tobruk	11	P	
	Misurata	11	P	
	Zuetina	20	P	
	Brega	20	P	
Possible Libya total of export plans		67		

Economic arguments against the development of refineries in the producing countries are also strong. In the first place the actual cost of construction is considerably higher, with all the specialist equipment requiring to be shipped from the developed countries, and with the cost of erection and provision of basic facilities considerably higher from the lack of infrastructure. In the second place the economic factor which has dominated oil companies' thinking in the location of refinery development has been the growth in tanker sizes and the economies in the cost of transporting oil that growth has brought. When the great refinery at Abadan was built and was functioning at its highest level there was little difference in size and cost between tankers carrying crude oil and those carrying products, and it made good sense to refine and make a series of products available for distribution according to the needs of different consuming countries. With the growing disparity in size between crude and product tankers the advantages of refining before shipping have virtually disappeared except for very short hauls. It now costs less than half as much to transport oil in a VLCC as in the largest product tanker afloat. Product tankers will undoubtedly grow in size but that in itself will present problems. Abu Dhabi for instance has seriously put forward a plan for an export refinery with products to be shipped in 250,000 ton tankers. It does not seem to be understood that only the largest of consuming countries, and the biggest distributors within those countries, could possibly afford the size of reception terminal and the elaborate network of piping and tanks that would be required on the arrival of tankers of such a size. Even the 60,000 ton product tanker which is generally expected to become an economic size for ocean movements will not be welcome in many oil-handling ports. The third difficulty is that in the advanced industrial countries the number of oil products required, each with exacting technical specifications, stretches into several hundreds and it is difficult to foresee any possibility of such a range being transported from the producing countries. Opinion now would appear to be that product tankers from the producing countries might be acceptable if they carried products in three or four broad ranges, resulting from primary distillation, to refineries in the developed countries for finishing to required specification. Such a development clearly implies a close cooperation which must mean cooperation with benefits to both sides.

It would seem likely the way such projects will develop, if they are to be achieved, will be to concentrate the refining operation which the oil producing countries can do best, and that is the production of low sulphur fuel oil. Even the best of Middle East crudes is heavily sulphurous by world standards. In the primary refining process most of the sulphur accumulates in the fuel oil, and the sulphurous fuel oil gives rise to pollution at a level which in some parts of the developed world is increasingly unacceptable. Special atmospheric conditions affect the industrial areas of Japan, and California and New York in the US, and the authorities are determined to reduce the level of pollution. In other countries the problem is not so acute but still causes concern, and limits on sulphur content are set. Therefore if fuel oil can be desulphurised at a location where the resultant pollution can be dispersed without seriously affecting the inhabitants it will command a premium price in the markets. The remaining products then, because they will be somewhat more expensive by the time they reach the consuming countries than competing products from refineries in those countries, may have to stand a small loss but that loss could be outweighed by the increased value of the sulphur-free fuel oil. The economics of a particular project will need careful examination but it is probable that some at least of those proposed would be able to go forward on these lines. The establishment of a refinery with no assurance as to the reception of its products is unlikely to be profitable, as Kuwait has learned.

For Libya the short haul to European markets would appear to offer conditions more favourable than for the Gulf countries. In the Mediterranean however competition is strong, with France, Spain and Greece all having surplus capacity designed for export, and cargoes regularly on offer from the Black Sea. Italy in particular has made product exports the keystone of its energy policy and with consumption just over 100 million tons has refinery capacity approaching 200 million.

Countries planning export refineries might consider further the figures for world capacity. With the long lead time in major projects, developments started in 1973 in expectation of a continuing growth rate of consumption will not be coming on stream until 1977. At the start of 1975 refining capacity outside the communist states was 2810 million tons, and is expected to reach 3250 million tons by 1977, while a survey early in 1975 showed over 600 million tons then unused, possibly one third for normal operational reasons and the rest surplus to current requirements.

Consuming countries both large and small have pursued a policy of building up their own refining industry, and while import duties on crude oil are rare they are almost universally applied to products. To a large extent product movements nowadays are a result of imbalance between product demand and refinery yield patterns, and duties may be reduced or eliminated it is mutually advantageous – free movement of products within the EEC being an example. If the share of products in world oil trade is to start expanding again, it maybe that prior agreement on the economic benefits would facilitate the process.

Natural Gas

Besides the refinery projects, almost all the producing countries are formulating large-scale projects for natural gas. Natural gas is a complicated subject. Statements in the press are seldom very clear precisely what is meant and even official speakers sometimes appear to be confused. When oil is produced there is, in all the oilfields of the Middle East, gas associated with it under pressure underground which automatically comes to the surface with the oil. Typically in a Middle East field the amount of gas reaching the surface with every barrel of oil may be around 500 cubic feet (at standard temperature and pressure, the basic state at which all volumes of gas are stated). This gas has been flared as all visitors to the Gulf are well aware.

Flaring of the gas was for long a bone of contention between the oil companies and the governments. The governments saw quite rightly that gas was a basic natural resource being simply wasted. The companies agreed but showed that its production was completely unavoidable, and that in the circumstances of the time the possible economic uses of the gas were limited. Over the years a number of minor uses for the gas were found; for instance almost all oil production and loading operations use the gas as fuel, quantities of it are provided for the power stations in the oil producing countries, and a certain amount has found industrial use. The governments also at one time were insistent that what was not used should be reinjected into the fields so as to be available subsequently, but for technical reasons the number of Middle East oilfields where this can be done without seriously reducing oil production is very small and when the governments had developed greater technical expertise they also realised the fact.

The first exports of liquefied natural gas on a commercial scale were shipped from Algeria to UK in 1964, and this gave rise to further claims from the Middle East governments. However the whole process of liquefying the natural gas at a temperature of minus 160° C, shipping it, keeping it in that condition and off-loading it still under control was extremely expensive and at that time the maximum range at which it was feasible was under 1000 miles. In due course the special techniques of building LNG carriers were developed and they became larger, so that the range of possible shipments was extended. It still however was not great enough to make shipments of LNG from the Middle East an economic proposition.

The natural gas associated with oil is not strictly a single gas but a whole range. Basically it consists of simple hydrocarbons which are generally referred to by the number of carbon atoms in the molecule, from C1, methane, up to C8, octane. Methane is natural gas as most

Diagram – 7A

THE PETROLEUM GASES

<table>
<tr><td>Names :</td><td>Methane</td><td>Ethane</td><td>Propane</td><td>Butane</td><td>Pentane</td><td>Hexane</td><td>Heptane</td><td>Octane</td></tr>
<tr><td>C_nH_{2n+2} :</td><td>C_1</td><td>C_2</td><td>C_3</td><td>C_4</td><td>C_5</td><td>C_6</td><td>C_7</td><td>C_8</td></tr>
<tr><td rowspan="2">Industry names:</td><td rowspan="2">lean gas
dry gas
LNG when
liquefied</td><td rowspan="2"></td><td colspan="6">natural gas liquids (NGL)</td></tr>
<tr><td colspan="2">liquefied petroleum gas (LPG)</td><td colspan="4">natural gasoline</td></tr>
<tr><td>Consumers' names:</td><td>natural gas</td><td>*</td><td colspan="2">bottled gas</td><td></td><td></td><td></td><td></td></tr>
<tr><td>Liquefaction temperature: °C</td><td>– 162</td><td>– 88</td><td>– 42</td><td>– 1</td><td></td><td></td><td></td><td></td></tr>
<tr><td>Main uses:</td><td>energy

fertilizer feedstock</td><td>chemical feedstock</td><td colspan="2">* energy</td><td colspan="4">petroleum blending</td></tr>
</table>

* "Natural gas" may containe ethane. Propane may also be used as chemical feedstock; so occasionally may higher fractions

consumers know it, with a slight admixture of C2, ethane. The next two gases in the series, C3 propane and C4 butane, are familiar to consumers as the bottled gases and known in the business as LPG, liquefied petroleum gases. They become liquid at comparatively low temperatures, minus 40° C for propane and zero C for butane, or under moderate pressures, and can be transported in this form. Originally small tankers with precisely constructed pressure vessels started the trade in propane and butane in liquid form, but parallel with the development of refrigeration techniques which made the shipment of methane possible it was found that by temperature control of propane and butane far larger containers were practicable, and the size of an economic carrier leapt from 1000 to 20,000 tons in a single stage. The remaining gases that are produced – pentane to octane – become liquid at the surface. Nomenclature is confusing, with some authorities referring only to this group as natural gas liquids while others include propane and butane, describing the higher fractions as natural gasoline.

The development of techniques for shipping propane and butane in ocean-going ships led to the start of a new production industry in the Middle East as early as 1963. Gas processing plants were set up, initially in Kuwait and later in Iran and Saudi Arabia, in which these fractions of the associated gas produced with the oil were stripped out and made ready for shipment overseas, while the methane remained to be used if possible or flared. The fractions of the different gases in the associated gas differ considerably between fields, but methane is always the primary constituent, typically 70 to 80 per cent, with all the other fractions making up the remainder. To produce economic amounts of LPG large plants and supplies of gas were needed, but they were developed. Propane and butane have always been popular fuels with users for both their cleanliness and the precision with which their burning can be controlled. There was already considerable experience in their use, because a certain amount of these gases is produced by normal refinery operations which, before there were shipping possibilities, had been the source of supply. The limits of demand were set by the rate at which the handling facilities on the scale of retail distribution could be set up. The natural gas liquids on the other hand found little use in their pure state, though they might be blended with the crude oil.

While the quintupling of oil prices has not made a great difference in comparative terms to the advantages of LPG and NGL it considerably improved the economics of shipping LNG. Many projects which could not previously have come into the reckoning can do so now, always of course provided that the price of the basic methane from the producing countries is not set too high. A further process has been developed as a rival to the liquefaction of natural methane, which is the conversion of it to methanol. The conversion process is comparatively expensive – estimates vary from a quarter to three-quarters more than the cost of the liquefaction process – but there is then the great advantage that the methanol can be transported in ordinary tankers and does not depend on special expensive carriers. On the other hand at the consumers' end methanol will also need more expensive conversion processes to bring it into use than does methane. At present the economic and technical arguments between the advocates of the two processes are far from being resolved. Either way the producing countries would have a market for their methane, but against that they are conscious that the gas would essentially be competing against their own oil, that the profits from it will be considerably less, and that they have a decision to make between their purely financial interests and their interests in the long-term conservation of their natural resources.

While most of the argument in the Middle East has been about associated gas, in the course of exploration various gasfields have been found which are capable of producing largely gas alone with very small amounts of entrained liquids. In some parts of the world there is an intermediate type of field which contains both gas and very light oils but in the Middle East there is only one field of significance of this type, Pazanun in Iran, and that is already under exploitation. Of the gasfields discovered, three have been claimed to be of giant size, although in each case further appraisal drilling needs to be done before the estimates can be considered reliable. Two of them are in Iran, one discovered by Egoco, the European Governments' Oil Companies' Consortium, containing ENI, ERAP and others, at Kangan onshore, which the Company claims to be of the order of 5000 billion cubic metres. Offshore the C field, originally discovered by Shell, is now claimed by the Japanese Nissho-Iwai, one of the group hoping to exploit it, to contain 2500 billion cubic metres. In Abu Dhabi, underlying the main Bu Hasa oilfield but physically separated from its gas deposits have been found which an Abu Dhabi government spokesman has claimed also to be of 5000 billion cubic metres. To put the size of these fields in perspective the total gas reserves in all the fields in the Middle East where gas is associated with the oil may be put at 6000 billion cubic metres while the Groningen field in Holland, at present supplying half of Europe's gas requirements, has reserves estimated around 2500 billion cubic metres.

There is however a little difficulty with these fields. In addition to the hydrocarbon gases they contain, gasfields normally bring a certain amount of water to the surface, which needs to be separated out, and they contain other non-hydrocarbon gases, of which nitrogen is common but in small quantities harmless. On the other hand hydrogen sulphide when it occurs is intensely obnoxious and corrosive. Of the fields mentioned at least the C field is known to contain a high concentration of hydrogen sulphide and its commercial prospects are thereby decreased.

In view of the quantities of associated gas available and the more pressing need to ensure that it is utilised as soon as possible the problems of the unassociated gasfields can wait. There is no urgency for their development, and possibly Iran and certainly Abu Dahbi may consider it advisable to keep them in reserve for use later rather than press ahead with exploitation in the near future.

Various of the oil producing countries are considering further extension downstream into the utilisation of gas and possibly some oil by-products to develop a chemical industry. It is some years since the oil companies dropped the use of the word "petrochemicals" and started to refer to the industry as simply "chemical". Although hydrocarbons now form the raw material for much of the world's chemical production many of the techniques were originally based on coal and the hydrocarbons took over as a matter of economics. It is interesting to note that processes were developed with natural gas as feedstock in the United States, where gas has been abundant and as mentioned earlier unnaturally cheap, whereas Europe often obtains the same product from naphtha, a surplus product where gasoline demand is much lower than in the States. Technically many organic compounds at present based on hydrocarbons could be produced from other materials. There are signs that the rise in price of oil and gas is causing industries in the States to think of reverting to coal, while in Europe other simple organic substances are again being looked at as possibly more economic sources of supply. Progress in the industry and development of processes have been so rapid in the past that although hydrocarbons hold the field today the possibility of a quick flank attack should not be ignored.

The simplest of the bulk chemical processes in the industry consists of converting a suitable feedstock – methane from natural gas is the obvious one for the Middle East – into ammonia and then manufacturing the ammonia into urea, ammonium sulphate or other fertilizers. Existing and planned fertilizer plants in the Middle East are shown in the table.

Table 7.2
ME FERTILIZER PLANTS

		Capacity tons per day		
		Ammonia	Urea	Other Fertilizers
IRAN	Shiraz	120	150	
	Shahpur		500	1730
IRAQ	Basrah	180	150	400
KUWAIT	KCFC	360	500	450
	KPIC	1600	1250	
SAUDI ARABIA	Dammam	200	400	
QATAR	Umm Said	330	360	
UNDER CONSTRUCTION / PLANNED				
IRAN	Shiraz: expand to	1200	1500	
	Shahpur	1000	1500	
	French Partner		?	
IRAQ	Basrah: expand to	800	1300	
	Plan		5500	
SAUDI ARABIA	Partners: ICI, Agrico (US), Taiwan F.C.	"3 Large"		
QATAR	expand to	660	720	
LIBYA	Brega	1000		

Sources: Hydrocarbon Processing and various

There is a great and growing need for fertilizers throughout the world especially in the less developed countries and the Middle East can play an important part in trying to satisfy this need. Economics still plays a part because in such a capital-intensive industry the cost of transport of process plant to the Middle East and erection there, together with the cost of skilled management and technicians, may outweigh the savings on cheap fuel, so that until recently it was still cheaper to supply fertilizer to India from Europe than from the Gulf. At one time India was proposing a partnership whereby the ammonia itself could be produced in the Gulf and shipped in liquid form, with the further processing into fertilizer being done in India and the capital cost of the scheme being shared. No producing country would then agree, but such an arrangement does offer a possible route for cooperation between the oil producers and some of the less developed countries.

The difficulties involved in the establishment of a fertilizer plant in the Gulf become accentuated when the manufacture of more complicated chemicals is considered. It does seem that the point is appreciated by Middle East governments, and the projects being discussed are not to be embarked upon in isolation but depend on finding a suitable partner both to supply the technical expertise and to provide a market. Production of simple chemicals such as caustic soda and sulphuric acid is already established in some countries, as are consumer plastic goods. Iran has a carbon black plant under construction, and both Iran and Saudi Arabia are interested in BP plants for making protein from oil. Sulphur and its derivatives have been exported and there are plans for methanol. The plans for major export plants however concern either the aromatics group, benzene and xylene, or the olefins, ethylene and derivatives such as polyethylene and propylene. In this field they may cause serious problems to the chemical industry in other parts of the world, but they could have problems themselves with greatly excess capacity. Cooperation at all stages from the tentative plan onwards is likely to repay all parties more surely than in any other activity.

The Arab oil producing countries are in the process of rapidly expanding their tanker fleets. They have for many years been preoccupied with the importance of carrying their own oil, with a concern that appeared to show little understanding of the freedom of the charter market, or of its frequently depressed state. The extreme

Table 7.3
MIDDLE EAST SHIPPING AT END 1974

	Tanker Fleet	Thousand deadweight tons
National Iran Tanker Co.	4	184
Kuwait Oil Tanker Co.	3	627
Kuwait Oil Tanker Co.	3	169
Iraq Maritime Transport Co.	7	247
Petroship (Saudi Arabia)	1	27
Arab Maritime Shipping Co. (Saudi Arabia)	2	120
Dubai National Shipping Corp.	1	19
Libyan General Maritime Co.	4	268
Abu Dhabi National Oil Co.	1	269
	26	**1930**

	Tankers on order	
National Iran Tanker Co.	2	460
Iraq Oil Transport Co.	9	1263
Kuwait Oil Tanker Co.	3	983
Kuwait Government	4	212
Petroship	2	80
Libyan General Maritime Co.	7	758
Abu Dhabi National Oil Co.	1	260
Arab Maritime Petroleum Transport Co. (OAPEC)	4	1176
	32	**5192**

Table 7.3 contd......

	Dry Cargo	
	Ships	Thousand GRT
Arya National Shipping Co. (Iran)	13	142
Iraq Maritime Transport Co.	6	51
Kuwait Shipping Co.	16	170
National Maritime Agencies (Kuwait)	4	60
Saudi Lines	7	19
Orri Navigation (Saudi Arabia)	2	9
	48	**451**

depression of 1975 certainly provides opportunities for acquiring tankers cheaply, but emphasises the risks of ownership. Ali Khawneh, chairman of the Kuwait Oil Tanker Company, has estimated that to carry sixty per cent of their oil exports the Arabs would need over 400 tankers at a cost of $12–15 billion.

In addition to the ships listed in the table there are further dry cargo ships on order. Libya has three LNG carriers and both Saudi Arabia and Iran may acquire some in relation to their gas projects. Two other private tanker companies, the Saudi Arabia Shipping Company and the Saud Maritime Company, have recently been formed. Iran has announced that it is to purchase ten tankers, both crude and product carriers, from BP which will then contribute an equal number to a jointly-managed fleet.

Industry

Some of the difficulties that confront the Arab states which are proposing to establish large-scale chemical industries are seen even more in various intentions for general industrial development. Cheap fuel is relied on to offset all the other advantages possessed by their potential competitors. It is necessary to distinguish schemes which aim at a country's desire to replace imports for itself, or possibly with sufficient regional cooperation for the region, from the projects which are aimed to export to the rest of the world. There is little doubt that various of the projects which aim at self-sufficiency can be justified and will be developed. With the upsurge of construction throughout the Gulf and the probable future needs of that industry the number of cement plants which have already sprung up appear to have a prosperous future. Similarly it is likely that in the iron and steel industry projects for manufacturing pipe to be used locally or for steel reinforcement rods are also likely to be successful.

The success of the Bahrain aluminium smelter has encouraged other countries to think of similar projects. That however was a special case with unexploited gas reserves, a very modest oil income and, at the time when the project was instituted, no other prospect of benefiting from the gas. In addition the Bahrain government took on partners in a strong marketing position and the intensive use of energy in the project has paid off. Similar projects are now proposed in other Gulf countries, but whether with the much higher prices for energy now prevailing they are in fact economically justifiable is a matter that will require careful consideration.

Another large scale project which depends for its viability on the supply of low cost energy is the Saudi design for a steel complex. The plan is to ship Saudi oil to Brazil and bring back in the same carriers an iron-ore slurry. The project to be economical depends both on the use of Saudi energy at low cost as opposed to the value of its sales elsewhere, and also on the provision of the basic raw material virtually free of transport costs, and it must be very vulnerable to any change in circumstances. If for instance the recent oil discoveries off the coast of Brazil are as large as some of its government spokesmen have been claiming the whole project will clearly call for reconsideration.

In the case of Iran it should be noted the size of the population means that projects can be designed to satisfy internal requirements which are on a very much larger scale than could be justified across the Gulf, but projects designed for export will still face problems of the same order.

Agriculture

Nobody listening to or reading the speeches of leaders of the oil producing countries can have failed to notice a certain degree of preoccupation with the future of their countries when oil has slowed to a trickle or been exhausted. One of the ways in which they wish to deploy their wealth is in the development of agriculture which if taken sufficiently far will provide them with an important insurance, even if no more, against difficulties in the future. Each government has laid great stress on agriculture in its development plans and, on the basis of what has been put forward, one can expect even in the most arid lands a considerable move towards self-sufficiency.

In speaking of the arid lands it is not the land itself, or more strictly the soils of which it is composed, that is the limiting factor for agricultural growth. Investigations in many parts of Arabia have shown soils with potential for production and, as may be seen in many areas after rain, the life that sprouts from the apparent desert is a delight to the inhabitants and an amazement to strangers. It is the lack of water which inhibits agriculture. There are parts of the Middle East where rain-fed agriculture is successful and productive. The northern belts of Iran and Iraq, the Asir province of Saudi Arabia, parts of Oman which catch the fringe of the monsoon, and the coastal belt of Libya are all fruitful. In the rest of the area, however, where rainfall may be as little as fifty millimetres a year, prospects are much poorer and only small patches irrigated from wells produce crops.

In each of the countries there are government experimental stations in which a variety of agricultural methods, various breeds of seed and additional soil nutrients are exhaustively tested. The experimental farms are managed with great expertise and enthusiasm and some fine results have been obtained. It is however a slow business to extend the tested practices to the general agriculture of the state. The farmer, like the sailor, in all parts of the world is notoriously conservative and takes much persuasion to alter his ways. He knows very well the strength of natural forces and the variety of conditions, which differ one growing season from another, and he is always suspicious – occasionally with reason – that the new methods which he is being persuaded to adopt may have gained official approval by a combination of lucky circumstances.

Planners and administrators who have been educated in the cities tend to be ignorant of the variety and power of nature, and they fail to be sympathetic with the conservatism of the countryman. Certainly the plans they form often seem to pose unrealistic targets for the growth of agriculture and, in the administration of the plans, the persistence and effort needed over a long period to achieve real progress in agriculture are seldom appreciated. There is a danger that in their impatience administrators may be tempted to enforce some form of collectivisation on the land, but as Arthur Lewis has pointed out in his *Development Planning* 'that is the surest way to reduce agricultural output. All countries which have tried it have found it a failure'.

Where farmers can well come together is in cooperative marketing, and several states have shown the wisdom of encouraging such ventures. While in production the sturdy individualism of the farmer may well pay off, marketing individually shows him at his weakest and the reinforcement of a cooperative will help him to remedy it. With reasonable management a cooperative can hardly fail to get better prices for the farmer than he can on his own in rivalry with his neighbours. If becoming accustomed to cooperation in marketing brings greater readiness among farmers to cooperate in productive operations it should improve the prospects for the future.

Country	**Report**	**Water Supply**
Saudi Arabia	Cressey	12,500 cubic metres/ hectare/year
Iraq	Salter	7,000 cubic metres/ hectare/year
Jordan	Huntings	9,700 cubic metres/ hectare/year
Iran	IVth Plan	10,000 cubic metres/ hectare/year

However there have been advances in technology which have produced some extremely interesting results. Two of the pilot schemes have been in Abu Dhabi where Shaikh Zayid's knowledge of the countryman's problems and deep interest in his welfare have given a special impetus to agricultural studies. For the intensive development of market garden produce glass or plastic housing has been erected, a controlled humid atmosphere applied, and nutrient elements fed to the plant roots. Obviously such methods at present are intensive in their use of capital, but as regards the use of water they may require as little as a tenth of normal irrigation methods. The Sadiyat plant north of Abu Dhabi which the University of Arizona piloted has produced yields as great as 180 tons per hectare, while in the Al Ain area a French scheme with simpler methods has produced 65 tons per hectare over a much greater area. One trouble with such methods besides expense is the skilled maintenance required as well as the farmer's touch, but their advantages in the climate are such that a great spread of such methods may be expected.

Animal husbandry plays an important part in the life of the Middle East and although the purely nomadic life persists only in remote corners pastoralism remains widespread. In the areas mentioned above where rain-fed agriculture is possible the flocks also flourish but in the more desert areas only the tough local breeds survive, without being very productive. Various attempts to introduce new blood have not been very successful, as the pure breeds fail to survive and the cross breeds soon revert to the original type. Further development on the animal side may depend on a pilot experiment currently being discussed in Saudi Arabia to try the effect of rearing animals in a protected and enclosed environment such as has been so successful with produce.

Communications

Successful development depends on the coordination of a large number of projects and in getting the timing right. Nowhere is this more important than in development of the infrastructure, the basic communications and facilities without which any other stages of development will be completely hamstrung. The oil producing countries have for a number of years been able to devote considerable revenues to infrastructural projects, but even so the great access of wealth in 1974 showed up neglected areas.

The principal deficiency now apparent is port capacity. Development of port facilities has a long lead time, and like other advances in the Middle East cannot proceed by small additions at a time but requires successive major construction works. In some of the countries the ports were operating with considerable spare capacity but others were already under pressure both for current needs and for development supplies. With some knowledge of difficulties of port handling which had already manifested themselves it was apparent that some of the import programmes that were announced could not be achieved. Equally the new or enlarged development plans that have been coming forward do not always appear to have considered the capacity of the ports to handle all the necessary materials.

Physical capacity is not the only limiting factor in port operation. It is a familiar enough story to those involved, but possibly not to

Table 7.4
CARGO PORTS IN ME OIL PRODUCING COUNTRIES

Ports	Existing			Developing	Planning
	No. of Deep Water Berths	Maximum Draught (ft)	Draught in Roadstead (ft)	No. of Berths	No. of Berths
IRAN					
Khorramshahr	9	27		3	
Abadan	3	32			
Bandar Shahpur	6	34		4	10
Bushehr	2	27	30		
Bandar Abbas	6	29	35		"large"
IRAQ					
Basrah-Maqil	9	29		4	4
Umm Qasr	3	32	34	(4)*	3
KUWAIT					
Shuwaikh	8	31½	35		12
Shuaiba	6	30			"improve"
SAUDI ARABIA					
Dammam	7	36		8	25
Jubail	—				"gigantic"
Jeddah	12	36		4	4
Yanbu	2	31	35		"improve"
Jizan	2	Coastal			2 deep
BAHRAIN					
Mina Sulman	6	30		2 (32′)	4
QATAR					
Doha	4	29			5
UNITED ARAB EMIRATES					
Abu Dhabi-Port Zayid	6	31		12	
Dubai-Port Rashid	15	33		22 (37½′)	8
Sharjah-Port Khalid	2	25		6 deep	
Ras al Khaimah-Khuwair				2 (41′)	
OMAN					
Port Qaboos	8	32			
Raysut	5	coastal			4 deep
LIBYA					
Tripoli	3	24		2	4
Benghazi	5	24			16
Tobruk	1	30			

* Special cargoes

the planners, that administrative difficulties can set back a whole import programme very seriously. It is not uncommon to walk along a quayside, with difficulty because of the goods that block it, only to be told they are all waiting for various forms of paperwork to be completed. Programmes of still greater imports will require some of the states to look more closely at their procedures. Methods which have been imported from Western areas where there have been generations of port operation and port staff may not be appropriate where the work is being undertaken in the first generation, however much care and attention have been given to the training of the supervisory and clerical staff. Nor is it an answer simply to enlarge the staff; indeed experience shows that this is likely to be counter-productive. If the simplification of procedures would seem to pose certain additional risks, or reduce the amount of information available to central government departments, it may be considered whether the present situation with goods of all kinds competing for clearance does not also pose similar risks, and whether the amount of information flowing to the central government is not already more than needed or than the offices there can handle competently. The whole of the development programme hinges on satisfactory operation of the ports and governments may perhaps find that attention to their administrative as well as their physical development will prevent serious holdups elsewhere.

Another aspect of port operation is the movement of goods away from the port. Possibly accumulation in the docks may be the result of unsatisfactory physical clearing procedures rather than administrative ones. However that is not a general experience, and probably the ports in the Middle East for which distribution forms a difficulty are those dependent on railways, which may often be as poorly equipped to meet sudden additional demands on them. For ports where distribution is a matter of trucking clearance seldom appears to present much difficulty, since truck driving is an activity to which Middle East nationals have taken easily. If there are shortages of trucks, the situation can be quickly made good when money is available. The requirements of special vehicles for heavy load movements will be known far enough in advance for provision to be made, and the industry is one which can be seen to flourish in all the countries.

Although there have been holdups and delays, road construction has gone ahead rapidly under all development plans and the question of access for the vehicles distributing goods from the ports or in other economic activities is seldom a problem. In the soil and climate of much of the Middle East indeed vehicles can move easily without made roads although wear and tear then becomes a serious problem. More difficult construction in mountainous areas remains to be done, but there are already large parts of the region where road development has advanced so far that new undertakings are a matter of convenience and amenity and not of necessity.

The Middle East was fortunate to be situated on the first of the inter-continental air routes and for forty years air travel has been familiar to some if not all of its inhabitants. The great development which took place after the Second World War again brought the Middle East in as a focal point for many services, and the growth of airlines in the countries themselves with inter-continental capacity soon followed. Airports were developed, a comparatively simple matter in much of the terrain, to take the largest commercial aircraft and airport facilities were installed in line with international practice. The progress has been continuous and no reduction has been seen in requirements for air travel in the Middle East, even when traffic growth in other parts of the globe has slowed down. Several airlines have specialised in regional services, and in the larger countries internal services, with great benefit to the feeling of unity within the Arab world. It sometimes appears from the difficulty of getting onto popular internal services that a country paying more attention to providing such facilities for its own nationals could make a greater contribution to the general benefit than by the wide extention of long distance services.

The scale on which communications need to be provided may not be immediately realised from an atlas map. Iran is as large as Germany, France, Spain and Italy put together. Saudi Arabia is half as large again, or as big as the United States east of the Mississippi.

In the field of telecommunications the Middle East has also long been a focus since the first cable and landlines were laid through the region over a century ago. With the advent of more technically-advanced systems coverage of the wide areas has been enormously facilitated, and microwave and satellite communications are now supplementing the earlier systems. The development has been somewhat piecemeal and not all centres are as well served as their business would make desirable. For international business in particular only Beirut is a fully efficient centre. However the enlargement of the telecommunications system is an important item in all development budgets, and the demands made on it according to experience elsewhere will expand commensurate with the expansion of the services, so that it is difficult to envisage a halt to the growth in the development of telecommunications.

Technically radio and television services fall to be described under the heading of communications. Radio in each country today has no trouble in reaching to all parts. There is scarcely a city that does not have television reception and services are extending to the towns and other populous areas; in the Gulf most transmissions are already in colour. The social aspects of the broadcasting services are perhaps of more significance than the technical. The importance of radio is well recognised and it has long been used in the region as an instrument of government – and occasionally against governments. The mere entertainment value of television should not be underrated; in outlying areas it offers daily a full and varied programme such as the occasional cinema never could, and with it a sense of immediate contact with the capital. On a more serious note, in country countries where many adults have had no formal schooling, even ordinary programmes can be of educational value, while some authorities are providing regular services for this purpose.

Social Services

Even before the rise in oil prices the producing countries had taken considerable steps in social progress. Comparatively speaking social services take little of the total expenditure made possible by the government oil revenues, even as they were, and the brake on progress was not money but administration and availability of appropriate skills. The development of education, of housing and of medical services has been limited only by the rate at which the basic facilities and staff could be provided. In Kuwait it has already reached the stage where there is scarcely any more to be done, and the other states are making rapid advances.

In education in particular the smaller of the surplus states have found it relatively easy to advance to almost complete provision of primary education. These states on the other hand are the ones in which it seems unlikely that education at university or polytechnic level can effectively be provided. For them it will almost certainly be better to plan to send students for university education abroad, and even in the much more populous state of Saudi Arabia it would seem this has been adopted as deliberate government policy, with such advanced education as is planned to be provided within the state being confined largely to technological courses. In the more populous states there is room for complete progress from the earliest to the top stages of education, but particularly for the higher stages it might be suggested there is a tendency for the authorities to concentrate too much on mere buildings.

Education however is to a greater extent a matter of personal abilities of the teachers if it is to be anything more than learning by rote. Here the oil producing countries are meeting at an early stage the trouble that is apparent among the already industrialised countries. As greater opportunities develop throughout a state's economy both the status and salaries of teachers appear to drop; hence, especially where there is a great demand for educated people in all branches of government service and private enterprise, an inadequate number of those qualified to be teachers choose the profession. Fortunately the world of education is more international than many other activities, and the shortages of teaching staff have been made good from other countries. Perhaps, though, this may tend to confirm to the pupils the impression that teaching is not a job for the best of them, and so the shortage of national teachers may be perpetuated.

The dilemma, between the needs of the state and the ambitions of the students, is a matter that needs the attention of the governments. Arthur Lewis in his book *Development Planning* emphasises 'The shortage of technicians is worldwide but most acute in the developing countries. It is impossible to have a surplus of technicians. On the higher level, most of the jobs which those who study the humanities take in administration and teaching can be done equally well by engineers or scientists, but the converse is not true'. On the technician level those states which have deliberately introduced technician training instead of more generalised secondary schooling would appear to be on the right lines. Even this however is no guarantee of success, nor is the policy always pursued as energetically as is desirable to produce the benefits in the long run. In announcing the complete takeover by the state of the Kuwait National Petroleum

Company the Minister of Oil Abd al Muttalib al Kazimi stated that one of the principal reasons for the step was that 'the company had failed to create the necessary expertise and form a new generation of technicians well versed in the industry'. It was not made clear how the government which had always held majority control of the company intended now to remedy the situation, and leaves open the question whether Kuwaitis suitable for technical appointments are not being produced by the educational system or are not coming forward. It is hard to over-emphasise the important part that men trained in technology must play if the oil producing states are not merely to maintain their present industrial level but to expand it.

Housing is another of the social services in which important progress has been made but much remains to be done. This is one matter of which all the states are well aware and they are putting great effort into housing development. Again it is less a matter of physical shortage of materials, which if not available locally can always be imported, but of the required organisation and supervisory staff. The rate of progress in the states is now being accelerated by the employment of outside experts or even whole organisations to undertake major developments, and the urgency with which governments regard the problem further use of these methods may be expected.

With the wealth of the countries increasing rapidly the flow to individuals is also on the increase and, while government housing schemes may well be the most appropriate solution for those who are on the sidelines of development, they are unlikely to satisfy the desires of those who are benefiting more directly. The development of housing associations, providing assistance on easy terms for those wishing to get their own homes built, may be a suitable method and there are interesting developments in most countries along these lines.

Medical services are looked on by all the oil producing countries as not simply a matter of providing for the inhabitants' needs but also as one of prestige. Some of the best modern architecture can be seen in various of the hospitals that have sprung up in recent years, as well as quantities of the most modern equipment inside them. Medical staff however cannot be developed with the speed of building, and for a long time to come the countries will need assistance from outside. Exchange of personnel, with nationals going for training to other countries and foreigners coming to work in the Gulf, is very desirable. Progress in medicine, in techniques and in standards, is continuous and without constant exchanges a country can easily be left behind in its medical services. While at the moment the countries are conscious of the need for outside assistance to expand their services to the whole population, it is to be hoped that in the future those in responsible positions will be equally aware of the necessity for constant retraining and further exchange of personnel, and not hinder the process by nationalistic attitudes.

In the provision of the less tangible social services the distinction between the populous and the surplus states is very marked. In the surplus states the rulers have seen to it that by one means or another all their native inhabitants who wish it have opportunities for gainful employment, so providing social security. The more populous states on the other hand, although they have already made progress are now faced with the demands of a population which has been led to expect a great deal from their new wealth. Whether some of the steps the governments are already taking, such as subsidising foodstuffs, are merely a stopgap policy or are part of their permanent plans is not clear.

These considerations lead to fundamental doubts whether the long-term planning of the states has so far been in sufficient depth. One of the contrasts which people from more mature states sense on coming to a developing country is the excessive concentration of power and influence in the capital, which serves to attract many of the under-employed and unskilled from the outside areas. In the developed countries provincial cities with strong traditions of their own and excellent facilities are to be found and, although their inhabitants may grumble about the powers of the capital, they can also feel themselves to be the equals of those who live there. In developing states there is a tendency for the capital to attract far too many of the skills and too many of the population and to ignore the need to develop alternative centres. This is understandable in view of the shortage of top-class trained men so that each of them in the early stages expects to reach an important position quite young in life and sees those positions in the capital. Among the development plans of the producers there appears little acknowledgement of the need for other centres of excellence to devlop and be powers in their own rights. Certainly there is some effort on a small scale, in for instance the provision of municipal amenities and in the diversion of particular industrial projects into various provincial centres, but the will to develop the provincial cities into attractive alternatives to the capital itself appears to be lacking. In Iran, of course, various citis have historically been centres of importance in their provinces, but the very rapid growth Tehran has seen compared with the other cities suggests that not enough attention has been paid to their all-round development. Saudi Arabia perhaps has come nearest to a deliberate policy on these lines, with the reservation of political power to Riyadh but the development of heavy industry and appropriate support, particularly in the educational field, taking place in the eastern province, while the importance of the western province, Jeddah in particular, in the field of commerce and light industry with social facilities to match has been emphasised.

Coupled with the lack of policy for developing alternative city centres comes a lack of policy for making it attractive for people to remain on the land. While the states acknowledge the importance of agriculture, they have been slow to devise plans and provide administrative support to make country life prosperous enough to attract back the shanty dwellers on the edges of the cities. It is far from easy and there are not many countries, developed or undeveloped, that can be satisfied with their achievements in this field. For the individual farmer to remain on the land it is clearly necessary that he can attain a reasonable degree of prosperity for himself, and governments can assist by various fiscal policies to ensure this is so. On the social side, both for the farmer and for his growing children, it is also of importance that the small towns in agricultural districts should be pleasant places and offer services which are not totally inferior to those of the cities. Governments which can see and take their opportunities in this sector are likely to be building a genuinely prosperous nation.

Power supplies are normally treated in the development plans as part of the industrial sector. Thereby it tends to be overlooked that good power supplies are an essential part of making a country town comparable in amenities to the capital, and power is therefore as appropriately considered in the social sector as in the industrial. This applies even more strongly to the provision of water supplies, while not forgetting the needs of industrial plants, and to sewerage systems. Sewerage, as those familiar with the Middle East know well, has been one of the last of social amenities to be developed and even so it is largely the capitals that have received attention.

In the strictly social services of education, housing and medicine the governments have already made considerable efforts to improve the standard of life throughout, and are continuing to do so. Greater priority for the physical services in outlying districts might be seen to confirm their policies and relieve the pressure of immigration to the capital. The capital however attracts the elite as well as the poor; more than half the doctors in a country, for instance, may be practising there. Only by strong and deliberate personnel policies, not least in the government service, could the trend be reversed.

CHAPTER 8

The Oil Producers Development Plans

IRAN

The 'white revolution' which the Shah inaugurated in 1962, with his thorough-going land reforms and the drive on a broad front to take Iran past the breakthrough point into a prosperous developed country, had been making steady progress even at the old level of oil revenues, supplemented by massive external borrowing. In the process much solid work had gone into the infrastructural facilities, as well as on the agricultural and social fronts, and the considerable experience that has been gained over a period of years has left Iran well placed to make the best of its present fortunes. Indeed, while the early stages of the 'white revolution' met with initial doubts, and from both extremist wings with open hostility, as the prospertiy of the country has increased and its achievements become visible the Shah's programme has gained the full support of all but a tiny minority, and his belief in the approaching breakthrough has gained wide acceptance.

One problem Iran has had to face in common with other developing states is that the increasing prosperity together with the reduction of under-employment in agriculture has brought waves of unskilled labour to the capital. Tehran now has a population of approximately four million or one-eighth of the whole country. One of the major objects of the revision of the fifth development plan, which was made possible by the increase in the expected oil revenues, has been to concentrate on the development of the provincial capitals with the deliberate intention of drawing the unwanted hands away from the capital. Already great progress has been made in communications, and the foundation of centres of advanced education and development of major industrial complexes in the provinces have been undertaken, but the latest plans have provided further support for this policy by developments to take place in provincial administration. Whether the central government will in fact dare to go far enough to enable the cities with their own great traditions, such as Tabriz, Esfahan and Meshed, to grow into centres with the real power to rival that of Tehran is rather debatable but the policies do imply a considerable shift in this direction.

A percipient visitor to Iran will find two things about it that may surpise him. One is the sense of national identity which pervades the country and has done for two-and-a-half millennia. Although some of its manifestations may raise a smile, the sentiment exists and is unmistakable, and in some of the ancient provincial cities it may be even more apparent than in Tehran. The other is that in Iran the universal sense of division between those who work with their hands and those who do not exist, but more than in most countries is bridged by a common respect for skill. The richer man values the products of the manual worker and the intellectual's respect is sincere and not mere lip service. The traditions of the country in carpet weaving and ceramics are a matter of pride and the products of pleasure to all, while the more mundane green fingers of a gardener or finishing touches of a cook are duly appreciated and understood.

With this background, Iran starts with the advantage that the higher levels of skill in science and engineering are also admired, if not understood, as too often they are not in other countries. In consequence today the technologists and technicians in Iran are coming into their own and are able to play a part in the country's development in which all take pride. One of the most encouraging features for the future of the country is the reverse brain drain that is now taking place, as men who have gained much experience and often reached high positions in other countries are finding that the prospects in their own country are attractive enough to make them glad to return.

Not that it will all be plain sailing. Agriculture, as so often in the schemes of planners, is proving difficult to develop at more than a gentle pace and production is rising only slowly, not at the rate necessary to meet demand. The government is conscious of this and by various means is endeavouring to improve the progress, but it is hard work. The most notable advances have been on the slopes confronting the Caspian where production of both tea and rice has improved considerably faster than agriculture elsewhere.

For much of Iran the difficulty facing agriculture is the scantiness of water supplies, and in each five year plan to date the building of dams has had high priority, designed as much to extend the areas of irrigation as for their value in the production of power. One idea being considered is whether, in connection with some of the new irrigation schemes, foreign development corporations should be brought in to provide a high quality of management for large-scale agricultural projects, on lines that have proved successful in other developing countries, and it will be interesting to see whether the idea makes progress.

The development of hydroelectric power is an indication of the long-term view Iran is taking as to its energy resources. Although still relying largely on conventional stations fuelled by oil and gas, it intends in the future that its hydrocarbons should be devoted to premium uses. The series of orders which Iran has been placing for nuclear power plants, at first surprising, is therefore seen as quite logical. In the important trade deal Iran has agreed with France the anxiety of Iranians to ensure nuclear fuel supplies has been met by their taking a ten per cent shareholding in the Eurodif plant for uranium enrichment which is being erected at Tricastin. Also in the French agreement Iran is to buy two nuclear power plants from Creusot-Loire while it has also been negotiating to buy two others from the German firm Kraftwerk. In its five-year trade agreement with the US nuclear generating stations are also included, the number not being settled yet but possibly as many as eight. In the next plan a start will also be made on the enormous project of a nationwide electricity grid.

For industrial development Iran is presently laying emphasis on the development of the steel industry. The Aryamehr steel plant near Esfahan has a nominal capacity at present of 600,000 tons a year but plans are in hand to double that rapidly and extend capacity to four million tons by 1980 and perhaps six or eight million subsequently. Steel complexes are also projected for Ahwaz, Bushehr, Bandar Abbas and Meshed, while the French firm Creusot-Loire is to produce a special steels plant with the needs of the motor industry particularly in mind. Altogether it is intended that the capacity of Iran to produce steel should be expanded to between fourteen and seventeen million tons a year by 1983.

The car manufacturing industry is at present represented by

Chrysler but under the French agreement Renault will erect a factory while on the heavier side the present plant, in which British Leyland holds the minority share, may also get a rival. Other industrial projects are numerous and will cover a wide range of the national requirements. Guest Keen and Nettlefolds for instance is designing a factory for car components and Pilkingtons a float glass plant.

There is a number of mineral deposits in Iran and some of them are apparently exploited on a small scale. Recently attention has been concentrated on the iron-ore deposits for feeding the Esfahan steel complex. There is a second iron-ore deposit in the Kerman district, and there have been discussions with Swedish interests about its exploitation. Great possibilities are offered by the Sar Cheshmeh copper deposits inland from Bandar Abbas. The find was made by Selection Trust in 1962 and its huge size was proved during the years in which discussions with the Iran government continued. These however eventually failed; more recent discussions have been held with American and Japanese metal companies; and now a viable operation may be about to get under way with the assistance of the Anaconda company. Many years ago George Canning, British Foreign Secretary, trying to negotiate a trade treaty, remarked:-

> 'In matters of commerce the fault of the Dutch
> Is offering too little and asking too much,'

and it is possible that the various company chairmen hold the same opinion of Iran. The recent breakdowns of all three of Iran's attempts to set up export refineries with Japanese, German and American partners seem to have stumbled on the same point.

In the social sector the large developments now scheduled include an emphasis on power supplies and on communications. While in most sectors the planned investments under the Fifth Plan were increased by two-and-a-half times, after the great increase in oil revenue, the allocation for electricity is four-and-a-half times greater. The plans for housing development are also considerably expanded, while those for education and health were comparatively high, considering the progress already made, and in this round of planning show only moderate increases. One really large new figure is that for government buildings, which has been specifically stated is for developments in the provinces and not in the capital.

Some of the major developments planned in the oil and gas sector have been referred to in the preceding chapter. The question of the three major export refineries is apparently being reconsidered but there are certainly to be further expansions to meet domestic requirements. In association with the gas projects there are plans for further gas processing plants, both within the consortium area and outside, to provide more LPG and natural gasoline for export.

The plans for gas export are also in an indecisive stage as there has been some rethinking in Iran about the country's own gas requirements for chemical uses. The existing trunk gas pipeline exporting ten billion cubic metres a year to Russia is already being expanded to a capacity of sixteen billion. The tripartite plan to lay another similar line alongside it to deliver gas to Southern Russia while USSR delivers corresponding amounts to Germany has been under debate for two years now, but although there may be commercial attractions in the project it seems doubtful whether the risks involved will prove acceptable to the parties. The other two large gas export schemes using the non-associated gasfields are also still under discussion with the National Iranian Gas Company. One involves El Paso of US and Distrigaz of Belgium and may be considering LNG exports at 20 to 30 billion cubic metres a year to be shipped to Europe via Suez, no fewer than 34 LNG carriers being required. The other scheme involves the Kalingas group including Chicago Bridge, Nissho-Iwai, Fred Olsen and others but at present there are few details except that requirements of 13 to 19 tankers have been mentioned.

In the fertilizer developments the existing Shahpur Chemical Company has plans for a considerable expansion and one large new plant is covered by the agreement with the French signed at the end of 1974. In the more complex chemicals there are plans for carbon black, polyester fibres and protein but the major development envisage is in cooperation with the Japan Petrochemical Company at Shahpur for which the aromatic section is to be designed to take feedstock of one million tons a year of naphtha from the Abadan refinery and the olefin section to be fed by 1.2 million tons a year of the heavier gases from plants processing methane for export to the USSR. A variety of developments is envisaged for the existing chemical plants. At present however there are more projects covered by letters of intent than by firm construction contracts and full details of the developments cannot be forecast, but in total the present plans are enough to occupy the resources available into the early 1980s.

IRAN DATA

Population	32.8 million (1974 UN estimate)	
Area	1,650,000 sq.km	
	Usable for agriculture	790,000 sq.km
	Annually cultivated	190,000 sq.km
	Irrigated	48,000 sq.km

Exchange Rate rial 82.2425 per SDR (March 1975 rial 66.64 per $)

National Accounts 1973/74 (Iran year 1352)

Sector		**billion rials**
Agriculture		213.6
Oil and gas		381.2
Industry		292.7
Services		512.1
GDP (at 1351 prices)		
Net factors income from abroad		–157.7
Indirect taxes net		+ 83.4
GNP	($ bn 19.44)	1325.3
Terms of trade adjustment		+237.9
National income		1563.2

Source: Central Bank of Iran Annual Report
1974 GNP at market prices $ bn 41.8 (rials bn 2850) – Union Bank of Switzerland

Budgets

billion rials

	1973/4 Budget Original	1973/4 Budget Actual	1974/5 Budget Original	1974/5 Budget Revised	1975/6 Budget
Revenues					
Oil and gas	227	311	445	1349	1473
Direct and indirect taxes	119	102	170		219
Other	143	52	188		97
Total	489	465	803	1603	1789
Expenditure					
General Operations	68		85	130	175
Defence	134	82	214	373	693
Social affairs	105		138	235	317
Economic affairs	133	163	230	376	425
Other	49		136		179
Total	489	497	803		1789
Total in $ billion	7.2	7.3	11.8	(23.5)	26.8
Subsidiary Budgets revenue & expenditure	204		283	478	656

Trade

$ million

Imports	1972/3	1973/4
Total	2570	3737
Food, beverages & tobacco	210	332
Chemicals	222	356
Manufactures classed by material	758	1252
(including iron & steel)	(321)	(583)
Machinery, non-electrical	603	804
Electrical machinery etc.	263	311
Transport equipment	234	288
Miscellaneous manufactures	75	128

Budgets **billion rials**

Imports by Source

	1972/3	1973/4	1974 March to Sept.
US	428	487	437
Japan	359	548	440
Germany	471	732	514
France	120	180	113
Italy	112	141	85
UK	297	351	226
USSR	71	214	88

Non-oil exports

	1972/3	1973/4	1974 March to Sept.
Traditional	337	529	
New industries	103	106	
Total	440	635	269

Development Plan 1973/78 revised

		billion rials
Government fixed investment		2619
Semi-government fixed investment		445
Non-fixed investment		472
Government loans for private investment		229
	($ bn 56.5)	3765
Private investment from own resources		1351

Sectoral Allocation

Agriculture and water	399	Government buildings	320
Industry and mines	414	Housing	230
Oil and gas	384	Education	130
Electricity	240	Rural and urban development	105
Telecommunications	91		
Communications	404	Other	130

IRAN
Some Major Projects

Oil-related

Three 12.5 million ton export refineries, with partners Deminex, a Japan group and a US group including Shell Oil – currently doubtful.

Domestic refineries at Esfahan (10 mn ton) and Tabriz (4 mn ton).

Gas export trunkline, either doubling that to USSR for onward delivery of 10 billion cubic metres a year to Germany, or possibly a line to Iskanderun.

Two LNG export projects, with Kalingas – Chicago Bridge and others – perhaps 8 billion cubic metres from C Structure to Japan, and with El Paso and others for over 20 billion cubic metres from Kangan to Europe.

LPG: doubling capacity (180,000 tons p.a.) of NPC/Amoco Kharg export plant.

LPG (1.6 mta) and methanol (5 mta) plant with US Transco Energy Corporation – currently doubtful.

Fertilizers: major expansions of plants at Bandar Shahpur (export) and Shiraz (domestic): possible third plant with French partner.

Chemicals: Abadan plant, expansion including increase of principal product PVC from 20,000 to 60,000 tpa (estimate $ 118 million).

Carbon black plant, 15,000 tpa, at Ahwaz ($ 10 mn) with Cabot Corporation.

Plasticiser – dioctyl phthalate – 40,000 tpa at Bandar Shahpur with Mitsubishi and Nissho-Iwai ($ 40 mn). Possible ethylene developments.

Major plant at Bandar Shahpur with Mitsui group for ethylene (330,000 tpa) and derivatives, benzene (154,000 tps) and Xylene (120,000 tpa). Estimated $ 433 mn.

Nylon 6 plants at Shiraz and Tehran (57 mn lbpa; $ 100 mn)

A number of further projects under discussion for aromatics and olefins, ethanol, methanol, DMT, caprolactam and isoprene rubber.

Mining

Development of iron-ore deposits to feed Esfahan steelworks.

Development of iron-ore deposits north of Bandar Abbas.

Development of Sar Cheshmeh copper deposits.
Small developments of zinc, lead and chrome.

Industry
Expansion of Aryamehr steel complex at Esfahan to 4 mta and later to 6 capacity, introducing direct reduction of iron-ore.

Special steels plant at Esfahan with Creusot-Loire, 200,000 tpa ($ 230 mn).

Four other steel plants, about 8 mta. Five more possible.

New aluminium factory (150,000 tpa)

Cement plants, raising total capacity to 23 mta.

New car and truck assembly plants and components factory.

Other projects include float glass, tyre plants and paper mills.

Agriculture and Water
Four major dams now in programme, primarily for power but irrigating some 600 sq.km.

Extension of village cooperative and larger corporations.

Mechanisation drive with output from new tractor plant.

Power
Eight nuclear plants from US, five French and two German have been announced. Further development of hydro and gas-fuelled conventional plants.

Transport
A major new port at Bandar Abbas and large expansion at Bandar Shahpur. Main railway links to these ports, and improvements between Tehran and Tabriz.

Underground railway system for Tehran, 60 km (3 billion francs).

Roads, over 6,000 km including incomplete projects.

New Tehran international airport, with Mehrabad reserved for domestic services.

IRAQ

Iraq is a country of unrealised potential. Many years ago it was estimated that Iraq could support a population of 15 million and even now the population has only topped the 10 million mark. Although in the fifties food imports were increasing there was always a surplus of agricultural produce for export giving a credit balance. Development of cultivable land then had priority, with investment in infrastructure, although long-term plans for other sectors were being made, but since 1958 stop-go changes of policy have adversely affected development.

Part of the trouble has been the internal dissension that has distracted the attention of governments for a number of years. Not only were many of the productive facilities allowed to run down, while the attention paid to growth of the economy was always greater on paper than in practice, but the proportion of the ordinary budget required for defence and security increased from 33 to 45 per cent and in such actual figures as are available the proportion appears to have been even higher. A part of the development budget was also put to military use while other parts were regularly needed to supplement the ordinary budget, so that development expenditure in practice has been running at around 55 per cent of the planned figures for the investment sectors.

With the present access of wealth there is a new spirit and greater prospect for real growth in Iraq. Some of the millstones of the past are however still round its neck. Military activity has been considerable and most of the armaments have been supplied by the USSR on long-term credits, with the amounts appearing in the budgets representing only annual repayments. The exact level of present debt is difficult to establish, but one estimate is of the order of $ 3500 million. Iraq has held an importance in the eyes of the USSR because it has been almost the only one of its client states which is able to settle its debts in hard currency, and in the past increased earnings by Iraq have been the signal for pressure by USSR for increased repayments. The position at present is not clear, but the failure to produce a full budget for the current year and the variations in figures each time future developments are announced may be indicative that the financial situation is still not as easy as it might appear.

Another legacy of the past is the grave shortage of executive and technological skills. The recurrent decimation of experienced administrators, for their obedience to previous regimes or suspected differences from those in power, has deprived the country of talent that was already scarce, even if it has provided some young ment with the opportunity to prove their ability. Moreover it has engendered a sense of insecurity among the staff who remain, so that virtually no administrative decision of consequence is made without higher reference, if possible to the Revolutionary Command Council itself. In a socialist country, with 90 per cent of all economic activity in government hands, the delays have been daunting.

The rulers are not unaware of the position. The success of the Iraqi National Oil Company in establishing oil exports from North Rumaila was achieved by granting the management freedom from the normal administrative procedures and top priority in all its requirements. Now that financial constraints have been removed, the government is determined on a crash programme of development in all sectors. For this purpose it has passed a law on the implementation of major projects, setting up an Oil Affairs Follow-Up and Agreements Implementation Committee with powers similar to those which INOC proved effective. The Committee can grant exemption to those engaged on a project from almost all laws and regulations, except for individual tax liabilities and the requirements of the security services. The ordinary ministries are required to give every assistance and officials are to be answerable for any dereliction.

Whether the system which made possible the rapid development of one sector can be applied successfully over the whole field of economic activities remains to be proved. The effective downgrading of all existing offices is unlikely to be accepted easily, although dissent will be muted under a regime not noted for its leniency. The open acknowledgment of the dearth of Iraqi skills by the invitation of foreigners to tender for projects on a complete turnkey basis is also liable to be unpopular, even though it is the only practical method of achieving the sudden growth desired. The emphasis on maximum speed which the government is stressing in all its contacts with foreigners may come from the need to demonstrate to the people that its policies work.

Oil and oil-related projects have for some years been given first priority by the present government and although other sectors are now showing a great increase in activity, oil projects remain at the heart of development planning. The government recently scaled down its plans for a production potential of 300 million tons a year by 1980 to 200 million, which is still a sizable target. More important for investment demand may be the gas project, which as at present formulated envisages the export of 3.8 million tons a year of natural gas liquids from associated gas produced in the fields in the Basrah district. Mitsubishi heads a consortium of Japanese firms which has been invited to tender and has itself contracted to take 1.2 million tons a year. Fertilizer production at the plant near Basrah will be greatly expanded and there are plans for a petrochemical plant at a cost of some ID 60 million to produce ethylene and related products.

Khor Zubair near Basrah is to be the site of an iron and steel complex to produce 400,000 tons a year for which a contract has been awarded to the French firm Creusot-Loire, while SECIM, another French company, is involved in a plant to manufacture aluminium ingots to be set up at Nasiriyah. Large increases in the number and capacity of textile factories, paper mills, cement plants and brickworks also feature among industrial developments planned.

As with other of the states wishing rapidly to expand their imports, Iraq has found that its present port facilities are quite inadequate and delays are currently over three months. The modern port of Basrah has been in existence for a long time but is restricted in the size of the ships it can take owing to the bars at the mouth of the Shatt-al-Arab and of the Karun. In the sixties a second port was developed at Umm Qasr on another inlet to the west which can take ships of deeper draught and the combined capacity of the two ports is 2.8 million tons a year of imports. Plans are being made to expand capacity of 4.7 million tons but the target date at present set is 1980. When the ports are busy there is congestion on the railway to clear the goods up-country and railway developments feature prominently in the investment programme. It is interesting to note plans to deepen the Tigris, which has always been used for light-draught barge navigation, to render it more suitable for year-round transit from Basrah to Baghdad or possibly even to Samarra. The Iraq Maritime Transport Company is planning to obtain a fleet of river craft to maintain the service and is to add to its fleet of cargo ships, while the oil tanker fleet is currently being expanded. Road construction is one activity which has seen continuous progress and the new plans are to accelerate it, with several important bridges also required. The Baghdad International Airport is scheduled for further expansion and completely new fields suitable for modern large aircraft are to be provided for Basrah, Mosul and Kirkuk. Improvements in telecommunications have also been given priority.

In the social field education takes the largest allocation with provisions for new schools at all levels and there is to be a concentrated programme of adult education to reduce illiteracy in the country. Housing has already consistently received attention over the years and the programme outlined will continue the progress. While Baghdad is well served with medical facilities the rest of the country has in the past been somewhat neglected and plans so far announced will only start to correct the position.

Agriculture remains a problem in Iraq. One difficulty is the fall of only 30 metres in the 500 kilometres from Baghdad to the sea, with the result that inadequate drainage of irrigated land develops salinity of the soil. Developments of barrages and new canals have only sufficed to keep the area of irrigated land under cultivation in Iraq steady at around 1.4 million hectares. The current plan envisages leaching out and restoring 0.3 million hectares and adding a further 0.3 of newly irrigated land. One major project affecting agriculture which is contained in the forthcoming plan but may be doubtful is the construction by the USSR of a big dam on the Euphrates near Haditha and development of irrigation from it. With the difficulties that have arisen from the Russian construction of the Syrian Tabqa dam still unresolved the USSR may be in no hurry over a commitment which it first undertook in 1961.

Implementation of the many projects will not be simple. In addition to the general difficulties mentioned regional differences are making themselves felt. The number of major projects designated for Basrah has aroused resentment in other parts of the country, but Basrah itself is conscious of having had no say in the matter. The concentration of the power of decision into a small circle in Baghdad deprives the regions of effective contact and Basrah with its ocean-going tradition has suffered from the land-locked views of the northerners. Although the list of projects is extensive there are imprecisions and possible duplications in it, suggesting that the ideas of the planners are somewhat sketchy. Much work needs to be done before the projects can be translated into contracts, and it is not yet sure if the sense of urgency which the government stresses to foreigners can be implanted in its own administration.

IRAQ DATA

Population 10.75 million (1974 UN estimate)

Area 438,000 sq.km

Agricultural holdings (591,000)	57,300 sq.km
Cereal plantings 1973	29,000 sq.km
Irrigated	14,500 sq.km

Exchange Iraqi dinar = $ 3.38

National Accounts – 1972

Oil	38%
Agriculture	22%
Manufacturing	10%
GNP	$ 3730 million

Source: UN

Iraq Source 1973 GNP: $ 6740 million

Budgets **ID million**

Revenue	**1973/4**	**1974/5 Original**	**1974/5 Revised**	**1975 April-December**
Oil	409	1800	1800	1200
Customs & Excise	87	80	80	85
Loans	25	28	28	25
Other	154	192	192	356
Total	675	2100	2100	1666
= $ million	2280	7093	7093	5631

Expenditure

Administration	90	134	162	140
Defence	168	306	878	406
Social affairs	76	124	129	106
Economic affairs	6	7	9	6
Other	39	86	181	156
Total ordinary	379	657	1359	814
Debt settlement	–	274	–	–
Development	296	1169	1169	988
Total government	675	2100	2528	1802

Government agencies

Revenue	615	921	927	1536
Expenditure	700	1107	1122	1839

Development **ID million**

Allocations	1973/4	1974/5	1975 April to Dec.	1976/80 Plan approx.
Agriculture &)				1715
Irrigation and Dam)	65	190	185	1295
Transport &)				735
Communications)	35	120	156	300
Industry	45	225	392	1400
Building & Social Services	35	175	188	1000
Investment Expenditure	180	710	921	6445
Other	116	459	67	1000
Total Allocations	296	1169	988	7445
= $ million	1000	3950	3340	25165

Trade	January – June 1973	**$ million** January – June 1974
Imports Total	430	664
Food, beverages & tobacco	83	213
Chemicals	33	51
Iron & steel	21	39
Other manufactured materials	104	147
Machinery & transport	167	190
Other manufactures	12	15
Imports by source		
USSR	35	46
China	22	27
US	13	68
Japan	30	41
Germany	21	38
France	47	42
Italy	16	24
UK	38	35

Non-oil exports 1973 111 including dates 39

IRAQ
Some Major Projects

Oil-related	**Estimates $ million**
Pipelines. Increase Kirkuk-Banias capacity by 10 million tons p.a.	60
Haditha-Basrah strategic 2-way, 45-49 mta to switch shipments if necessary, with parallel gas fuel line.	650
Kirkuk-Dortyol (Turkish Mediterranean) 35 mts.	550
Baghdad-Basrah products line.	90
Kirkuk-Batman (Turkey) gas line.	
Refineries: Export: 10 mta at Basrah, Umm Qasr or both.	250
Domestic: 1½ mta Mosul, 12½ mta Kirkuk.	

Gas processing: near Basrah to produce 3.8 mta LPG and natural gasoline for export.		
Chemical: Fertilizers: expand present plant to 500,000 tons pa.a. urea.		100
New plant 2 million tons p.a. urea		200
Ethylene and consumer plastics 130,000 tons p.a.		200
Plan 700,000 tons p.a. plant		750

Industry

Two sponge iron plants, 0.75 mta for export and 0.4 mta for steelworks; ore from India, Brazil and Sudan.		200
Steelworks at Khor Zubair; 0.4 mta with four 70 ton furnaces and two rolling mills.		160
Aluminium smelter at Basrah: 0.1 or 0.2 mta; bauxite from India.		85
Aluminium manufacturing plant at Nasiriyah, 32,000 tons p.a.		125
Paper mills: three, total 140,000 tons p.a.		500
Textile factories: six		150
Assembly plants for cars, trucks, buses and tractors		
Volkswagon car factory		
Cement plants: ten, raising capacity to 7.5 mta		400
Flour mills: four		
Sugar plants: three		

Agriculture

Irrigation: eight major schemes, total 16,000 square kilometres.		1300
Dams: Euphrates – Haditha.		700
Tigris – north west of Mosul.	65	650
Four barrages for irrigation		
Research stations and farms.		330

Transport

Shipyard, Basrah, for river and coastal.	50
Port, Basrah Ma'qil, 4 berths, 4 more planned.	20
Port, Umm Qasr, berths for containers and liquid sulphur.	55
dry-dock and 3 more berths planned	
Tigris navigation improvements and barges	65
Railways, new lines over 1800 kilometres	over 1250
conversion metre to standard gauge and modernisation.	over 250
Baghdad rapid transport system.	
Roads, over 2500 kilometres.	950
Bridges, ten major.	520
Airports, Baghdad extension, new at Basrah, Mosul and Kirkuk.	100

Communications

Baghdad radio and TV centre.	300
National microwave system.	35
Earth satellite station.	

Construction

Housing, 25,000 units.	500
Baghdad university further stages	80
Hospitals, six new	1000
extensions, Baghdad Medical City and others.	75

Services

Power stations, nine, at least 3,000 MW.	over 800
Rural electrification and water supply	600

KUWAIT

Kuwait is now by any standards a fully developed country; indeed it has gone beyond that point and, as one correspondent neatly put it, has become the world's first rentier state. Everything needed in the way of physical development has now been done. Roads, schools, hospitals, whatever is taken as the criterion, Kuwait has everything it requires and all that remains is to add the odd touch of luxury. Even though it tries, it cannot use internally more than a quarter of its current revenues. The government has taken a close look at investment possibilities in the country and apart from a few minor consumer industries has decided that there is nothing that offers a worthwhile return except the final stages of oil-related investment.

The project it has formed for this purpose gives rise to an interesting paradox. Already Kuwait is using a comparatively high proportion of the gas associated with oil production. In providing for the government needs for power generation and desalination, which are still growing at a rapid rate, the technical requirement for gas to be reinjected into the fields for pressure maintenance and the existing plant for processing natural gas liquids for export, the minimum gas requirements of the state necessitate a minimum rate of oil production which is fast approaching 75 million tons a year. It is to be noted that this is less than half of the installed capacity for oil production, but is the figure which some members of the National Assembly have been trying to establish as the maximum rate at which Kuwait should produce; the government appears to consider that the limit should be between 100 and 110 million tons a year. What is now being proposed by KOGEC, the newly-formed Kuwait Oil Gas and Energy Company combining several state companies, is a much larger processing plant for NGL which will require the gas from approximately 60 million tons a year of oil production. This together with the existing requirements is more than the government appears to desire, but questions about the way in which the difference is to be resolved are not answered.

Kuwait has another problem. For its native citizens there are direct and indirect provisions to see that all share in the prosperity of the state and there is always a job for anyone who wishes. There have never been enough nationals for all the work that has to be done, and so almost 50 per cent of the inhabitants of Kuwait are foreigners who have come to work and form around 75 per cent of the working population. Although they may prosper, foreigners have no civil rights and are offered no hope of obtaining Kuwaiti citizenship. They have been called helots by some writers, but a more apt comparison from ancient Greece is with the metics who were encouraged to settle in Athens and seek their fortunes by undertaking tasks which the citizens felt beneath their dignity. In modern times another parallel comes to mind, with the Uitlanders in South Africa. Whether the strains of the situation may come to a head is something the Kuwait government worries about, but seemingly the foreigners find that the economic attractions of their life outweigh the political disadvantages.

Although there are some Kuwaitis who are content with sinecure posts there are many who retain the drive and energy which for centuries made their small city famous around the oceans. Some find outlets for their energies in political or industrial affairs within the state, but others still look outwards and are drawn to work in a wider field. The original foundation of the KFAED and the growth of institutions for the use of Kuwait's capital round the world are surely evidence of the breadth of their interests.

Although the powers of the KFAED have now been widened to include non-Arab countries, there is little question that the other Arabs will remain the principal recipients of the Fund's assistance. Ahmad Duaij the director of the Kuwait Planning Board has indicated as much and has said that Kuwait regards long-term investment in productive assets in the Arab world quite as safe as those made in the west. Projects such as the establishment of a glass factory in Egypt using Pilkington's technology with Kuwait finance appear to set the likely pattern for similar developments in the future. While the Kuwaiti financial institutions will undoubtedly remain very active in the international field, the suggestion put forward in some quarters that Kuwait will be an international financial centre of great importance must be doubtful, because of the government prohibition on foreign companies establishing themselves in Kuwait to engage in financial activities.

In the flurry of attention that was paid to the finances of the Middle East states at the start of 1974 it was sometimes overlooked that the reserves of Kuwait which are normally published are only those of the Central Bank, maintained at a level to cover import and immediate development requirements. Much larger sums go into the government reserve, figures for which appear only infrequently. Kuwait has been building its reserves over many years and the Minister of Finance 'Abd al-Rahman al-'Atiqi has rightly pointed out that Kuwait shares the common interest in the stability of the international financial system, and has always been careful not to jeopardise it by taking part in short-term exchange operations. On the contrary much of Kuwait's investment has gone into long-term holdings, without the publicity that its recent purchases of Daimler-Benz stock and the St. Martin's Property Company recently excited. In fact property has always been one of the favourite investment sectors for the government funds.

Kuwait is a small country without natural defences on its frontiers and under the astute guidance of the Al Sabah family has always reckoned its security to lie in diplomacy and financial generosity. Nevertheless it hss been sufficiently affected by the large expenditure on arms being undertaken by other Gulf states to allot a record sum of KD 42 million to defence this year, which still does not begin to compare with the spending of its neighbours.

In development planning the ever-increasing demands for electricity and water call for corresponding investment, and other public works feature prominently. The productive investment contemplated on the NGL plant has already been mentioned. Kuwait was unfortunate in that its sophisticated Shuaiba refinery opened only a month before the Suez Canal closed in 1967 and the loss of its potential European customers gave rise to considerable difficulty in its early years. It is not surprising therefore that apart from minor additions to this plant Kuwait has not proposed export refinery plans on the lines of others in the Gulf. On the other hand Kuwait's tradition of maritime enterprise is being maintained by orders for four LPG tankers for the shipment of its products, by continuing enlargement of its tanker fleet, much the largest in the Arab world, and by the aim of the Kuwait Shipping Company to double its present fleet of sixteen cargo ships and treble its tonnage. Kuwait has also played a leading part in joint Arab projects for a tanker fleet and dry-dock scheme, as well as being prominent in non-maritime joint schemes.

Students of the Gulf are aware how in the last thirty years events in Kuwait have later been paralleled by similar developments further down the Gulf. In the preceding chapter (p. 123) reference has been made to the difficulties which the Kuwait National Petroleum Company has experienced in attracting recently qualified technical graduates and technicians. It may be, as the Minister of Oil hopes, that a completely nationalised company will be more successful. On the other hand it is possibly an indication that the new generation of Kuwaitis does not feel the urge to participate in work of such nature, and indeed the movement of labour away from the oil industry has been a notable feature of Kuwait employment statistics. Many of the existing well-trained and capable staff in the industry are approaching retirement; how to replace them is a problem Kuwait and later other governments will have to face.

KUWAIT DATA

Population:	800,000 (government estimate 1975)
Area:	19,000 sq.km.
Exchange:	Kuwait dinar = $ 3.41 (1974 average)
GNP:	1973 $ 4300 million (official). 1974 $ 10,000 million. (Union Bank of Switzerland)

Budgets				**KD million**	
Revenue	**1974/5**	**1975/6**	**Expenditure**	**1974/5**	**1975/6**
Oil	920*	1687	Ordinary	394	552
Customs & Excise	10	15	Development	180	274
Income from services	25	30	Reserves	386	911
Other	5	5			
Total	960	1737		960	1737
			($ million)	(3270)	(6080)

* Expected oil revenue not included in 1974/5 budget KD 2080 million.

Expenditure Allocations

Ordinary	**1974/5**	**1975/6**	**Development**	**1975/5**	**1975/**
Administration	64	78	Public Works	59	87
Defence	42	69	Electricity & Water	51	86
Economic	49	72	Land acquis.	35	90
Social	116	165	Others (net)	5	11
Semi-government	123	168	Contingencies	30	–
Total	394	552		180	274
($ million)	(1344)	(1932)		(614)	(959)

Trade

Imports	**1973/4**	**$ million**
Total	1050	
Food, beverages & tobacco	200	
Machinery & transport	345	
Manufactured goods	210	
Imports by source		
US	142	
Japan	188	
UK	107	

Non-oil exports and re-exports 1973/4 $ 235 million

Principal Project: Gas processing plant to produce 5.5 million tons p.a. of LPG for export ($ 600 million).

SAUDI ARABIA

Saudi Arabia is trying to take a giant leap forward with a heavy weight attached to one leg. Its rulers wish to bypass all the gradual development that has occurred in other states and to see the country take its place as an industrialised and modern state working in the forefront of technology, compressing all the intervening stages of learning within one generation. At the same time they intend to avoid what they see as the moral degradation of other industrial states and retain their traditional spiritual and social values. While this deliberate policy stems largely from the highest in the state it commands wide support even among the young men who are often impatient with what they see as the slow progress in development.

The Saudis are quite willing to admit that their diverse aims can have some curious results. The King Faisal Memorial Hospital opened in May 1975 in a magnificent new building with every item of equipment that technology has developed and money can buy, but it is at the moment staffed by foreigners. Nearby the first generation of home-trained Saudi doctors are approaching their final examinations in a cramped old building with equipment that the poorest training school in the west would consider inadequate. Furthermore these doctors are being trained to treat only half the population, since at no stage have they been permitted to examine a female patient. The first course for training women doctors has recently started, a development which has surprised some and delighted others, but training for them will be even more circumscribed since they are permitted to see no male, either patient or lecturer.

The emphasis the Saudis place on advanced technology even at the start of development comes in part from what they have seen in the states around them. They have made it clear that they do not intend to encourage pauperism with a system of regular handouts. Already a considerable proportion of manual workers consists of immigrants from the Yemen and to a lesser extent from Oman and the Sudan, and the government does not wish to establish industrial operations which will require a considerably greater influx. At the higher levels they are confident of their own abilities, and the numbers of the educated elite, including members of the royal family, who have proved themselves by hard work and competence in government posts support their belief. Westerners who have been lucky enough to have friends among the bedouin do not doubt their innate intelligence and remarkable ability to master details of technical operations. At the higher levels therefore the Saudis are more ready to admit foreigners in the confidence that in due course they can be replaced. They are placing a handicap on their own progress and on their ability to recruit a suitably broad range of training staff by over-rigid insistence on paper qualifications, without regard to the different standards which may apply or to the value of practical experience, but they are not alone in this narrow outlook. More to the point they have shown a degree of flexibility and judgment in reconciling their own puritan version of Islam with practices required in the operations of a modern state. Reference has already been made to the reconciliation of Wahabism and western methods in the banking field while the success of Aramco in training Saudis for high-level posts also shows how two cultures can work together.

The Saudis are realists enough to know that the development of capable staff in every sector of the economy cannot all be accomplished at once. In the discussions on the national take-over of Aramco it has been made quite clear that a number of Americans will still be required, and a similar understanding is shown in planning for other major developments. To some extent this may not be entirely voluntary. The published statistics of Saudi population have shown a growth to over eight million but a census – enumeration might better describe it – was carried out in the summer of 1974 and the failure to publish the results in any way has given rise to speculation. It is believed however that it revealed a population between five and six million, while one report puts the figure at only four million. It is not surprising therefore that some doubts appear to be creeping in about the country's ability to carry out and maintain in operation all the large-scale projects which have been planned.

The plans are ambitious for the director of the Central Planning Organisation Hisham Nasir has spoken of developing the industrialisation of Saudi Arabia to such an extent that in thirty or forty years' time the whole of its present oil revenues will have been replaced by those from other state enterprises. Shaikh Yamani has been speaking in similar terms since his seminal address at the American University of Beirut in 1969, and has maintained his view that oil should be supplied only in return for an equivalent supply of high technology equipment and know-how. The plans that have been and are being developed for this end are on the largest scale. In the oil-related field the first aim is a system to collect all the associated gas not at present being used, currently between 40 and 50 billion cubic metres a year and provision may be made for 60. The existing Aramco facilities for the extraction of natural gas liquids is to be expanded to a capacity of 11.5 million tons a year and a new government plant is to be set up to extract the remaining 19 million tons a year that would be available. There are plans to dispatch the liquids by a pipeline 1300 kilometres long, which will be paralleled by a crude oil pipeline of 48-inch diameter, to Yanbu on the Red Sea for further processing and export. Meanwhile from the remaining gas the ethane will feed a chemical plant for processing into ethylene and further derivatives while the methane will be taken for power generation and for a fertilizer plant. There is a proposal for the construction of a methanol plant in which Houston Natural Gas is concerned with a capacity of 1.8 million tons a year, but it has not yet been decided whether there will be enough gas remaining to supply it. Besides the gas plans it is intended to construct three export refineries, of which one may be at Yanbu, each with an initial capacity of 12.5 million tons a year and each designed in due course to be doubled. While other Arab states have plans for a government-owned tanker fleet, it is interesting that in Saudi Arabia three private companies have already been established.

Developments in the eastern province are to be centred on Jubail some 50 kilometres north of Ras Tanura where Saudi plans envisage a giant industrial complex. In addition to the oil and gas facilities, the principal item is to be an iron and steel plant with a capacity of 3.5 million tons a year of metallised pellets and one million tons of steel. The plans to supply the ore for this plant from Brazil have been mentioned above. There is also in the programme an aluminium smelter, while plants for processing copper, zinc and lead are to be considered. The complex will require heavy investment in power generation and in water desalination besides all the ancillary construction of houses, schools, hospitals and other services. It is planned that agriculture in the neighbourhood should also be developed, together with a food processing industry.

The western province now contains the consumer-oriented industries, as well as 45 per cent of the working population, and it is intended that development will continue along these lines. The oil-related facilities to be developed around Yanbu are an exception, but there are no plans at present for instance to expand the existing steel mill at Jeddah which produces 45,000 tons a year of reinforcing bars. Jeddah is the centre of population for the region and the most important port of Saudi Arabia with a capacity of 1.8 million tons a year out of a total of 2.3. The great harbour development planned in association with the Jubail development will alter the proportion, but Jeddah and Yanbu as well as Dammam are included in port development projects.

The south-west of the country features in projects for agricultural development as it receives an average of 300 mm of rainfall compared with the country average of 50 mm, and in the districts of Asir and Tihama lie the best prospects for doubling the land under cultivation, which is at present some 4,000 square kilometres or 0.2 per cent of the area of the country. In Hejaz and the Nedj more attention is to be paid to animal breeding and grazing management and there is hope that the expansion of animal husbandry will enable the country to be self-supporting in meat.

Although most announcements and dicussions of plans concern the major projects in the public sector the government itself lays emphasis on the development of private activity. In 1974 the Ministry of Finance issued an important statement on industrial policy, part of which reads –

> 'The government considers that competition which serves the interests of the local consumer is the best way to ensure that industrialists achieve the highest levels of profitability in production and marketing. Similarly the government considers that competition is the best regulator of the level of returns in relation to market demands, production incentives, lowering of overheads, and the fixing of fair prices for both producer and the consumer'.

The policy statement lists the incentives the government is prepared to offer, which include –

Loans on favourable terms and government participation with investment capital.

Assistance in selecting industrial projects, the provision of finance and carrying out economic and other useful studies.

Assistance in technical and financial fields and in hiring employees.

The exemption of initial imported equipment and components from import duties.

The exemption of foreign shareholders' dividends from company profits tax in accordance with foreign investment laws.

Favoured treatment for locally-produced commodities.

The imposition of protectionist import duties on competitive imported goods.

The provision of sites in industrial zones.

Assistance in training Saudi employees.

Assistance in exporting products.

Dominating all discussion is the consideration of how much development is feasible. Reports say that Saudi Arabia has some sixty firms of international consultants at work at the moment; even to piece so many recommendations together into a coherent whole will be an administrative feat. The rapidity with which development can be expanded is still dependent on past development, both of physical facilities and of personnel of appropriate calibre. As in most of the Middle East countries, budgetary provisions and planned allocations are well publicised but details of actual results are scarce. With Saudi Arabia there is the difficulty that the figures available of allocations to the various ministries combine both current and capital expenditure, with little indication of the division between the two. The table of the Saudi Arabian budgets includes some of the few actual figures which have appeared. After growing at an annual rate of 15 per cent in the sixties, recently government expenditure has advanced at a rate of 18 per cent, with capital rather faster than current. There has rarely been a time when the income available would not have permitted faster growth, quite apart from any reserves that were held. In contemplating the acceleration of growth rate that is now possible these figures should be borne in mind, and so should the habit of some spokesmen in referring to expenditure on development while quoting figures that in fact are the total for both current needs and projects. The five-year plan which was scheduled to start in January 1975 had still to be published at mid-year, and whereas in the middle of 1974 a total five-year expenditure of \$ 45 billion was contemplated the sum became \$ 60 billion in the autumn and \$ 150 billion in the spring of 1975. Actual capital investment in 1973/74 is estimated to have been just on \$ 2 billion; the first of the plan figures would require a sustained annual growth rate of 25 per cent and the last would require 55 per cent. The latter figure may be considered improbable but the former may well be attainable with the present resources of the state.

SAUDI ARABIA DATA

Population: perhaps 5.5 million – see text. Higher estimates are published but appear to be based on incorrect assumptions.

Area: 2,400,000 sq.km.
Area under cultivation perhaps 4,000 sq.km.
Area irrigated 1,200 sq.km.

Exchange: SDR = 4.28255 Saudi riyals
Average 1974 dollar = 3.55 SR (end March 1975
$ = 3.511 SR

National Accounts

GDP	**1974/5**	**1979/80**	**$ billion target**
Oil sector	36.4	73.8	
Government sector	1.0	2.8	
Private sector	4.6	13.4	
	42.0	90.0	

Source: Five-year plan.

Budgets **SR million**

Revenue	**1974/5**	**1975/6**	**Expenditure**	**1974/5**	**1975/6**
Oil	94 432	87 160	Current	14 698	32 428
Customs & Excise	493	378	Capital	26 397	74 380
Government Services	333	332	Aid	4 648	4 127
Other	2 989	7 977			
From reserves	–	15 088			
Total	98 247	110 935		45 743	110 935
($ billion)	(27.7)	(31.8)		(12.9)	(31.8)
Defence allocation, both current and capital				10 109	26 337
Independent government establishments				2 710	21 741

Previous Years Actual	**1970/1**	**1971/2**	**1972/3**	**1973/4**
Revenue – budget	6380	10782	13200	22810
Revenue – actual	7940	11120	15368	
Expenditure Budget allocations				
Current	3946	5146	6400	8547
Capital	2596	5036	6800	14263
	6542	10182	13200	22810
Expenditure actual			(estimates)	
Current	3483	4262	5310	7000
Capital	2273	3378	4178	7150
Aid	662	662	660	660
	6418	8302	10148	14810
$ mn	1720	2226	2720	4172

Trade

Imports	**1972**	**$ million**
Total	1136	
Food & tobacco	295	
Chemicals	59	
Iron & steel	32	
Other manufactured materials	84	
Machinery	252	
Transport	155	
Miscellaneous manufactures	177	

Source: SAMA

Imports by origin	**1972**	**1973**
US	346	486
Japan	265	427
UK	124	158
Germany	91	139
Italy	59	85
France	56	62
Lebanon	66	91

Source: IMF

SAUDI ARABIA
Some Major Projects

Oil Related

Gathering and treatment system for natural gas up to 60 billion cubic metres a year. New plants to produce 12 million tons a year of NGL (propane, butane and higher factions) (estimates $ 5 billion)

Pipelines to carry from the eastern province to Yanbu on the Red Sea 8 mta of NGL and 115 mta of crude oil.

Three export refineries, one at Yanbu and two at Jubail, each with initial capacity of 12.5 mta, later to be doubled. (estimates $ 3 billion).

Expansion of refineries for domestic consumption. (estimates $ 0.8 billion).

Seven chemical plants, most based on ethylene and derivatives, one or two perhaps methanol. (estimates $ 4 billion).

Three large fertilizer plants.

Industry

Steel plant at Jubail to produce 3.5 mta.

Aluminium plant possible.

Cement plants to raise capacity from 1.5 to 10 mta.

Car assembly plant.

Agriculture

Irrigation of 500 square kilometres.

Transport

Increase port capacity to 13 mta with major developments at Jeddah and Dammam.

Roads: 1300 kilometres surfaced roads.

Construction

Principal target 122,000 housing units.

Services

Increase desalination capacity by 600,000 tons p.a.

Increase electrical generation and distribution including over 3500 kilometres transmission lines.

Health

Provide 115,000 new hospital beds.
Double local dispensary services.

QATAR

The man in the street would still be hard put to it to say where Qatar is or to pronounce it, yet as a member of the United Nations since 1971, of the IMF and other international bodies and with an income from oil of about $ 15,000 per head, Qatar is far from negligible on the modern scene. With the accession of Shaikh Khalifa bin Hamad al-Thani a new spirit and sense of direction came to the country and a coherent strategy for its future has emerged. Oil production is expected to last into the twenty-first centry, but much larger quantities of natural gas are believed to be available though not as yet proven. The future of the country is to be based on industrialisation utilising natural gas.

The population of Qatar is estimated at 130,000 – it was 5,000 when oil was discovered in 1940 – of whom only some forty per cent are Qatari nationals, as are only twenty per cent of the labour force. This disproportion is accepted without the doubts that affect the plans of other Gulf states, and the industries being developed will continue to need large foreign staffs. There is ample time for full and detailed examination to be given to the feasibility of various projects, and without a formal development plan a series of major investments is expected over the next ten years.

In spite of the considerable advances that have been made in the social field Qatar is still faced with the need for comparatively large expenditure in the fields of education, housing and medicine, but with its present income it is only a matter of time before its inhabitants are catered for on the Kuwaiti scale. Other infrastructural activities also require investment as in all of the other Gulf states. The demand for electricity and for water to be supplied by desalination plants grows at a rapid rate. The major road network is complete but further development is required and the existing port facilities at Doha are to be doubled, besides the special facilities for loading that will be needed for products from the gas-based plants at Umm Said.

There is no surface water in Qatar and successive hydrological surveys have shown the potential underground supplies to be limited, with the result that there has been a severe restriction on the development of agriculture in Qatar. Nevertheless some 1500 hectares are under cultivation and with careful development of appropriate methods Qatar is now self-sufficient in vegetables besides producing fodder crops. Although experiments are in progress, this is one field in which the prospects of further development are small.

The principal industrial investments to date in Qatar besides the oil industry are a cement plant with a capacity of 300,000 tons a year and a fertilizer plant in which the government participates with Norsk Hydro, Power Gas and Hambros. This has a capacity of 330.000 tons a year of ammonia of which one-third is exported and the remainder goes to the making of 360,000 tons a year of urea. Under the new development scheme the capacity of the fertilizer plant is to be doubled and that of the cement plant trebled. The Qatar natural gas liquids project using gas from the onshore Dukhan field was inaugurated in May 1975 and the government has formed a 70/30 partnership with Shell for the development of further gas projects, of which the first is to be an NGL plant using gas from offshore production. A start has been made on a project with CDF Chimie on a petrochemical plant to produce ethylene and derivatives and with Kobe Steel of Japan on an iron-ore production plant, with a capacity of 300,000 tons a year, of which it is expected internal demand will take one quarter. An export refinery possibly with a capacity of ten million tons a year is under study and an aluminium plant has been discussed.

Qatar has been taking a full part in the various joint Arab investment companies formed as well as its share in providing aid. Nevertheless there is a limit to all that it can spend and the probability remains that well over fifty per cent of its income will remain for investment under an investment board of which the Shaikh himself is chairman.

QATAR DATA

Population: estimated 130,000

Area: 10,000 sq.km

Exchange: SDR = 4.7619 Qatar riyals
1974 average \$ = 3.96 QR; end March 1975 3.80 QR.

Budget QR million

	1973	1974	1975
Expenditure			
Current	763*	1000	2200
Capital	249*	581	1800
including budget provisions for			
Heavy industry			305
Housing water & electricity	114	182	602
Communications & agriculture	93	181	477
Education, health & information	43	102	275
Justice & security	48	51	144
Aid	357	350	(?)
Total	1369	1931	4000
(= \$ million	352	488	1053)

Oil revenue \$ million 408 (actual) 1900 (estimate)
* actual

Source: Ministries of Finance and Information

Trade \$ million

Imports by sources	1973	1974
Total	197	270
US	20	28
Japan	22	48
UK	54	38

1974 By category – incomplete, leading items in each classification only.

Food and tobacco	39
Steel	33
Non-electric machinery	15
Electric machinery	9
Transport	27
Oil company equipment	23

Source: Ministry of Information

QATAR
Some major projects

Oil-related

Expand recent domestic refinery to one mta
Export refinery 10 mta
Gas processing plant, with Shell
Chemical: ethylene (300,000 tpa) and polyethylane plant ($ 200 mn) with CDF Chimie – also partner in Dunkirk project.
Fertilizer plant: double capacity to 720,000 tpa urea.

Industry

Steel plant (400,000 tpa) with Kobe Steel ($ 200 mn)
Aluminium smelter (75,000 tpa)
Cement plant expand to one mta ($ 20 mn)
Pharmaceutical factory.

Transport

New Doha international airport
Conversion main roads to dual carriageway
Doha port: 5 new berths.

Other

New hospital
Sewage treatment plant
Earth satellite station

THE UNITED ARAB EMIRATES

The seven states which now federally comprise the UAE had each of them long independent trucial relationships with Britain. The first formal cooperation between them was the institution of the Trucial States Council in 1952. In 1965 Britain with the cooperation of the states set up the Trucial States Development Fund and although in the early days finance was restricted the habit of working together and considering the problems of their neighbours bore fruit in economic planning when the UAE itself was established.

Four of the states have no oil production, while that of Sharjah started only in July 1974 and the limited revenues to be expected in its first years are likely to be required by Sharjah itself. Dubai has been established as a producer since 1969 but its yield remains comparatively small. By far the most important producer and therefore revenue-earner has been Abu Dhabi and in the finances of the UAE it officially contributes ninety per cent, and by the personal generosity of Shaikh Zayid a rather larger share. Before the formation of the UAE, Kuwait made considerable contributions to the setting up of educational and health facilities in all the states, and its share in the foundation of the present community is by no means forgotten.

With the assistance of UAE funds social development in the five northern states is making rapid progress while the infrastructure of roads and power stations is also receiving support. In Ras al Khaimah an experimental station at Digdaga originally founded by Roger Huntingdon has been operating since the mid-fifties. Starting with research into the improvement of agricultural methods it has spread into the field of plant experiments and now of lifestock breeding and with support from the Federation serves the whole community. Ras al Khaimah has also an established cement plant and a new port Khor Khuwair is to serve both that and developing oil research requirements. Ras al Khaimah is also developing a small port for local craft and an airfield of its own.

The oldest airfield in the UAE is that at Sharjah established by the then Imperial Airways early in the thirties, and although restricted for modern international traffic it still performs a useful function. After the discovery of oil offshore near Abu Musa Island – itself the scene of one of the earliest industrial enterprises in the southern Gulf in the extraction of red oxide – Sharjah started to develop its own port facilities for ocean-going ships and is now enlarging its capacity from two berths to six. The social sector is also to benefit from the first oil revenues; discussion of developments to follow is still at an early stage.

The ruler of Dubai Shaikh Rashid bin Sa'id al Maktum would have made his mark in any country or sphere of activity. When the consultants for building a new port for Dubai proposed four berths and then reluctantly seven, he personally insisted that fifteen should be provided at the first stage. Now with congestion causing long delays at every port in the Gulf Dubai is able to assist as an entrepot as well as meeting its own needs, and Shaikh Rashid's judgment has been vindicated. Construction has already started on the addition of twentytwo berths, a measure of his ambition to maintain the position of Dubai as the premier port in the Gulf. Duabi believes in free trade, in every sense of the term, and Shaikh Rashid considers that its reputation, together with the establishment of a free zone for manufacturing and storage, will play a key part in the future of the state. The decision to go ahead with Dubai's £91 million dry-dock scheme, to accommodate tankers up to one million tons, was not popular with the other Arab states who were still engaged in the prolonged discussions for the establishment of a similar project in Bahrain, but the present crisis in the tanker world must throw some doubt on the viability of both projects. The Shaikh ventures his own money on projects with which he agrees, and keeps only a small but competent staff to vet all development plans and enable those approved to proceed without bureaucratic delays.

It is typical of Dubai that while a tunnel to connect the two halves of the community separated by the Dubai Creek is scheduled for completion by the end of 1975, plans are already in hand for a bridge to be ready before the traffic can exceed the capacity of the tunnel. The oilfields of Dubai are offshore a hundred kilometres from the town. Plans are now in hand for the construction of a pipeline to bring the associated gas ashore to be used in industry and power generation. It is not at present certain whether the quantity available will justify the construction of a plant for the extraction of LPG for export. Dubai has ambitions to become the financial centre of the Gulf; the encouraging atmosphere for business may favour it but its size and dependence on the personality of the present ruler may tell more heavily against it.

ABU DHABI

Abu Dhabi is the largest state of the UAE, but the town itself on its sandy island with a brackish water supply was one of the poorer until the accession of Shaikh Zayid in 1966. Since then its growth has been remarkable and continuous. The five-year development plan 1968/72 was more a catalogue of the many things that needed to be done to found a modern state than a settled orderly plan. So many of the necessary tasks were undertaken simultaneously that in 1969/70 some strain was experienced and a slow-down was required. The brake was applied merely temporarily and activities soon surged ahead again. It appears that at the end of 1974 there was a further slight pause for consolidation, due largely to the flood of aid which Abu Dhabi had poured out to various Arab states, but again it will probably be only temporary.

The most essential of the development projects was the new port of Mina Zayid and until it was available the use of lighters for offloading was a handicap on other developments. The port was opened in 1972 with three berths and three more were soon added; construction in progress will add another six berths and the total planned is seventeen. There is an international airport at Abu Dhabi; a second one is planned and one inland at Al Ain, the principal Abu Dhabi town in the group sometimes referred to as the Buraimi Oasis. Road development has been continuous and, besides the network within the state, a main road now runs along the coast connecting the emirates, and to the west is pushing towards a link-up with Qatar. The interland of Abu Dhabi is largely covered with sand dunes ranging up to 150 metres in height, and the easing of communication problems by new roads has had an important effect in bringing the communities together.

Shaikh Zayid believes that the desert should rejoice and blossom, and has taken steps to make it do so. If the project for a forest alongside the road between Abu Dhabi and Al Ain is not of practical value, the experiments in cultivation by hydroponics which have been made at Sadiyat and Mazaid are taken seriously in scientific circles. The ruler's long residence at Al Ain has given him great understanding of and sympathy with the small farmers, and much is now being done to encourage and assist them by agricultural research stations, by extending the area of land under cultivation, by providing new strains of seed and by developing services in the rural areas. It is hoped to avoid the depopulation of the land which other developing countries have experienced, and to draw into the capital only those who have a special contribution to make there.

At the present stage of growth of the federation cooperation is greatest in the social sector. Education and health are joint responsibilities and, although housing is not, Abu Dhabi has been receptive to requests for assistance. There have been consultations on the provision of technical and industrial colleges so that hopefully the need for immigrants in many jobs can be reduced.

The problems of development where ten years ago only a few received even primary education are recognised, and the dependence of Abu Dhabi on foreigners for some time to come is accepted; unlike some Gulf states Abu Dhabi has plans to grant naturalisation to suitable immigrants. The Oil Minister Mana al Otaiba has said that for some time Abu Dhabi will have neither the administrative nor the the technical staff to run its own oil business, and industrial developments being planned will face similar difficulties. On a lower level most of the manual work is being done by Baluchis, Pakistanis and others and although it is hoped that there will be a turnover of individuals there seems no escape from dependence on foreigners in the foreseeable future.

Among projects in the oil sector pride of place goes to the plant on Das Island for processing the gas from the offshore fields and shipping liquefied natural gas to Japan, in which the National Oil Company has taken shares with Mitsubishi and the partners in ADMA. Plans to use the onshore gas are not so far advanced, although part of it is already being provided to generate power for industrial use in Abu Dhabi; at the moment the favoured export project is for LPG while Abu Dhabi's own needs for methane or the possibility of finding a customer for LNG receive further consideration. While discussions have been taking place with a French group on the possibilities of a chemical plant based on ethylene the government is going ahead with the project for a 0.75 million tons a year domestic refinery on Umm al Nar Island – incidentally the scene of discovery of a culture nearly 5000 years old. The possibility of a second export refinery on Zirku Island using the offshore fields is being discussed, while in April 1975 Abu Dhabi took possession of its first tanker and another is on order.

Abu Dhabi has plans for a direct reduction steel mill and so has

Dubai. With building construction unlikely to flag the completion of the 250,000 tons a year cement plant at Al Ain is awaited, although with the plants at Dubai and Ras al Khaimah the capacity of the UAE is probably approaching requirements. The danger of all the Gulf states, with few natural resources apart from oil, all endeavouring to carry out the same kind of development at the same time, with resultant considerable over-capacity, is recognised in the UAE and plans for an aluminium smelter appear now to have been dropped. It is possible that with further consideration of labour problems Abu Dhabi may follow the pattern of Kuwait, that is confining industrial development to the oil-related field and then moving abroad to find other opportunities. Already with the help of the Investment Advisory Board established in 1967 Abu Dhabi has long-term investments which are believed to have been increased by $ 1.25 billion in 1974, in addition to current reserves, and has started to make loans denominated in dirhams both to the World Bank and privately. In looking abroad Abu Dhabi's close ties with Pakistan are to be noted, with the current development of a fertilizer plant at Multan financed by Abu Dhabi and the possibilities of a refinery and other industrial development there. Abu Dhabi has taken a full share in the various combined organisations of the Arab countries for development and has directly aided Syria. The Abu Dhabi Fund for Arab Economic Development is committed to loans for a range of countries from Zaire to Bangladesh, although actual disbursements to date have been restricted. At present the lending policy appears to be a matter of impulse rather than of planning but if there is to be greater cooperation between the funds granting aid, as some hope, Abu Dhabi is likely to continue to take a full share.

UNITED ARAB EMIRATES DATA

Population:	estimated 350,000 (Abu Dhabi 120,000)
Area:	80,000 sq.km. (Abu Dhabi 67,000)
Exchange:	$ = 3.95 UAE dirham

Budgets are presented rather confusingly and inconsistently, making year-to-year comparison difficult.

Federal Budget 1975 **Dirham million**

Total Dh 2778 mn ($ 703mn)

Abu Dhabi contribution Dh 2500 mn of which 500 will be returned for federal projects in education etc. within the state.

Development expenditure Dh 970 mn ($ 245 mn) including 770 for further work on projects already in hand.

Reported 1974 actual expenditure total Dh 785 mn, of which 80% current, 20% development.

Abu Dhabi Budget 1975

		Reported 1974 actual
Revenue	13084 ($ 3912)	13500
Total expenditure	12878 ($ 3260)	8000
including		
Current	3278	
Development	3500	1000
Contribution to UAE net	2000	
Capital Commitments (ADFAED etc.)	600	
Aid	3500	4000

Trade **UAE** **$ million**

Imports	**1973**	**1974 estimates**
Total	849	1402
Food, beverages & tobacco	100	178
Pharmaceutical	17	44
Manufactured goods		356
Transport equipment	184	385
Oil company equipment	111	137

Imports by source

Japan	158	291
US	163	160
UK	163	179
Germany	38	66
France	34	47
Italy	16	54

UAE
Some Major Projects

Federal

Roads: complete link to Qatar, mountain road to Fujairah and enlarge coast road Abu Dhabi – Dubai – Sharjah to four-lane dual carriageway.
Hospitals: six new
Education: complete primary facilities for all – 60,000 pupils, plan 'Open University of the Gulf'.
Fisheries: refrigeration plants.

Abu Dhabi

Oil-related

Domestic refinery 0.75 mta on Umm al Nar
Export refinery on Zirku or Jabal Dhanna, up to 15 mta
LPG extraction and export
Chemical – ethylene plant
Fertilizer plant

Industry

Complete Al Ain cement plant 250,000 tpa
Steel bars mill 25,000 tpa

Tranport

New international airport for Abu Dhabi, and one at Al Ain
Port Zayid: 5 new deep-water and 4 coastal berths

Dubai

Oil-related

Pipe gas ashore from Al Fateh oilfield
Possible LPG extraction/export

Industry

Complete cement plant 500,000 tpa
Steel strip mill using sponge iron from India

Transport

Port Rashid 22 new berths, 8 more later, making 45 in all.
Dry-dock to take million ton tanker
New bridge over creek

Sharjah

Transport

Port Khalid 2 berths immediate; 4 to follow
New international airport

Ras al Khaimah

Industry

Complete cement plant 700,000 tpa

Transport

Khor Khuwair 2 deep-water berths
Ras al Khaimah local craft harbour

OMAN

Oil production in Oman started in 1967 in the shadow of the June war, but the fields are only of moderate size and the revenues do not match the country's needs, welcome as they would be to many developing countries. Oman has also been put to considerable expense by the guerilla warfare in the southern province of Dhufar which is supported from bases across the border in the Yemen People's Republic. It was also hampered by the conservatism of the late Sultan and only started real progress in 1970 under Sultan Qaboos bin Said. The development of port facilities was first priority and Port Qaboos opened in 1974 with berths for nine ocean-going ships. At Salalah, where only the most primitive lighterage arrangements had existed, a new port nearby at Raysut adequate for small craft has been developed to provide sheltered offloading, and it is already apparent that deep-water berths are required there. With the coastal strip of the country divided from the desert inland by a range of mountains reaching 10,000 feet road development is both important and difficult, and while rapid progress was made on a system of graded roads to provide a reasonable connection between the towns the next stage of all-weather surfaced roads requires a long programme. The mountains can also pose problems in telecommunications and Oman, developing such facilities only recently, has been able to take advantage of the most modern equipment.

The mountains catch the fringe of the monsoon and in the season rainfall can be heavy. Much of it goes to waste in the flash floods, although primitive dams retain some for irrigation, and in other areas the water table is tapped by a falaj system. As a result, in the district there is a series of small patches intensely cultivated. Among many feasibility studies at present in progress in Oman perhaps the most important relate to the availability of ground water and plans for using it agriculturally. Along the coast a cultivated belt, nearly 500 kilometres long but only one or two wide, relies on shallow underground water, but owing to its brackish nature the date is the only crop that really flourishes. Experiments are necessary to improve the productivity of the Batinah coast and the state has established a major research station at Rumais, as well as smaller ones in the districts. Agricultural extension centres in the farming areas are trying to communicate the results of research and help the cultivator to get better results. Fishing has always been important in the local economy and a research station is in operation, while another group is experimenting to improve the design of the local fishing craft. On the industrial side consumer industries have already been started and a large cement plant to produce 600,000 tons a year has been established. The most important industrial project is the completion of a gas pipeline from the oilfields through the mountains to a site near Muscat where LPG will be extracted, while the methane will be used for a fertilizer factory, as well as providing the fuel for power generation and water desalination.

The late start on social development in Oman and a large but scattered population, mean that the tasks ahead are large and will take years to be accomplished. Nevertheless there is already progress in the infrastructural developments already mentioned and in the provision of power facilities around the small towns. Housing is a great problem, but the construction industry at all levels has responded enthusiastically to its opportunities and has already achieved surprising results. The government is mindful too of education and medical development and, although the resources are so limited compared with the needs, there has already been a great spread of activity. A new school is opened nearly every month and so is a new hospital, while for the remoter areas there is a system of travelling clinics. In Dhufar particularly the medical staff combine with other social and educational workers, and the benefits they have brought to the small settlements have played their part in reducing the field of activity of the guerillas, as has the programme of drilling water wells in the desert area.

With so much to be done Oman has welcomed assistance from a number of bodies: the World Health Organisation, Food and Agricultural Organisation and various governments, consultants, commercial firms and universities. At the same time, although not a member of OPEC, it has joined with the other Arab oil producers in granting aid and in particular has contributed to the funds to assist the even poorer countries which have been hurt by the rise in oil prices. Iran has given military aid to Oman and may continue to help in its peaceful development, while Sultan Qaboos has reestablished good relations with Saudi Arabia. Certainly the country can make use of greater resources than its own oil revenues are likely to provide.

OMAN DATA

Population: estimated 750,000

Area: approximately 300,000 sq.km, including 95,000 Dhufar

Exchange: Rial Omani = $2.895

Budget Allocations **RO million**

	1974	1975 reported
Oil revenue	212	
Total revenue	220	420
	($638 mn)	($1220 mn)
Capital expenditure	107	
Current expenditure	94	
including Defence	58	160

Trade

Imports in 1973, excluding those by government and oil companies, totalled $ 118 million, of which 29 were from Arab countries and 22 from UK.

OMAN
Some Major Projects

Oil-related

Gas processing plant near Muscat, with gas piped 320 km from fields, to produce LPG, with Tesoro of US ($ 100 mn).
Fertilizer plant to produce 720,000 tpa of ammonia and urea with Gazocean of France ($ 400 mn).

Industry

Complete cement plant 600,000 tpa.
Various consumer industries.

General

At the present early stage of development all sectors require large investment and are receiving a proportion.

LIBYA

The position of Libya resembles that of the Gulf oil producers much more closely than it does that of the other populous OPEC countries. Apart from oil there are few natural resources. There is a sparse population inhabiting a large country, and there is a shortage of water which has given an emphasis to the development of the combined power station and desalination plants similar to that seen in the Gulf. Libya particularly lacks trained technical and administrative personnel at all levels and has been fortunate that her neighbour Egypt has numerous well-qualified men to spare. When Libya expelled all its skilled Italian inhabitants only an influx of Egyptians enabled further progress to be made. Recently a number of inducements, including naturalisation, has been offered to attract any skilled Arab.

Libya has an asset in the comparatively wide tracts both on the coast and inland with agricultural potential. Four areas are receiving particular attention; the Jefara plain west of Tripoli, Jabal Akhdar in the bulge of Cyrenaica, the Fezzan district in the south-west and the Kufra oasis in the south-east, where the discovery in the mid-sixties of plentiful artesian water transformed the scene. Australian experts together with Spanish and Turkish are assisting developments. It is not easy under the present regime to understand what progress is actually being made behind the public pronouncements about various allocations, but it would seem that the advances in the sector have been sufficiently encouraging for it to be allotted a good proportion of the increase in planned investment which followed the 1974 oil price rises.

In the oil-related field Libya was able to profit from her geographical position by the installation of a large plant at Brega for processing and shipping liquefied natural gas. The project however ran into a number of technical difficulties, and when they were eventually solved there were political ones, so that the plant has only briefly operated near to its designed capacity. The plans for its enlargement appear to have been shelved following the latest period of difficulties. Libya's first export refinery at Zawia is now open and a contract has been awarded for doubling its capacity, but it remains to be seen whether Libya's plan to have refineries totalling 66 million tons a year of export capacity in 1980 is a feasible one. Perhaps by then the present worldwide surplus capacity may have been eliminated and Libya with its short haul to the European market would be well placed for new developments. It will not however be the technical advantage but commercial talent of the management which will be needed to ensure success and that is a talent which at present is clearly lacking in Libya. Plans for chemicals are still at a formative stage but after the troubles of the LNG plant potential partners may need convincing evidence of Libya's intentions before committing themselves, although the simpler type of fertilizer plant appears possible.

In general industry several projects are in progress directed to the consumer market, such as shoes and clothes, flour milling and canning factories. One plant for the manufacture of line pipe is under construction and the capacity of cement plants is to be greatly increased.

Ports are at present a severe limitation on progress and have not been able to meet the increased demands of an accelerating import programme. Construction at Benghazi to increase the present five berths to sixteen is expected to start in 1976, while the doubling of the comparatively restricted capacity of Tripoli is in hand. Road building has already seen considerable progress but a large amount remains to be done to provide adequate links between all centres of population.

On the social side there has been a great advance in the provision for education, and housing and medical facilities also take large shares of the development allocations. One type of development the Libyan government has firmly set its face against is tourism, since its insistence on the elimination of European languages and alphabet, not to mention alcohol, seems bound to restrict severely the number of people who might be interested in visiting the country. The future of Libya cannot easily be foreseen in the present secretive atmosphere, but the growth of its imports suggests developments greater than had seemed probable.

LIBYA DATA

Population: estimated 2.25 million

Area: 176,000 sq.km
Area cultivable estimated 24,000 sq.km
Area under cultivation estimated 5,000 sq.km

Exchange: Libyan dinar = $ 3.38

National Accounts	**LD million**
	1972
GDP	1599 ($ 4730 mn)
including	
Oil sector	920
Government	131
Construction	125
National Income	1266 ($ 3750 mn)

Source: UN Monthly Bulletin of Statistics

1974 GNP estimate $ 11,100 million (Union Bank of Switzerland)

Budget Allocations		**LD million**
	1974 revised	**1975**
Current	310	437 ($ 1477 mn)
including		
Defence	50	60
Local authorities	117	167
Development	859	1110 ($ 3750 mn)
including		
Agriculture	186	231
Industry	111	139
Oil	65	84
Municipalities	55	96

Trade — $ million

	1972	1973 first half
Imports	1038	790
including		
food	161	133
transport equipment	137	70
non-electrical machinery	137	180

Source: Libya

Imports by origin	**1973**
Total	1723
Italy	446
Germany	178
France	141
UK	123
Japan	115
US	94

Source: UN Direction of Trade

LIBYA
Some Major Projects

Oil-related

Export refineries at Zawia, being doubled by SNAM to 6 mta ($ 54 mn)

Tobruk, 11 mta to be built by Foster Wheeler, estimate $ 340 mn,
Misurata 11 mta.
Zuelina 20 mta and possibly Brega 20 mta.

Chemicals, at Brega, methanol plant, 365 tpa,
estimate $ 88 mn started by Uhde.
Ethylene plant 400,000 tpa, $ 200 mn, Stone and Webster.

Fertilizer plant, ammonia 365,000 tpa.

Industry

Steel pipe plant, 75,000 tpa

Cement plants, including tripling Benghazi capacity to 600,000 tpa.

Various plants for consumer needs.

Infrastructure

Roads, 2,000 km, estimate $ 300 mn

Desalination and electrical plants, estimate $ 675 mn.

CHAPTER 9

Aid

The subject of aid has become a playground for propagandists who, often with some inconsistency, use the word with a wide range of meanings from outright grants to mere portfolio investment. The Development Assistance Committee of the OECD has over the years evolved a system of classification giving its members a fair basis for comparison of their efforts. The essential aim of all aid as the DAC employs the word is to promote the economic development of the third world. Recipients may value other forms of aid, military for instance, and other definitions may well be used or implied; it is merely that such assistance will not be aid in the sense used by members of the DAC.

The narrower classification of Official Development Aid means in DAC usage concessional aid including a large grant element. Outright grants form a comparatively small proportion; they may be given on some special occasion or on a regular basis, one of the commoner of which is the provision of experts to give technical assistance. Most ODA consists of 'soft' loans which contain three elements; a grace period before any repayment, an extended maturity and a low rate of interest. The DAC assesses the value of these factors to arrive at the concessional element in loans by its members, and the target rate is 84 per cent, which most members exceed.

Multilaterial aid is usually given through the International Bank for Reconstruction and Development, IBRD, more commonly known as the World Bank, and its offshoot, the International Development Authority. The latter was instituted to make loans on very easy terms to the countries most in need; it offers correspondingly low terms to lenders, who have channelled only a small proportion of their aid through it. Kuwait has joined the DAC countries in subscribing to four loans, with a total of $50 million. The loans granted by IBRD have a grace period but are at market interest rates, and lenders have been more numerous. Bilateral aid may be without strings or in part tied to purchases in the lending country. Although IBRD and DAC endeavour to discourage tied loans, most aid takes this form and is still reckoned as ODA if it is largely concessional.

Governments may provide aid with a concessional element which is not great enough to place it in the ODA category. The most common form is in export credits, from which incidentally the OPEC countries still benefit. On the non-governmental side are reckoned gifts by charities and individuals, and so are investments in productive facilities by commercial organisations. The latter admittedly are looking for a non-concessional return, after a grace period, but meanwhile bring to receptive countries investments and technical skills in larger amounts and at an earlier period than would otherwise be possible, and undoubtedly promote the economic development of their hosts.

The DAC calculates the aid disbursed by its members and proceeds to express it in terms of their GNP. The industrialised countries form a fairly homogeneous group but the DAC warns that differences in measurement of GNP mean that comparisons should not be pressed too far. The position of Portugal for some years at the head of the table of donors, in GNP terms, might raise a suspicion that the composition of GNP may also be a factor in capacity to grant aid. When it is observed that in 1974 some 85 per cent of GNP in Kuwait and Saudi Arabia was composed of government oil revenues, that is in economic terms of rent received from abroad, the suspicion may be reinforced.* For 1974 the DAC has recorded the aid contributions of the oil producers, so far as it has been able to ascertain them, on a comparable basis excluding, with the same proviso, military assistance.

Footnote:

*Thomas Stauffer (in Schurr and Homan 1971) is one of the few economists to recognise publicly the distortion which the system of oil payments has caused in the standard calculations of economic data such as Balance of Trade. All GNP data are similarly affected.

Table 9.1
AID IN 1974

$ billion

	Aid Commitments Bilateral and Multilateral Funds	International IMF Oil Facility	International World Bank Bonds & Loans
Iran	2.42	0.70	0.35
Saudi Arabia	2.04	1.21	0.89
Kuwait	0.86	0.48	0.05
UAE	0.81	0.12	0.08
Qatar	0.16		
Iraq	0.49	–	–
Libya	0.42	–	–
ME-OPEC	7.20	2.51	1.37
Other OPEC	0.34	0.66	0.76
OPEC	7.54	3.17	2.13
Oman	0.02	0.02	0.03
ME-OPEC			
Actual disbursements	2.54	1.48	1.37
of which concessional element (57%)	1.45		
Other non-concessional and portfolio investments	2.21		

Recipients of bilateral aid commitments

Egypt	1.800	India	0.907
Syria	0.783	Pakistan	0.897
Sudan	0.139	Bangladesh	0.165
Jordan	0.122	Others	0.428
Lebanon	0.120		
Other Arab	0.579		
Total Arab	3.543	Total non-Arab	2.397

Commitment to multilateral funds 1.595

Source: OECD

The figures show a considerable effort by the oil producing countries, but it might be thought that the actual disbursements are somewhat out of proportion to the additional oil revenues which the producers have received from the LDCs. The total of commitments announced has been very much larger than actual aid, and it has been assumed in some quarters that grants of aid on a massive scale were naturally slow to start because of administrative delays and that they will build up into a much larger annual figure corresponding with the commitments. A closer look does not support this argument. On the contrary, the commitments already made are likely to be spread out over several years, and the annual rate of disbursement does not seem likely to rise far, while from some countries it may actually fall. Iran for instance has stated that by 1977 it expects to be able to employ all its oil revenues domestically and that although it has been one of the foremost in granting aid in 1974 there will be little addition to the total to which it is committed. New commitments undertaken by other producers in 1975 have also been scarce.

Another feature of the aid that has been granted is its very uneven distribution and the fact that only minor sums are connected with the additional oil costs of a country. Over 75 per cent of bilateral commitments have been made to four countries, Egypt, Syria, India and Pakistan. Egypt and Syria together with Jordan have received over 60 per cent of actual aid payments. The whole of black Africa, contributing nearly a thousand million dollars a year to the oil producers, has received pledges of 437 million and actual aid estimated at 60 million dollars.

Of the formally constituted funds for distribution of aid which are listed in the accompanying table, the Kuwait KFAED has much the longest history and record of achievement. In the twelve years to March 1974 it had loaned a total of KD 134 million ($420 million) to twelve Arab countries for various projects, of which the principal beneficiaries were Egypt with 27.8 million, Sudan with 22.3 million, and Tunisia with 17.3 million. Accounts for the year 1974/75 may show an increase of nearly fifty per cent in actual disbursements. Commitments of $850 million have been made to Egypt and the wider authority to invest outside the Arab countries has brought promises to Tanzania, Uganda, Bangladesh and Malaysia.

Table 9.2
AID FUNDS

NATIONAL	Founded (at)	Authorised Capital millions	Equivalent $ million	
Kuwait Fund for Arab Economic Development – KFAED	1961	KD 200	560	
enlarged and extended	July 74	KD 1000	3400	
Abu Dhabi Fund for Arab Economic Development – ADFAED	Aug 71	BD 50	105	
enlarged and extended	May 74	Dh 2000	506	
Iraq Fund of External Development – IFED	June 74	ID 50	169	
Saudi Development Fund – SDF	Sep 74	SR 10,000	2817	
MULTILATERAL				Pledged $ mn
Arab Fund for Economic and Social Development – AFESD (HQ Kuwait)	1972	KD 100		
AFESD special fund for Arab oil importers	Jan 74 (Cairo)		80	
Islamic Development Fund (HQ Jeddah)	July 74 (Cairo)	"Islamic Dinars" 2000	2400?	900
Arab Fund for Industrial and Agricultural Development in Africa	Nov 73 (Algiers)		206	231
Arab-African Technical Assistance Fund	Jan 74 (Cairo)		15	6
Special Arab Fund for African oil importers *	Jan 74 (Cairo)		200	200

* To be administered by the African Development Bank on behalf of the Organisation for African Unity.

The other national funds which have been established have still to make much mark on the scene of international aid. For Abu Dhabi the primary area of concern has been the other members of the UAE, contributions to which do not go through the Fund, but assistance has been provided to Bahrain and Syria. The Iraq Fund has started with small loans to Afghanistan and Tunisia, and the Saudi Fund is reported to have lent 169 million dollars by mid-1975.

The senior of the multilateral funds, the Arab AFESD, has also required time to consider projects but loans to Somalia and Mauritania have been recorded. Its special Oil Fund is understood to have been more active and may have granted $48 million. The Islamic Development Fund was a particular project of the late King Faisal and Saudi Arabia has been supported by Libya and the UAE. There was a certain confusion among early reports about the Fund due to its being quoted in 'Islamic Dinars', a currency which was not familiar, but as more about the Fund's constitution has appeared it would seem to be equivalent to the pre-1971 dollar, or SDR. The Fund's aims are to support economic and social development in Islamic countries, but it is also authorised to assist Muslim communities in any country. Pakistan is the country likely to benefit most from the Fund but no commitments have yet been reported.

The several funds to assist African countries have been the subject of conflicting reports, perhaps due simply to variations in translation. The one that has definitely been making disbursements is the fund for assisting African states to pay for the additional cost of their oil imports, which was founded at the beginning of 1974 at a meeting in Cairo between seven ministers of OAU countries and ten of OAPEC. The administration of the fund was handed over to the Organisation of African Unity which adopted a very precise method of calculating the entitlements of its members. By the end of 1974 the fund appeared to have provided some $60 million to fourteen African countries, each receiving exactly half of its entitlement with the other half to follow in 1975. The remaining funds appear to be still at the stage of gestation.

The multiplicity of the formally constituted funds has already attracted some criticism in the Arab world as well as outside it. The Kuwait Fund itself has indulged in some self-criticism, reporting that the obstacles it has met in achieving its objects lie partly in the countries it wishes to help, which lack staff competent to formulate and put forward projects worthy of support, and partly in Kuwait where the administrative procedure for consideration and discussion of projects takes far too long. If this is still the situation in the Fund which has been established since 1961 and has accumulated both experience and competence, it is certainly a question whether the other funds can operate effectively until several years have passed. With the grave shortage of trained administrative talent in the various Arab countries, and the priority of their own developments, those who have argued for some form of merger would seem to have a case. The generous initiative and justifiable pride of the originators of the funds are to be respected, but they might reconsider whether the route they have chosen will take them to their goal. Much more effective aid could surely be achieved by greater cooperation of the donors with each other and with organisations in the rest of the world. At one time Iran proposed a combined OPEC fund, by which some of the deficiencies of the multiple organisations could have been avoided, but the proposal met with a completely negative response and Iran has proceeded to grant aid without finding the necessity for formally established funds.

In fact the Arab governments have provided much greater sums through direct government channels than through the formal funds. For many years the Kuwait government has been accustomed to making grants and loans to various of the Arab countries – in the eyes of the recipients there often appears to be little difference between a grant and a loan – and its activities have continued since its wealth increased. The scale of its assistance is difficult to assess especially as a proportion of its grants has been towards the rearming of other Arab states.

In 1967 the Arab League countries agreed that the oil producers would subscribe to a fund, at that time £135 million per year, to compensate Egypt for the loss of revenue from the Suez Canal and also benefiting Syria and Jordan; with intermissions the aid has continued. Following the war of October 1973 an Arab League fund was proposed at Algiers to re-equip the front line countries and an amount of one billion dollars was the aim. A year later a meeting at Rabat fixed a total of 2.5 billion dollars for 1975. Kuwait, Saudi Arabia and Libya were the principal contributors to the 1974 fund but all offered a share and UAE is one of the large donors in 1975. The Arab League has been active in following up the promises made, so the relation between commitments and disbursements may be closer than in other funds. In addition to the regular provision of military aid there has been a series of *ad hoc* presents for the same purpose, notably from Shaikh Zayid.

By no means all grants have been for military purposes. The plight of the Sahel countries stricken by drought attracted donations from most of the oil producers, and floods in Bangladesh and an earthquake in Pakistan also brought rapid contributions. The sums given are counted in millions, even if they are small compared with the total of aid commitments. Libya has pursued its own policy of granting aid to 'revolutionary' movements everywhere including the IRA, the Uganda government and what its announcement called the Rhodesia National Front. However in April 1975 Colonel Qaddafi stated that Libya had stopped all forms of aid to Arab and African countries 'because they are always a source of trouble'. His action may serve to underline the point that not all commitments will be fulfilled.

Iran in 1974 was very ready to lend from revenues which it could not immediately use, although the concessional element in its loans was small. After OPEC had turned down proposals for any reduction in the price of oil for the LDCs Iran took a lead in arranging concessional terms. In return for future supplies of trade goods or capital equipment it is giving to India credit on payments for oil which may have amounted to some 940 million dollars in 1974, and to Pakistan credit of perhaps 190 million, while Bangladesh and Sri Lanka have received similar benefit. Iraq has assisted India with oil credits worth perhaps about 110 million dollars and has also helped Bangladesh.

A Pan-Arab investment company has been established to finance joint petroleum projects in OAPEC countries with an authorised capital of SR 3600 million ($1000 million) and headquarters in Dammam; Egypt is likely to be favoured. On similar lines an Arab investment company for the development of Arab resources has been established with an authorised capital of $200 million, and its primary target may be the development of the Sudan.

Some of the Middle East producers have contributed to the oil facility established by the Managing Director of the International Monetary Fund, Dr. Witteveen, lending SDR 2100 million out of a total of 3055 million. The Fund started to make loans only in

Table 9.3
IMF OIL FACILITY 1974/75

Lender — SDR Millions

	Commitment Total	Lendings at end Dec. 74	Lendings at end March 75
Canada	254.9	140.7	191.3
Iran	580.0	374.1	479.8
Kuwait	400.0	225.0	333.7
Oman	20.0	11.6	15.1
Saudi Arabia	1000.0	561.8	822.6
UAE	100.0	63.8	78.0
Venezuela	450.0	252.0	361.4
Netherlands	150.0	87.0	122.0
Nigeria	100.0	–	80.8
	3054.9	1715.9	2484.6

Borrowers

	At end Dec. 74		March 75	
Developed Areas (7)	951.4		1469.6	
including Italy		675.0		675.0
Spain		–		296.2
Latin America (8)	156.1		234.1	
including Chile		41.5		118.5
Uruguay		46.6		46.6
Asia (6)	462.7		520.3	
including India		200.0		200.0
Pakistan		97.9		125.0
Korea		90.0		100.0
Africa (14)	130.0		181.2	
including Kenya		32.0		36.1
Tanzania		28.4		31.5
Sudan		28.7		28.7
Others (3)	15.7		79.4	
TOTAL	1715.9		2484.6	

Table 9.4
IMF OIL FACILITY – 1975 INCREMENTS

Lender	SDR million Commitments to June 1975
Iran	410
Kuwait	200
Saudi Arabia	1000
Venezuela	200
Netherlands	200
Belgium	100
Germany	300
Austria	50
Norway	50
Total	2510
Target for 1975	5000

September 1974 and remains to be drawn on until the end of 1975. Meanwhile Dr. Witteveen has been trying to establish a second fund for 1975, the target for which has been gradually reduced to SDR 5000 million ($6000 million) but it is still far from being achieved. Apart from the oil facility the ME producers have made loans to the World Bank amounting to $1400 million, as well as other market placings.

It will have been apparent that loans form a very large proportion of the aid given by the oil producers, as they do in aid from the developed states. The concessional element in the latter was however 87 per cent in 1974 whereas it was 57 per cent in aid commitments by the producers. The practice some of the states have adopted of recording all aid in the budgets under the heading of current expenditure is misleading; much of it is to be repaid in due course even if rescheduling may sometimes be necessary. Interest is received even if rates are low, and it may be noticed that the Kuwait budget shows the KFAED due to receive 22 million dollars in 1973/74 and 28 in 1974/75 in interest on its loans.

The future of the various forms of lending by the oil producers is a matter for conjecture. It would appear that unless steps for reorganisation of their administration are taken the special funds are likely to make only slow progress. The Arab donations for military purposes appear likely to continue at a high level unless there is further progress towards a settlement of the Palestine problem. The reluctance of the oil producers to provide aid through multilateral channels may set a limit to what can be done by these means, although they rightly point to the preference which the developed countries have always shown for bilateral aid. Iran has stated that it expects its own requirements to overtake its oil income by 1977 and in fact is already returning to borrow on the international market. The secretary of the OAU Mansour Khalad has drawn attention to the wide difference between the amounts which the African states have had to contribute to the oil producers and the amount of aid which they have received. If aid from the oil producers is to be of more than marginal assistance to the less-developed countries, a more consistent and sustained programme will be needed, with a much greater degree of cooperation.

CHAPTER 10

The Challenge to Countries & Companies

The oil producing countries appear to be sitting on top of the world. The rise in prices which they have been able to impose has brought revenues greatly exceeding their capacity to spend. The populous countries with reserves of manpower and natural resources to be exploited have been able to make plans for their development and in two or three years will be making full use of their revenues; meanwhile a safety cushion is being built up. The surplus countries have been able to formulate development plans on a grand scale and know that their reserves will still accumulate. Current government expenditure has been freed form financial limitations, so that the increase in income of the state is reflected in that of individuals. The demand for imports of capital and consumer goods, by government and private sector, has risen steeply and is restrained only by physical inadequacies. Yet in public the leaders of the countries have little to say of their good fortune and much of the difficulties they face.

In part the intention is to create a public image rather than describe facts. For instance much play has been made with the rising costs of the producers' imports due to the rate of inflation in the industrialised countries, and the consequent justification for further increases in oil prices. The UN index of export prices of manufactured goods shows that the increase from 1973 to 1974 was 27 per cent. The government oil revenue on a barrel of the marker crude was \$10.12 at the start of 1975 compared with \$7.00 which was described as the right level at the start of 1974, an increase of 44 per cent. The real increase was somewhat less, only because government revenues had risen at the start of 1974 by more than was admitted at the time. Responsible OPEC leaders are well aware of the position, even if the statisticians are kept busy producing different figures for the public.

The actual price debate within OPEC has nothing to do with index numbers. In the short to medium term there is no substitute for oil and most of the populous states led by Iran and Algeria wish to take advantage of their power. Maximum revenues now will enable them to make such progress in development as to make them at least partly independent of production from their limited oil reserves. Saudi Arabia and other surplus countries, in spite of their development plans, will depend on oil revenues well into the next century, and do not wish to push prices so far as to hasten the day when they will no longer be indispensible. There is common although not public recognition that the price rises of 1974 were a little too steep and in part responsible for the recession in the western economies on which the producers depend. There is also relief that the early determination of the consumers to develop alternative energy sources seems to have weakened. The other producers have learned that they cannot maintain prices much out of line with those of Saudi Arabia, so prices will rise generally by the amount which the Saudi government judges to be politic. Since 1971 however the producers have no longer been content to accept equitable terms; there is constant competition to obtain some advantage which can be presented publicly as an improvement on the neighbours' terms, and it may be that the present Saudi government will not be confident enough to maintain a firm line.

The great concern of the producing countries is the consciousness that their oil wealth is a wasting asset. The exact situation is not clear in every case although most experts would probably say that the politicians are at present exaggerating the dangers. It should be remembered that their concern is of recent origin, as throughout the sixties and into the seventies there were repeated OPEC resolutions and demands by individual countries for ever-increasing production. It may be no bad thing that realisation has now come that the growing demand for oil, with forecasts that it would double every ten years, was becoming insupportable and it was time for the brake to be applied. There are some in the producing countries who now say that they should limit their output to a level sufficient only for the national need of oil revenues, rather than produce at a level to satisfy the demands of consuming nations. For the populous producers there is no real difference, as they foresee that the developments which they are planning will require all the oil revenues they can earn, even if for two or three years some of those earnings are held temporarily in reserve. For the less populous producers, who see themselves in surplus for as long as they continue to produce, the problem is a real one and eventually, whatever others may decide, comes down to a question of what Saudi Arabia will do. Fortunately the Saudis take their responsibility very seriously and are unlikely to endanger the economy of the whole world, as would be implied if the more extreme demands to limit production were heeded. Such a step would be tantamount to a declaration of war, a fact of which statesmen in both producing and consuming countries are conscious even if public mention of it has occasionally been intemperate.

In the producing countries there is now a strong feeling, which leaders of the oil industry share and have expressed over the years, that the world's assets of petroleum are too valuable in the long run to be dissipated simply as fuel. The slow progress of nuclear power after its early promise in the fifties has been a disappointment to many, since electricity generating stations waste two-thirds of the energy in the fossil fuel supplied to them. There is much support for the renewed concentration in the west on reducing dependence on oil for fuel purposes, and reserving it for premium uses in transportation and as chemical feedstock. However, the enormous redeployment of investment and resources that are required to bring about the desired change can only be made over a period of years, and during this period oil fuel will remain in great demand in the economy of the world.

The producers consider with some justification that they have not been given sufficient credit for the sense of responsibility they have shown in the management of their finances. Some of the more dire predictions at the start of 1974 have indeed been made to look absurd. The lifting early in the year of the cutbacks in production and of the embargoes may have had an element of self-interest, in that the producers were finding that even the states they considered friendly were beginning to show some irritation at the difficulties being caused, but it was also a practical expression of their realisation that the running of the world's economy is still dependent largely on adequate oil supplies. In currency matters there have been remarkably few of the difficulties that were forecast, the so-called recycling question which occupied the western press for months. As the Kuwait financial minister has put it, the producing countries have as much interest in the stability of currencies and of the world economy as has any other country, and they have no intention of taking actions which might wreck it. Indeed from the statistics available they seem to have gone out of their way to spread the placement of their funds, even if they have not been permitted to do so quite as freely as they might have wished, for instance by greater deposits in Germany and Switzerland. As regards helping the less-developed countries, their stated aims and promises have been more generous than their actual performance to date. Allowing for the practical difficulties of redeploying resources on the scale that is desirable, criticism would be premature, but more convincing evidence is needed that they are conscious of the damage they have done to every one of the developing countries.

They are well aware of their new importance in the economy of the world and power in the monetary field, and consider that it must now be recognised in formal arrangements. One consequence of the quadrupling of oil prices was that the Committee of Twenty of the IMF which had been examining the reformation required in the world's monetary system, as a result of the weakening dollar and floating currencies, broke up in the realisation that the new reserves which the oil producing countries would accumulate and their decisions on holding them would be fundamental to any new arrangements; until more was known the Committee could hardly make recommendations. The oil producers want a much larger say in any successor that is appointed to take up the subject again, and as a preliminary a greater say in the International Monetary Fund itself. The justice of the claim is recognised, and the Fund which has seen adjustment of its shareholdings in the past is ready to make further changes although there will no doubt be difficulty over the details.

Much of the discussion that had taken place on the accumulation of wealth in the hands of the oil producers is vitiated by the tacit assumption that it will all be held in the form of official reserves, i.e. cash or short-term money. That may be true for countries such as Iran which expect soon to be employing those reserves, and temporarily true for the surplus countries while they consider their policies. As Kuwait has done and the others have already started to do, they will then move their short-term holdings into investments offering better prospects, such as loans, equities or properties. A fall in official reserves does not necessarily imply greater expenditure; it may mean more long-sighted investment.

The great worry of the oil producing countries is how to preserve the value of the revenues they are receiving which are surplus to their present needs. They have seen the erosion of their financial assets as a result of inflation, and an argument heard frequently is that oil remaining in the ground is a better investment than money in the bank. The oil producers tend to see themselves as unique in this situation, but in fact their position is shared not only by others engaged in the extractive industries but by manufacturers and others who use equipment which wears out and must be replaced. The producers are only beginning to realise that the general response to the problem is to treat financial assets as merely temporary holdings and to take steps to transform them into real producing assets. Companies in the west which at one time were satisfied to sit on a stock of financial assets found themselves sitting targets for takeover by companies which had a more active outlook and were prepared to use those assets productively. Kuwait might be said to have been a takeover target on two occasions, and it may not be without significance that the first of them saw the foundation of the KFAED, although the generous impulses which played their part in it are also to be recognised.

Some Arab economists appear to maintain that a country cannot be said to truly invest in productive assets unless they are within its own borders. What they are really expressing is a view widely held in the producing countries that any investment overseas means placing resources in jeopardy. Governments of countries where such assets are placed may at any time expropriate them, nationalise them with derisory compensation, or enforce control in their operation in ways which ignore the interests of the investors. The comparative favour with which investment in other Arab countries has been regarded may in part be due to the many common interests and other financial ties between the Arab states which make less likely an action by one of them harmful to the investments of another. The difficulties of resolving differences between a host country and a foreign investor are well recognised, and a little-known department of the World Bank, the International Centre for the Settlement of Investment Disputes, was founded to assist. It is little known because its first duty is to try conciliation, which has been effective with all disputes put to it so far and none has reached the public stage of formal arbitration. Most industrial countries and a large number of the LDCs have ratified the convention under which the Centre operates, with the Latin-American countries and the oil producers being the principal absentees. It is possible that now the producers are becoming large investors in their own right they may begin to appreciate the advantages the convention offers.

In earlier years the populous countries had few funds to place in reserve even for current requirements, and had borrowed on a large scale to assist development. The present surpluses are expected to be temporary, and the countries remain unconcerned in the search for long-term foreign investments. Saudi Arabia was at one time believed to hold its reserves largely in short-term securities, but recent reports indicate that funds are spread among eight equity and three property portfolios, each under separate management. Kuwait on the other hand has shown considerable sophistication in its investment policy, and holds a broad range of government securities, Eurodollar issues, property and industrial shares. It is now believed that the extent of its equity holdings is considerably greater than had earlier been supposed, but has been masked by the wide spread of the investments and by the care taken to avoid reaching a level in any one holding at which an open report to the authorities may be required. The other surplus states made an early decision to take expert advice on building up a portfolio but until recently their impact has not been felt as much as that of Kuwait. Perhaps the most interesting new development in the situation has been the large minority shareholdings taken by Iran in Krupps and Eurodif. The decision obviously has a dual purpose, the first of simply being a good investment for Iran and the second of making it probable that large subsidiaries, importing the latest in technology, will be established in Iran and help the development of the country directly. It may be that further investments of this nature will be made by Iran, and possibly similar moves may be considered by other producers.

All investors would like to place their money with low risk and high returns. The oil producing countries are asking that such funds should be provided for them, combined with guarantees that the price of their imports should rise no faster than the value of their investments, and the price offered for their oil no slower. In spite of the producers' power such an ideal state of affairs does not seem to be practical politics. It may be hoped that there will be greater cooperation between producing and consuming countries in the provision of opportunities for placing the surplus funds, but it is unlikely to come about unless risks and benefits are shared.

The perplexities of the governments over the ways their funds should be used are shared by private investors in the producing countries. It is to be observed that there is already a number of individuals who have been able to make investments on a large scale while others, it has been indicated, are still placing money with the Swiss banks in spite of penal charges. As internal expenditure by the states grows sharply, both on current and capital account, so will the wealth accumulating in the hands of individuals. Perhaps some will feel that investments inside the country will be secure but, if only for the lack of opportunities, most will be looking overseas. They will still face the dilemma of choosing between safety and a good return, and the Arab idea of a good return is high. The salesmen of IOS were very successful in the Gulf. Western financial institutions with the professional attitude of caring for the client's interests may have some prejudices to overcome but should be able to do much to assist and gently to educate the private investor.

Much of the aid which has been given by the producers is effectively long-term investment, although most of it is on less than commercial terms. It appears that the rate of commitments entered into in 1974 has not continued in 1975, although there has certainly been no diminution in the needs of the LDCs. It is increasingly being said by the Arabs themselves that there are now too many funds, all with the same general intent, for the number of experienced administrators available to run them. However it is one thing to state the obvious, it is quite a different matter to get the governments to cooperate to do something about it. Among the developed nations forming the DAC there is a strong preference for bilateral aid rather than multinational, as the donors do not like the anonymity of the latter, and it must be equally plain that the individual Arab states want the credit for their own generosity. Agreement, formal or informal, on a division of activities seems more likely than a direct amalgamation of the funds. In such case the shortage of suitable staff would not be alleviated, and it could be in this field that the financial institutions may have a contribution to make. The foreign partners in the consortium banks have usually considerable knowledge of various parts of the world, familiarity with the problems of the LDCs and some experience in assisting them, as well as the ability to marshal the appropriate resources from the developed countries. The Middle East partners will probably have contacts among the directors of the funds and be in a position to explain the potentialities of projects which have been located among the LDCs. Such an approach could perhaps discover more efficient ways of putting aid to work where it is most needed than the direct contacts between government and government which normally initiate the search for projects suitable for aid.

On the domestic front each of the producers has now been able to make very large plans for investment, as outlined in chapter eight. In the surplus countries however there is the recurrent theme of the non-availability of skills and of manpower which all the plans for education and training seem unlikely to overcome, and even the populous countries may have problems. It will be necessary to rely on foreigners for a number of years to come and the welcoming or grudging spirit in which a government accepts the inevitable is likely to affect the success of its plans. It will affect the speed of development of infrastructure, domestic industry and the social sector, but in any case there will be great progress. Agriculture will probably still lag in most countries until their governments learn greater wisdom than they have so far shown. The questions still to be answered concern the large plans for export industries. After the initial euphoria of assuming control of the oil industry, the countries have come to realise that they still need the companies both for their technical expertise and the market they provide. The same will be true of other advanced industries, as most of the governments understand. With the other disadvantages of the plants that are scheduled only the supply of almost free energy will prevent them making considerable losses, and it remains to be seen what attitude will be taken by countries with similar industries of their own to competition which is in effect heavily subsidised. Already there is talk of tying purchases of oil to accepting the products of the new plants, but by the time they come into operation the bargaining power of the producers may not be as strong as it is at present. The countries which wish to assure a future for their new industries may think it advisable to start discussions with the consumers soon, and to be prepared to offer some share of the anticipated benefits.

Consumers

The industrialised countries have had a healthy shock even if some of the reactions were more shocked than healthy. It has been made clear to them that their energy policies, or more strictly lack of policy, could not be allowed to drift on as they had over a number of years but that some difficult decisions must at last be faced. A warning had been given in 1967 and voices were heard then to point out that the increasing dependence on imported energy could be dangerous in the future and that rapid further development of indigenous energy resources was necessary. As that crisis died away so did the urge to take practical steps. Early in the seventies a general realisation began to grow that the continual increase in demand for oil imports could not for ever be met by increases in production, but reception of the message was marred by overstatement on the part of many of its proponents. To careful analysts it was becoming clear that the end of the seventies or the early eighties would see oil production facilities under pressure, if demand continued to grow unchecked, and practical moves to develop new energy facilities were already due, given the long lead times for construction. However no government wanted to be first in admitting the possibility of future difficulties and undertaking large-scale investment in more expensive forms of energy while its competitors might continue to obtain their requirements cheaply. The events of autumn 1973, however unwelcome, came therefore at the right time for forcing attention on long-term energy plans.

After the immediate threat to supplies was lifted, and with consumption falling in response to the rise in prices, less urgency than the situation requires is again to be seen. The elaborate American Project Independence formulated by President Nixon's government has already shed some of its priority applications and although President Ford has tried to maintain progress he has received little support from a Congress whose constituents are much more aware of te cost in the future. France's grand plan to attain independence appeared from the start to exceed its capabilities and not surprisingly has been scaled down. The British government clings to its hope of attaining self-sufficiency in oil from the North Sea, while throwing up a number of obstacles in the way, and has taken little action in developing alternative energy resources. Other European countries have been making plans in the nuclear field with no great sense of urgency; so has Japan which has also been cultivating relations with China, Indonesia and other potential suppliers of oil outside the Middle East. Althogether there is less likelihood than at first seemed possible that a significant reduction of the importance of oil from the Middle East in meeting energy demand will be achieved by 1980, although from then on progress will be more rapid.

Several of the OECD countries are at present acting in a way that may put these forecasts at risk. In Canada and Australia mining developments have been brought almost to a halt by the competitive greed of federal and state governments, supported by ignorance and nationalism. In the energy field the same Canadian policies are reducing the amounts available to the US, while the Australian government has ensured that gas, which Australia does not want but Japan does, will stay in the ground. In the North Sea the British and Norwegian governments are competing to discourage further exploration, and the selfish group demanding that development be restricted to national requirements may not be numerous but is loud. It is fortunate that the OPEC countries are governed by more generous men.

In the autumn of 1973 no country was feeling generous. M. Borschette, the EEC commissioner for competition, later reviewed the evidence and praised the oil companies for their allocation systems, which had foiled the efforts of each of the nine governments to grab more than its share. The formation of the International Energy Agency by eighteen of the larger industrialised countries may now be a hopeful sign that the lesson has been learned. It has in a short while made more progress than the EEC did in many years on cooperation between the countries, both in emergency planning and in coordination of long-term plans for energy development. Like OPEC itself, it is in an organisation for constructive progress and it may be suggested that cooperation between these two strong bodies is the most likely way in which the advance of the world's economies can be fostered and the weakness of the LDCs best be protected.

An important result of the oil crisis has been a renewal of concern for the LDCs among the industrialised countries. The EEC has concluded the Lomé Convention with a number of former colonies and their neighbours, marking an important advance in opportunities for them, and further meetings of the British Commonwealth and of the IEA have pursued that theme. The principal progress has been in matters of trade, taking up the developing countries' own slogan 'trade not aid', but aid to them is not to be neglected. The LDCs however generally have too high an expectation of what can be achieved immediately, and there is considerable disillusionment in the industrial countries about the progress made by the LDCs with the huge quantities of aid already received. There is growing realisation that some degree of stabilisation in the incomes of the primary producers is the most important immediate target and would provide a base from which further advances could be made.

One of the great questions at the start of 1974 has resolved itself considerably more easily than was then expected, partly due to the prudence of the oil producers. The surplus funds which they have been receiving have been accomodated in the world's monetary system with comparatively little strain. The deficits in balance of trade of the industrial nations have been less than expected, because of a larger rise than was thought possible in the imports of the oil producers. The surplus funds were still large but necessarily they have had to be placed with western countries and institutions, so offsetting the deficit in the industrialised countries' balance of payments. Naturally the funds were not placed in a way which corresponded with the needs of individual consuming countries but the recycling problem has proved less formidable than was expected. To some extent the countries helped themselves by sound policies, and even Italy, which was expected to show one of the largest deficits, has been able to adjust its balance. The only failure has been the UK, because the inflow of OPEC funds has relieved the government of the necessity to adopt firm but unpleasant policies. In view of the general weakness and the falling value of the pound the support it has been given by the oil states has been unexpected, perhaps to be explained by Britain's reputation. Privately Arab leaders have been heard to express surprise at the way the UK has not indulged in retaliatory measures, even in cases such as Libya's nationalisation of BP's oilfields where it was definitely expected. In their search for a safe home for their money the OPEC leaders may assess the likelihood of sequestration in the UK as perhaps the lowest in the world, and the low risk compensates for the comparative erosion of value.

The industrialised countries have been learning to take account of their common interests in the IEA and in the monetary field, but competition between them is still strong in matters of trade and development contracts with the Middle East countries, to the great advantage of the latter. Although conscious of their lack of skilled staff, the Middle East countries have suffered on occasions in the past by allowing themselves to be persuaded into projects by advice that was far from disinterested. Now in planning to deal with the flood of wealth, they have gathered around them consultants of the highest reputation from various of the western nations and are employing them to study, advise on and supervise the desired developments. By now most of the governments have discovered for themselves which firms are the more reliable, and have been able to eliminate some of the less conscientious, but in view of the vast expansion in their programmes they must necessarily take on untried partners. In choosing between various bidders, the advice of consultants whom they have also learned to trust can be invaluable, although there are still times when for some reason advice is not asked for or not taken, and there will undoubtedly be projects which will not turn out to be the success that the governments hoped. Nevertheless the growing area of trust between the Middle East governments and western nationals affords the best hope that the mistrust with which western governments are regarded can be overcome. The latter in turn owe a duty to the less experienced Middle East governments to utter a quiet word of advice if there are serious doubts of the ability of their nationals to fulfil engagements they wish to undertake, while lending their support on every reasonable opportunity. The governments which are sensible of their responsibilities are likely to be those whose words will be listened to in the future.

There is one disquieting feature about the approach of the west to the redeployment of the oil revenues. A large part of the productive facilities in the world stems from investments which the developed countries have made in other countries, not least the whole growth of the prosperity of the Middle East oil states. Western governments encourage their nationals to invest both in other industrialised countries and in those of the third world which permit it, and in the process of the investment all parties should benefit. Yet almost every investment which the oil producers since their new prosperity have made in industrial or commercial assets in the west has been greeted by a certain amount of public disapproval, if not outright obstruction. Certainly one of the advantages which investments by the developed countries in the less-developed countries brings is a gain in technology and training in skills, whereas the reverse now is thought of as bringing no comparable advantage. That is surely a short-sighted view; experience gained by Middle East nationals in the management of firms in which they participate, with the backing of funds to which they have access, should enable a genuine partnership to develop and perhaps assist the less fortunate countries. It is interesting that the principle of participation appears to be already accepted in the financial world, where as a result of the partnerships that have been formed many Middle East nationals are gaining experience and expertise which will be of value both to their own countries and to others of the third world. The response of some governments to ignorant popular pressure, by attempting to restrict the investment of the Middle East money in enterprises within their country, must surely in the long run work to their disadvantage.

The developed countries then have a clear twofold strategy. Firstly they must plan and invest in the development of alternative energy resources which will alleviate dependence on Middle East oil and increase their indigenous supplies, both to assure their own security and to reduce the waste of a resource which technology has not so far discovered how to replace. Secondly, while accepting that the surplus funds have of necessity been returned to the western financial system, they need to gain the cooperation of the oil producers in the redeployment of those funds. The liquid assets would be better transformed into real assets, in part at home and rather more around the world, so as to provide the producers with a solidly backed income for the future.

The Less-Developed Countries

The less-developed countries are not a homogeneous group, nor can the effects of the increase in oil prices on them be summed up simply. There are a favoured few Arab states who have received or been promised assistance, both direct to pay for their oil imports and indirect through greater investment and other financial aid, which outweighs the increased cost of oil. There were in 1974 producers of other primary commodities for whom the boom in demand for their exports and the rise in prices provided a welcome surplus of income enabling then to cope more easily with the oil deficit. The slump which followed means that 1975 will be a much more difficult year for them. The third group consists of the countries whose normal exchange earnings, with little hope of significant increase, left them with no prospect of meeting the increase in costs of essential oil imports. This group has been dubbed by the IMF the 'most seriously affected', or MSAs, and in themselves form a heterogeneous group, from India with a population of nearly 600 million down to small African states of 300,000.

Aid from the DAC countries increased considerably in money terms but slightly failed to do so in real terms, and the additional aid that was given by the OPEC countries only went a small part of the way to help meet the additional cost of oil imports. Unless a completely new programme of aid can be mounted, the MSAs have now little hope of development, and it is estimated that those which had planned for a six per cent growth rate will at best achieve one per cent. The commodity exporters will be in difficulties in 1975, although if an upturn takes place in the economies of the United States and Germany before the end of 1975, as is forecast, and in other industrialised countries in 1976, it may be that the difficulties will be temporary and their reserves sufficient to tide them over. They also have the hope that cooperation with the industrial countries will develop and achieve a greater stabilisation of commodity prices. The MSAs on the other hand will be relying entirely on increased aid, and the IMF and the DAC are both recommending to the donor countries that their efforts should now be concentrated on the group.

In spite of the damage to their economies by the increased cost of oil, and the firm refusal of the OPEC countries to offer them any reduction of price, the LDCs have continued to show a solidarity with the OPEC countries, both in UNCTAD and in the attempts to hold an international conference on energy and raw materials. Observers in the west have been surprised at this, and while some have suggested that a combination of fear of oil shortage and hopes of OPEC generosity in the future are enough to account for the behaviour of the LDCs, others see in it an ingrained distrust of the industrialised countries, which has been so much part of their thinking over the years that it is almost impossible for them to look at a situation with open eyes. It has been percipiently remarked that many of the LDCs were former British colonies, and that a significant proportion of the present ruling elite was educated at the London School of Economics soon after the end of the Second World War, when that organisation was going through an extreme socialist phase.

The practical policies of many of the LDCs are a discouragement to the aid which they claim to be their right. For thirty years the DAC countries have watched slow progress on capital projects for which massive aid has been given while unproductive expenditure has rapidly grown. The countries need investments, but take pains to frustrate the value of investments made in the past. Lingering anti-colonialist suspicions may be in part to blame for developments failing to match the flow of aid from the DAC countries. Perhaps, if it can avoid the neo-colonist tag, aid from the OPEC countries may be accepted less grudgingly and put more consistently to productive use.

The OPEC countries have an important lesson to communicate to the less fortunate. They now know much better how multinational companies function, and even the most socialist realises their usefulness, whereas many LDCs have not advanced beyond the stage of vague and irrational suspicions. There are companies which could make a considerable contribution to the growth of most of the LDCs, given fair conditions in which to do so, and greater cooperation between officials of the OPEC and developing countries may help indirectly to dispel come of the obstacles to growth.

There is little doubt of the willingness of the oil producers to provide aid in development of the LDCs. At present a very high proportion of aid is committed to a few countries, Egypt in particular, but besides the ties of Arab and regional interests which make it natural there may be the simple reason that the donors are better informed about their requirements than they are about those of remoter countries of Africa and Asia whose needs are equally great. The DAC countries have always preferred to give aid for specific projects but at times have responded to need by making grants for current expenditure. The OPEC countries also are more concerned to aid development by project loans, and most have said they will give priority to developments in their region, but it is to be hoped that with greater experience they will recognise and assist other of the LDCs.

The sums which the governments of the oil producers have at their disposal are very large. It is probable that development projects to attract their participation will also need to be on a large scale, if only for the administrative difficulties which a number of small projects is likely to cause. The developing countries will welcome such aid, but also need many smaller productive ventures, which could attract wealthy private investors from the producing countries. There are financial institutions capable of identifying the needs and bringing potential partners together, and also arranging the technical assistance necessary. Despite the drain on their resources which the imports of oil are now causing, the prospect of increasing real assets in the developing countries have greatly improved, if their governments are wise enough to see the opportunity and provide the conditions for progress.

APPENDIX A

Currencies and the SDR

Early in March 1975 there was a series of announcements from the Gulf states that henceforward they would consider their currencies in no way linked with the dollar. Kuwait was reported to be thinking of quoting its dinar in terms of a basket of currencies selected by itself, but Saudi Arabia and Qatar have decided to use the SDR and Iran had confirmed to the IMF the SDR value of the rial in February.

Special Drawing Rights were instituted by the International Monetary Fund in July 1969 'to influence the total of world reserves' and the first allocations made to participants in the Fund on January 1, 1970. The SDR was defined as equivalent to 0.888671 gram of fine gold, i.e. the same as the par value of the US dollar as it had been maintained since 1946. The values of the SDR and the dollar started to diverge in August 1971 when the US suspended gold convertibility and continued with the dollar devaluations of December 1971 and February 1973.

The first usage by the IMF of SDR for the denomination of borrowings and loans was in 1970. Most notable has been the SDR 2750 million oil facility – 'the Witteveen Fund' – to which nine countries had lent SDR 1716 million by the end of 1974 and on which thirtythree countries had drawn.

In June 1974 the IMF decided to re-define the SDR, effective from July 1, in terms of a basket of sixteen of the world's principal trading currencies. The list is:-

		Units of currency in one SDR	Weighting used in determining base
US	dollar	0.40	33
UK	pound	0.045	9
Germany	deutschemark	0.38	12.5
France	franc	0.44	7.5
Japan	yen	26	7.5
Canada	dollar	0.071	6
Italy	lira	47	6
Netherlands	guilder	0.14	4.5
Belgium	franc	1.6	3.5
Sweden	krona	0.13	2.5
Australia	dollar	0.012	1.5
Denmark	krone	0.11	1.5
Norway	krone	0.099	1.5
Spain	peseta	1.1	1.5
Austria	schilling	0.22	1
South Africa	rand	0.0082	1
			100.0

The SDR is merely a unit of account, not a currency, as the new definition emphasises. However some of the oil producing countries have announced that they intend in future to quote the price of oil in SDR instead of dollars although the latter will be needed for actual payment. The idea is not unfamiliar; the Geneva agreement of January 1972 introduced a form of indexing by movements in the exchange rates of the dollar against nine other currencies. Price changes took place accordingly, until the Kuwait meeting in October 1973 adopted unilateral price-fixing – it may have been mere coincidence that strengthening of the dollar had two weeks earlier brought the first fall in the dollar price under the indexing agreement.

It is not only the proposed use by the OPEC countries that has prompted reference to SDRs in this book but also the advantages in the use of the SDR as the unit of account for international comparisons. Simply for comparison at one time any one currency unit would be satisfactory and give immediately comprehensible results. Since 1970 however floating exchange rates and de- and re-valuations have brought such relative changes between currency units that a time series expressed in one currency may appear to be markedly and misleadingly different from the same series expressed in another currency unit. Employment of the SDR as unit brings out the average in international value over a period, expressing it clearly and distinguishing it from the fluctuations caused by the vagaries of an individual currency.

The currencies of the Gulf states have shown considerable stability in recent years, and the SDR would be a more suitable unit for expression of their economic progress than a more volatile currency. The increasing statistical use of SDR by the World Bank, as may be traced through issues of International Financial Statistics, and reference use by the OPEC countries may soon prompt greater familiarity with the SDR among many who are now barely acquainted with it.

Currency units per SDR

US dollar	
Until December 17, 1971	1.00
to February 12, 1973	1.0857
to June 30, 1974	1.20635
end December 1974	1.22435
end June 1975	1.23641
Pound Sterling	
Until June 23, 1972	0.41667
end December 1972	0.46237 approx.
end June 1973	0.46722
end December 1973	0.51920
end June 1974	0.59454
end December 1974	0.52133
end June 1975	0.56252
Iran rial	
Until April 1972	75.75
then	82.2425

Saudi Arabia riyal	
Until August 1973	4.5
Then	4.28255
Iraq dinar	0.357143
Kuwait dinar	0.357143
Bahrain dinar	0.47619
Qatar riyal	4.7619
UAE dirham	4.7619
Oman rial	0.4167
Libya dinar	0.357143

CURRENCY COMPARISON
Example : OECD exports to the Middle East

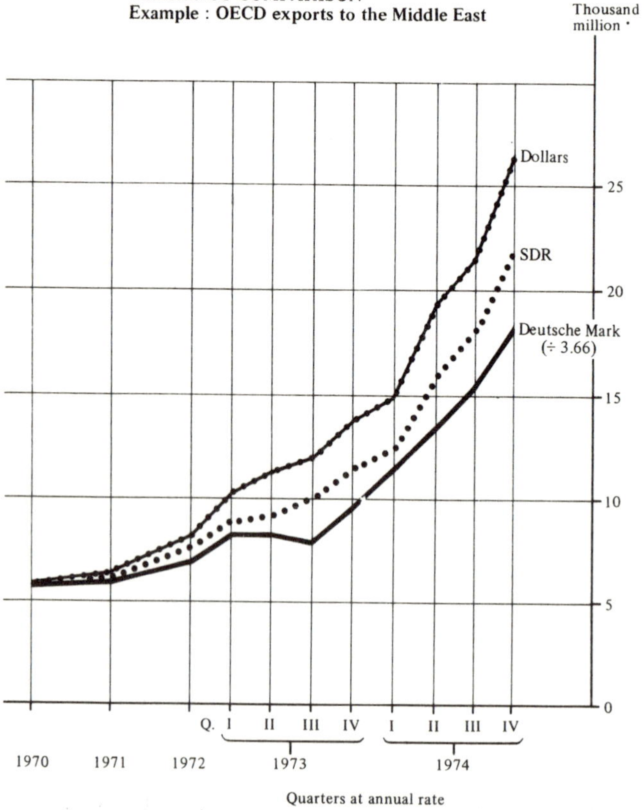

APPENDIX B

Fiscal Years

In most countries the fiscal year is not the same as the western calendar year, the Gregorian, and regular official publications normally give both years of the overlap, e.g. 1974/75, and similarly where the Muslim year is in use. In occasional official use, in journals and elsewhere, it is often referred to as a single year, e.g. 1974, generally it seems that in which the greater part of the fiscal year falls, but not always. When the fiscal year is cited at second- or third-hand, or when translations are made between the Gregorian and Muslim years, anything can happen and frequently does.

Statistics compiled by the UN and its agencies are frequently consulted, being readily accessible. In general the information submitted by national authorities for inclusion are on the Gregorian year basis, but in some cases the published notes show that it is not and there are other instances which have escaped attention. Quantitive oil statistics almost always refer to Gregorian months or years, but financial statistics may be found to refer to fiscal periods. A few notes may be of assistance in cases of apparently conflicting information about statistical or fiscal matters.

In IRAQ the fiscal year hitherto ran from April 1 to March 31. The government has made 1975 a nine-month fiscal year, from April 1 to December 31, and presumably the fiscal year will in future coincide with the Gregorian year.

LIBYA made the same change in 1973 and is now using the Gregorian year.

In KUWAIT the fiscal year is from April 1 to March 31.

ABU DHABI from the inception of formal budgets has used the Gregorian year as its fiscal one. The UNITED ARAB EMIRATES as a federal state was formed on December 2 1971 and has followed the same practice.

The Muslim or Hijra year is dated from the flight of Muhammad from Mecca to Medina, July 16 AD622. It is a lunar year, some eleven days shorter than the solar one, with months alternately of 30 and 29 days and *kabishah* years extended by one day. Year AH 1395 began on January 14 AD1975 and AH 1396 will begin on January 3 AD1976.

QATAR uses the Muslim year for fiscal purposes, running from Muharram 1 to Dhu'l Hijja 29 (common years) or 30 *(kabishah* years).

SAUDI ARABIA observes the Muslim year but starts its fiscal year in the middle of the calendar one. The fiscal year thus runs from Rajab 1 to Jumada-al-Thani 29, which for AH 1394–95 gives equivalent dates AD July 20 1974 to July 8 1975.

The epoch of IRAN is also dated from the Hijra but the year is solar, starting with the spring equinox, March 21 or Nahruz. The fiscal year corresponds and year 1354 runs from March 21 1975 (Farvadin 1) to March 20 1976 (Esfand 30). There are six months of 31 days followed by five of 30 and one of 29 or 30 (in leap years); the months, being more regular, start on dates from 20th to 23rd of Gregorian months. Monthly figures issued from Iranian sources are normally based on the Iranian month, even for oil, and annual ones probably cover the period Dey 1 (December 21) to Azar 30 (December 20) rather than the strict Gregorian year.

APPENDIX C

Index of Banks and other Financial Institutions

Mentioned in Chapter 6. References are to sections of that chapter.

	Section
Abu Dhabi Fund for Arab Economic Development – ADFAED	16c
Abu Dhabi Government	16d
Adcom Bank (Advances & Commerce Bank)	12b
Agricultural Bank (Syria)	13
Agricultural Credit Bank (Saudi Arabia)	5c
Agricultural Development Bank (Iran)	2c
AK Holdings (Luxemburg)	16e
Alahli Bank	4b, 16b
Algemene Bank Nederland	2b, 5b, 7, 12b
Almana Trading Company (Qatar)	17
American Express	18
Amsterdam-Rotterdam Bank	16a, 16c
Arab African Bank (Egypt)	7, 8, 11, 12b, 16b
Arab Bank (Jordan)	5b, 6, 7, 8, 12b, 14, 15, 16b, 16e
(Subsidiary: Arab Bank Overseas)	
Arab Financial Consultants Company	4d, 20
Arab Finance Corporation (Beirut)	17
Arab International Bank (Egypt)	11, 16c
Arab International Finance Company – ARINFI	16e
Arab Libyan Tunisian Bank	12b
Arab & Morgan Grenfell Finance Company	14, 16e
Arbuthnot Latham	4d, 7, 19, 20
Asseily family (Lebanon)	12d, 17

BAII – see Compagnie Arabe et Internationale d'Investissement

Banca Commerciale Italiana	2b, (12c), 16c
Banca Nazionale del Lavoro	16b
Banco Atlantico	(12c)
Banco Central (Spain)	16d
Banco di Roma	12b, 16b, 18
Banco do Brasil	16d
Banco Urquijo	16a
Bank Al-Mashrek	12b
Bank Bazargani Iran	2b
Bank Bimeh Iran	2b
Bank Dariush	2b
Bank Handlowy for the Middle East	12b
Bank Markazi Iran (Central Bank)	2
Bank Melli Iran	2, 2b, 2c, 5b, 7, 8, 15, 16e
Bank Misr: see Banque Misr	
Bank of Alexandria	11, 18
Bank of America National Trust & Savings Association	2b, 2c, 12b, 16e, 19
(Subsidiary: Bank of America)	
Bank of Bahrain	16a
Bank of Bahrain & Kuwait	15, 16b
Bank of Baroda	7
Bank of Beirut	12b
Bank of Credit & Commerce International (Lebanon)	7, 8, 12b
Bank of Iran & the Middle East	2, 2b
Bank of Jordan	14, 16b
Bank of Kuwait & the Arab World	12b
Bank of Kuwait & the Middle East	4b, 16d
Bank of Montreal	(12c)
Bank of Nova Scotia	12b
Bank of Oman	6, 7, 16a
Bank of Oman Bahrain & Kuwait	8
Bank of Sharjah	7
Bank of Sudan	16c, 16d
Bank of Tehran	2b
Bank of the Near East	12b
Bank of Tokyo	2b, 2c, (12c), 16b, 16e, 17
Bank Omram	2b, 7

Bank Pars	2b
Bank Saderat Iran	2b, 6, 7, 12b
Bank Sepah	2b
Bank Tedjarat Kharedji Iran; see Foreign Trade Bank of Iran	
Bankers Trust Company	(12c)
Banque Arabe et Internationale d'Investissement: see CAII	16d
Banque Arabe Libyenne Mauritanienne pour le Commerce Extérieur et le Développement	16b
Banque Arabo-Africaine: see Arab African Bank	12b
Banque Audi	12b, 16b, 17
Banque Beyrouth pour le Commerce	12b
Banque Centrale Populaire (Morocco)	16d
Banque de Beyrouth et des Pays Arabes	12b
Banque de Bruxelles	2b
Banque de Crédit Agricole	12b
Banque de Crédit Agricole Industriel et Foncier	12b, 12d
Banque de Crédit National	12b
Banque de Crédit Populaire	12b
Banque de Financement	12b
Banque de la Bekaa	12b
Banque de la Mediterranée	12b
Banque de la Société Financière Européenne: see SFE	16d
Banque de l'Essor Economique Libanais	12b
Banque de l'Indochine	5b
Banque de l'Industrie et du Travail	12b
Banque de l'Union Européenne	(12c), 17, 19
Banque de Paris et des Pays-Bas (Paribas group)	2b, 6, 7
Banque de Suez et l'Union des Mines	4d, 20
Banque de Syrie et du Liban	12, 12b
Banque de Tunisie	16a
Banque d'Investissement et de Financement–INFI	17
Banque du Caire	5b, 7, 11, 15, 18
Banque du Liban (Central Bank)	12
Banque du Liban et d'Outre-Mer	5b, 12b, 16d

Banque du Maroc 16b
Banque Etebarate Iran 2b
Banque Européenne pour le Moyen-Orient 17
Banque Extérieure d'Algérie 16b
Banque Française du Commerce Extérieur 16b
Banque Française pour le Moyen-Orient 12b
Banque Franco-Arabe d'Investissements Internationaux: FRAB 16a, 16c, 17
Banque G. Trad – Crédit Lyonnais 12b, 16b
Banque J. Lati et fils 12b
Banque Joseph Geagea 12b
Banque Libanaise des Emigrés 12b, 12d
Banque Libanaise pour le Commerce 12b, 16c
Banque Libano-Bresilienne 12b
Banque Libano-Française 12b
Banque Majdalany 12b
Banque Marocaine du Commerce Extérieur 16c
Banque Marocaine pour le Commerce et l'Industrie 16d
Banque Mebco 12b
Banque Misr 11, 12b, 16c 18
(Subsidiary: Banque Misr-Liban)
Banque Nasr Libano-Africaine 12b
Banque Nationale d'Algérie 16c
Banque Nationale de Paris 12b, 16d
(Subsidiary: Banque Nationale de Paris Intercontinentale)
Banque Nationale de Tunisie 16d
Banque Nationale pour le Développement Economique (Morocco) 16d
Banque Nationale pour le Développement Industriel et Touristique (Lebanon) 12b
Banque Pharaon et Chiha 12b
Banque Sabbag 12b
Banque Saradar 12b
Banque Tohme 12b
Banque Worms 4d, 20
Barclays Bank International 2b, 2c, 16e, 18

Index of Banks and other Financial Institutions

Bayerische Hypotheken-und Wechsel – Bank 2b
Bayerische Vereinsbank 2b, 16b
BBME – see British Bank of the Middle East
Beirut-Riyad Bank 12b, 17
Berliner Bank 2b
British Bank of the Lebanon 12b, 12d
British Bank of the Middle East 2, 2b, 4a, 4d, 5b, 6, 7, 8, 12b, 12d, 15
Byblos Bank 12b

CAII: – see Compagnie Arabe et Internationale d'Investissement
Cairo Barclays International Bank 18
Caisse Centrale de Banques Populaires 17
Canadian Imperial Bank of Commerce 16d
Capel, James 7
Carr, W.I., & Sons 7
Central Bank of Egypt 11, 16a
Central Bank of Iran: see Bank Markazi Iran
Central Bank of Kuwait 4a, 4b, 4c
Central Bank of Lebanon: see Banque du Liban
Central Bank of Libya 9
Central Bank of Oman 8, 16b, 16c
Central Bank of Syria 13, 16c
Central Bank of Yemen 16b
Ceskoslovenska Obchodni Banka (12c)
Chartered Bank 2b, 6, 7, 8, 12b, 15, 16, 19
Chase Manhattan Bank 2b, 4b, 5d, 7, 12b, 15, 18, 19
(Subsidiary: Chase Manhattan Overseas Corporation)
Chase National Bank of Egypt 18
Chemical Bank (US) 12b, 12d
Citibank: see First National City Bank
Commercial Bank of Dubai 7, 19
Commercial Bank of Iran: see Bank Bazargani Iran

Commercial Bank (Iraq)	3
Commercial Bank of Kuwait	4b, 16a, 19
Commercial Bank of Syria	13, 16b
Commerzbank	2b, (12c), 16b, 19
Commerzbank International (Luxemburg)	16b
Compagnie Arabe et Internationale d'Investissement – CAII	16d
(Subsidiary: BAII)	
Continental Illinois National Bank & Trust Company	2b, 12b
(Subsidiary: Continental Development Bank)	
Cooperative Agricultural Bank	3
Credit Bank of Kuwait	4c
Crédit Commercial de France	12d
Crédit Libanais	12b, 16c, 17
Crédit Lyonnais	2b, 4b, 12b, 16b
Crédit Suisse	2b, 12b, (12c), 16c
Creditanstalt-Bankverein	16c
Crocker National Bank	(12c)
Deutsche Bank	2b, 2c, (12c), 16c, 16e
Development Bank (Lebanon)	12d
Development Bank (UAE)	7
Development & Investment Bank of Iran	2c
Distributors Cooperative Credit Bank	7
Dresdner Bank	2b, 2c, (12c)
Dubai Bank	7, 19
Eastern Bank (later Chartered)	15
Egyptian American Bank	18
European Arab Holding	16c
(Subsidiaries: Europaisch-Arabische Bank European Arab Bank (Brussels)	
European Banks International Company – EBIC	16c
Export Bank of Iran: see Bank Saderat Iran	

Federal Bank of Lebanon 12b
First National Bank of Boston 2c, 5d, (12c)
First National Bank of Chicago 7, 12b
First National City Bank – FNCB 2b, 5b, 6, 7, 12b, 15
Fleming (Robert) & Company 4d, 20
Foreign Trade Bank of Iran 2b
FRAB – see Banque Franco-Arabe
d'Investissements Internationaux 16a
Frankfurter Bank (12c)
Fuji Bank (12c), 16c

Gillett Brothers 7
Grindlays Bank 2b, 6, 7, 8, 15, 19
Groupe Renault (France) 17
Gulf Bank 4b, 16d
Gulf Citicorp – see FNCB 7
Gumhouria Bank (Libya) 9

Habib Bank 2b, 7, 8, 12b, 15
(Subsidiary: Habib Bank Overseas)
Hambros Bank 16b, 17, 19

Imperial Bank of Iran (later BBME) 4a
Imperial Bank of Persia (later BBME) 2
Industrial & Mining Development Bank
of Iran – IMDBI 2c, 16e
Industrial Bank (Iran) 2c
Industrial Bank (Iraq) 3
Industrial Bank (Syria) 13
Industrial Bank of Japan 2b, 2c, 16a, 16c, 16e
Industrial Bank of Kuwait 4c, 4d
Industrial Development Fund
(Saudi Arabia) 5c
INFI: see Banque d'Investissement et
de Financement
International Bank of Iran & Japan 2b
International Bank (Washington) 2b,4d
International Financial Advisers 4d, 20
International Marine Banking
Company (UK) 16e

Intra Bank 12, 12d
Investment & Finance Bank (Lebanon) 12b
Investment Promotion Group (Lebanon) 17
Iran Chase International Bank 2b
Iran Industries Bank 2b
Iran Overseas Investment Bank
 – IOIB 2c, 16e
Iranians' Bank 2b
Irano-British Bank 2b
Istituto di Credito per le
 Imprese di Pubblica Utilita 16b
Istituto Ligure Interessenze
 Industriali e Commerciali 16b

Jammal Investment Bank 12b
Janta Bank 7
Jordan National Bank 12b, 14, 16b
Jugobank (12c; Tripoli)

Kent (William) & Company 4d, 20
Kidder Peabody 4d, 12d
Korea Exchange Bank (12c)
Kuwait Financial Centre 4d
Kuwait Foreign Trading, Contracting
 & Investment Company – KFTCIC 4d, 16a
Kuwait Fund for Arab Economic
 Development – KFAED 4c
Kuwait Insurance Company 16a
Kuwait International Bank 4c
Kuwait International Investment
 Company – KIIC 4d, 16e, 17
Kuwait Investment Company – KIC 4d, 16a, 16d, 17
Kuwait Investment Office (ex Board) 4c, 4e
Kuwait Real Estate Bank 4c

Lebanese Arab Bank 12b
Liberal Bank (Lebanon) 12b
Libya Insurance Company 16a
Libyan Arab Foreign Bank – LAFB 9, 16b

Litex Bank (Lebanon) 12b
Long-Term Credit Bank of Japan 2c, 16b

Manufacturers Hanover Trust Company 2c, 11, (12c), 16e, 17
Marine Midland Bank (US) 16e
Masraf al Gumhuria: see Gumhouria Bank
Mellon Bank 2c
Mercantile Bank of Iran & Holland 2b
Merrill Lynch 4d, 7
Middle East Banking Company – see
  Banque Mebco 12b
Middle East Finances (BBME subsidiary) 7
Midland Bank 2c, 16b, 16c, 16e
Midland & International Banks
  – MAIBL 16b
Misr International Bank 18
Mitsui Bank 16b, 17
Morgan Grenfell Holdings 11, 14, 16e
Morgan Guaranty Trust Company 5d, (12c)
Mortgage Bank (Iran) 2c
Moscow Narodny Bank 12b

National & Grindlays Bank: see Grindlays Bank
National Bank for Investment &
  Development (UAE) 7
National Bank of Abu Dhabi 7, 16b
National Bank of Bahrain 15
National Bank of Dubai 7, 19
National Bank of Egypt 11, 16c, 18
National Bank of Kuwait 4b, 16a, 16c, 19
National Bank of Oman 8
National Bank of Pakistan 5b
National Bank of Yemen 16b
National Commercial Bank (Libya) 9, 16c
National Commercial Bank (Saudi Arabia) 5b, 5d, 12b, 16c, 16d
National Insurance Company (Iraq) 3
National Investment Bank for
  Industrial Development 16a

National Investment Company (Libya)	16d
National Westminster Bank	15
Nomura Securities	16b, 17
Osterreichische Länderbank	2b, 16d
Oman Currency Board: see Central Bank of Oman	16b, 16c
Oman Housing Development Association	8
Oryx Investments	7, 19
Paribas: see Banque de Paris et des Pays-Bas	2b
Philadelphia National Bank	4d, 20
Phillips & Drew	4d
Popular Credit Bank (Syria)	13
Property Development Bank (Dubai)	7
Prosperity Bank of Lebanon	12b
Qatar Ministry of Finance	16b
Qatar Monetary Agency	6
Qatar National Bank	6, 16d
Rabiya Bank	12d
Rafidain Bank	3, 12b, 15, 16b
Real Estate Bank (Iraq)	3
Real Estate Bank (Syria)	13
Rif Bank	12b
Riyad Bank	5b, 16b
Royal Bank of Canada (Middle East)	12b
Sahara Bank (Libya)	9, 16a
SAMA – Saudi Arabian Monetary Agency	
Sanwa Bank	2b, 16b
Saudi Arabian Monetary Agency	5a, 5b, 5d
Saudi Credit Bank	5c
Savings & Credit Bank (Kuwait)	4c
Schroder (J. Henry) & Company	17
Schroder Wagg (J. Henry)	12d, 17
Shahryar Bank	2b

Singer & Friedlander 2b
Societa Finanziamenti Idrocarburi 16b
Societa Finanziari Telefonica
per Azoni 16b
Societa Italiana per Condotte
d'Acqua 16b
Société Bancaire du Liban 12b
Société Financière Européenne : SFE 16d
Société Financière pour le Moyen-
Orient – SOFIMO 17
Société Générale (France) 2b, 2c, 16a, 16c, 16e, 17
Société Générale de Banque
(Belgium) 16a, 16c
Société Générale d'Investissement 16a
Société Générale Libano-Européene de Banque 12b, 16c, 17
Société Nouvelle de la Banque de
Syrie et du Liban 12b
Société Tunisienne de Banque 16b
Somali National Bank 16b
Standard & Chartered Banking Group
– see Chartered Bank 19
Sudan Commercial Bank 16b
Swiss Bank Corporation (12c), 16a
Syrian Lebanese Commercial Bank 12b

Taiyo Kobe Bank 4d
Toronto Dominion Bank (Middle East) 12b
Trade Development Bank (12c)
Trans-Orient Bank 12b

UAE Development Bank 7
Umma Bank (Libya) 9
Union Bancaire pour le
Commerce et l'Industrie (Tunisia) 16d
Union Bank of Switzerland 12b, 15, 16d
Union de Banques Arabes et
Françaises – UBAF 16b
Associates:
Union de Banques Arabes et Européenne – UBAE 16b

Union de Banques Arabes et Nippon – UBAN	16b
Unione di Banche Arabe ed Europee – UBAE Roma	16b
UBAF Ltd	16b, 18
UBAF Financial Services Limited	16b, 18
United Bank	2b, 6, 7, 15
(Subsidiary: United Bank of Lebanon & Pakistan)	12b
United Bank of Kuwait	4d
United California Bank	(12c)
Vereinsbank in Hamburg	2b
Wahda Bank (Libya)	9
Wardleys	7
Wells Fargo Bank	19
Westdeutsche Landesbank Girozentrale	(12c), 16b
Westfalen Bank	(12c)
Williams & Glyn's Bank	2c, 12c
Yemen Bank for Reconstruction & Development	16b

Select Bibliography

ADAMS, M (Editor) The Middle East, Anthony Blond 1971.
ADELMAN, M.A. The World Petroleum Market, John Hopkins 1972
BRICAULT, G. (Editor) Major Companies of the Arab World and Iran, Graham & Trotman, Ltd, 1975.
DEAM, R.J. et al. World Energy Modelling, Energy Policy, June 1973
DEAM, R.J. et al. Energy Modelling, Energy Policy (special no.) 1974
FENELON, K.G. The United Arab Emirates, Longman 1973.
FRANKEL, Paul H. Oil – The Facts of Life, Frank Cass 1962
FRANKEL, Paul H. Oil Prices – Causes and Prospects, Platt's Oilgram Jan. 29 1971
FRANKEL, Paul H. and NEWTON, W.L. Comparative Evaluation of Crude Oils, Institute of Petroleum 1969.
GRIPAIOS, H. International Oil Prices, London 1964.
HARTSHORN, J.E. Oil Companies and Governments, Faber 1967
HARTSHORN, J.E. Oil Diplomacy: the new approach, The World Today, July 1973.
HILL, P. and VIELVOYE, R. Energy in Crisis, Yeatman 1974.
HITTI, S. and ABED, G. Saudi Arabian Monetary Agency, UN Staff Paper XXI-2 July 1974.
ION, D.C. The Availability of World Energy Resources, Graham & Trotman Ltd, 1975.
LEWIS, W.A. Development Planning, Allen & Unwin, 1966.
LONGRIGG, S.H. Oil in the Middle East, Oxford, 1968.
LUTFI, A. OPEC Oil, Beirut, 1966.
MALLAKH, R. el and McGUIRE, C. (Editors) Energy and Development, Colorado, 1974.
MIDDLE EAST MARKET RESEARCH BUREAU Marketing to Middle East Consumers, Graham & Trotman Ltd, 1975

MIKDASHI, Z. Financial Analysis of Middle East Oil Concessions, 1901-1965, Praeger 1966.

MONROE, E. and MABRO, R. Oil Producers and Consumers: Conflict or Cooperation, Bailey & Swinfen, 1974.

NASMYTH, J.A. The Cost of Oil, Petroleum Review, February 1972.

PENROSE, E.T. The Large International Firm in Developing Countries, Allen & Unwin, 1968.

POSNER, M. Energy at the Centre of the Stage, Three Banks Review, December 1974.

SAYEGH, K.S. Oil and Arab Regional Development, Praeger, 1968.

SCHURR, S.H. and HOMAN, P.T. (Editors) Middle Eastern Oil and the Western World, Elsevier, 1971.

TUGENDHAT, C. and HAMILTON, A. Oil, The Biggest Business, Eyre Methuen, 1974.

TUNLEY, J. Oil Payments and Debts, Lloyds Bank Review, July 1974.

TURNER, F.C. Methods of Crude Oil Valuation, OPEC Seminar, 1969.

WARRINER, D. Land Reform in Principle and Practice, Oxford 1969.

MIDDLE EAST ECONOMIC CONSULTANTS (Beirut) The Market for Financial Services in the Middle East, Graham & Trotman, 1975.

FIRST CITY NATIONAL BANK Saudi Arabia, a new economic survey, December 1974.

ORGANISATION FOR ECONOMIC COOPERATION AND DEVELOPMENT Energy Prospects to 1985, Paris 1974.

UNITED ARAB EMIRATES Third Anniversary, Ministry of Information, December 1974.

Publishers' Note : A complete catalogue of all Graham & Trotman books on Middle East business opportunities and Oil Affairs is available on request from Graham & Trotman Ltd, 20 Fouberts Place, Regent Street, London W1V 1HH, England UK

Index

* See also under individual countries in Chapter 8.

	Page
Abadan refinery	102, 131, 135
Abdullah Saudi	82
ABU DHABI	164ff
Aid	168, 186
Banking	80
Finances	59, 168
See also UAE	
Abu Musa Island	164
ADMA – Abu Dhabi Marine Areas	167
AFESD – Arab Fund	186
Afghanistan, aid to	186
Africa, aid to	184, 207
Agriculture*	114
Ahmad Duaij	147
Ahwaz	129, 135
Aid	181ff
Airports*	120
Akins, James	2
Al Ain	116, 166, 170
Al Fateh oilfield	171
Al Sabah, Ruling family of Kuwait	148
Al Sabah, Shaikh 'Ali Sabah Salem	75
Alaska	18
Algeria	ii, 63, 105
Aluminium*	114
Ammonia	110
AMOCO	135
Amuzegar, Jahangir	71
Anaconda	130
Animal husbandry*	117

	Page
Anwar Ali	76
Arab League Fund	187
Aramco	21, 77, 152
Arizona, University of	116
Aryamehr steel plant	129, 136
Asia, aid to	207
Asir	115, 154
'Atiqi, 'Abd al-Rahman al	74, 148
Baghdad	139, 140
Bahrain, aid to	186
Banking	88
Bandar Abbas	136
Bandar Shahpur	135, 136
Bangladesh, aid to	168, 184, 188
Banias (Syria)	143
Barrel	ii
Basrah	139ff
Batinah Coast	172
Batman (Turkey)	143
Benghazi	176, 178
Billion	ii
Borschette, M	202
Brazil	7, 41, 114, 153
Brega	175, 178
British Leyland	130
British Petroleum	111
Bu Hasa	108
Budgets*	51
Buraimi Oasis – see Al Ain	
Bushehr	129
Butane	107
Cabot Corporation	135
CDF Chimie	161, 163
Cement plants*	113
Chase Manhattan study	25
Chemical industry*	109

	Page
Chicago Bridge	131, 135
China	40, 202
Chrysler	130
Coal	10
Communications*	117
Consortium banks	89
Creusot-Loire	129, 136, 139
Cyrenaica	175
DAC – Development Assistance Committee	181, 206
Daimler Benz	148
Dammam	154, 159
Das Island	167
Deam, Professor R.J.	22
Defence expenditure*	49
Deminex	135
Development plans*	50, 99
Dhufar – see Oman	172
Distrigaz	131
Doha	160
Dortyol (Turkey)	143
Dry docks	165
DUBAI	164ff
Banking	80
Dukhan	161
Dunkirk	163
Ecuador	15
Education*	121
EGOCO	108
Egypt, aid to	184, 187, 188
Banking	83
El Paso	131, 135
ENI	13, 108
ERAP	108
Esfahan	128, 135, 136
Euphrates	140, 144

	Page
Eurodif	129
Europe	5, 17, 36
Faisal, H.M. King Faisal bin Abdul Aziz	76, 186
Fawzi al Kaissi	72
Fertilizer plants*	110
Fezzan	175
Finances*	
Oil revenue	41ff, 193
Reserves and surplus	8, 57ff
Financial centres	
Beirut	84
Cairo	83
Dubai	165
Kuwait	147
Tehran	72
Fiscal year	46, 213
Foreign workers	60, 146, 151, 167, 175
Foster Wheeler	178
France	4, 11, 104, 201
Frankel, Dr. P.H.	13n
Fujairah	164ff
Banking	80
Gabon	15
Gas – see Natural Gas	
Gazocean	174
Germany	11, 22, 131
Gholam Reza Moghaddam	71
Greece	104
Groningen	109
Guest Keen & Nettlefolds	130
Gulf rupee	73
Haditha dam	140
Hambros	161

	Page
Hamza Abbas	73
Hisham Nasir	152
Housing*	123
Houston Natural Gas	153
Imports*	52
Indonesia	63, 202
India	7
Aid to	60, 184, 188
Fertilizers for	110
Interest, Muslim views on	76
International Bank for Reconstruction & Development (IBRD) see World Bank	
International Development Authority (IDA)	181
International Energy Agency (IEA)	56, 204
International Monetary Fund (IMF)	7, 68, 188, 196
IRAN	127 – 136
Aid	184, 187
Banking	69
Exports, non-oil	60
Finances	58, 63, 198
IRAQ	137 – 145
Aid	186
Banking	72
Finances	58, 63
Iraq Maritime Transport Company	112, 139
Iraqi National Oil Company	138
Iron & steel projects*	114
Irrigation – water requirements*	116
Irving Trust	63
Isfahan – see Esfahan	
Iskanderun (Turkey)	135
Islamic Development Fund	186
Italy	13, 23, 53, 104, 203
Jabel Akhadar	175
Jabal Dhanna	170

	Page
Japan	18, 40, 55, 202
Japan Petrochemical Company	131
Jeddah	125, 154, 159
Jefara Plain	175
Jordan	
Aid to	184
Banking	87
Jubail	153, 159
Kalingas Group	131, 135
Kangan	108, 135
Kazimi, Abd al Muttalib al	123
Kerman	130
KFAED – Kuwait Fund for Arab Economic Development	147, 184, 186, 190, 197
Khalifa bin Hamad al-Thani, Shaikh of Watar	79, 160
Kharg	135
Khawneh, Ali	113
Khor Khuwair	164, 171
Khor Zubair	139, 144
King Faisal Memorial Hospital	151
Kirkuk	140, 143, 145
Kissinger, Dr. Henry	56
Kobe Steel of Japan	161
KOGEC – Kuwait Oil Gas & Energy Company	146
Kraftwerk	129
Krupps	59, 198
Kufra Oasis	175
KUWAIT	146 – 150
Aid	181, 187
Banking	73
Finances	8, 58, 196, 197
Kuwait Oil Tanker Company	112
Kuwait Shipping Company	113, 148
LDC – Less-developed countries	7, 37, 99, 184ff, 198, 205ff
Lebanon banking	84

	Page
Levy, Walter J.	63
LIBYA	175 – 179
Aid	186, 188
Banking	82
Finances	63
LNG – Liquefied natural gas*	105
Lomé Convention	202
LPG – Liquefied petroleum gas*	107
Malaysia	41
Aid to	184
Mansour Khalad	191
Mattei, Enrico	13
Mauritania, aid to	186
Mazaid	166
Medical services*	123
Mehdi Samii	71
Meshed	129
Methane	105
Mexico	41
Middle East – definition	i
Misurata	178
Mitsubishi	135, 139, 167
Mitsui	135
Morgan Guaranty	63
Mosul	140, 145
MSA – Most seriously affected	206
Multan (Pakistan)	168
Muscat	172
Nasiriyah	139, 144
Natural gas*	30, 104ff
in US	13
Netherlands	4
Nigeria	15, 63
Nissho-Iwai	108, 131, 135
NGL – Natural gas liquids	107

	Page
Norsk Hydro	161
North Sea oil	40, 201
Norway	40
Nuclear energy	18, 30, 129, 195
OAPEC – Organisation of Arab Petroleum Exporting Countries	3, 186
ODA – Official development aid	7, 181
OECD – Organisation for Economic Cooperation and Development	37, 53, 181, 202
OEEC (later OECD)	11
OIL demand	33ff, 63, 201
Exports	17, 22, 61
Prices, posted	16, 19ff, 42
Prices, real	22, 29
Products	22, 100
Products taxes	2, 11
Revenues	2, 44
OIL PRODUCERS' need to export	61
Olsen, Fred	131
OMAN	172 – 174
Banking	81
OPEC – Organisation of Petroleum Exporting Countries	15, 25
Aid	187, 207
Finances	7, 45, 61, 193
OPEC MEETINGS – Baghdad Nov.60	16
in sixties	194
Tehran Feb. 71	16
Geneva Jan.72	210
Vienna Sep. 73	3
Kuwait Oct.73	3
Tehran Dec.73	5
Vienna Sep.75	31
Organisation of African Unity	186
Otaiba, Mana al	167

	Page
Pakistan	168, 184, 188
Pazanun	108
Petroleum Economist, The	41, 46
Pilgrims' receipts	76
Pilkingtons	130, 147
Ports*	117
Posted prices	16, 19ff
Power Gas	161
Power supplies*	125
Propane	107
Qaboos bin Said, Sultan of Oman	172
Qadaffi, Colonel	188
QATAR	160 – 163
Banking	78
Railways	119, 136, 145
Ras al Khaimah	164ff
Banking	80
Rashid bin Sa'id al Maktum, Shaikh of Dubai	81, 165
Raysut	172
Refineries, export*	100
Surplus capacity	31, 104
Renault	130
Reuter, Baron de	69
Riyadh	125
Roads*	119
Robinson, Professor A	11
Rumaila, North	138
Rumais	172
Sadiyat	116, 166
Sahel countries, aid to	188
St. Martin's Property Company	148

	Page
Salalah	172
SAMA – Saudi Arabia Monetary Agency	76
Sar Cheshmeh	130
Saud Maritime Company	113
SAUDI ARABIA	151 – 160
Aid	186, 188
Banking	76
Finances	58, 63
Influence on oil prices	30, 31n, 194
Saudi Arabia Shipping Company	113
SDR – Special drawing rights	43, 209
SECIM	139
Selection Trust	130
Sewerage	125
Shah of Iran, H.I.M. Mohammed Reza Pahlevi	127
Shahpur Chemical Company	131
Sharjah	164ff
Banking	80
Shell	25, 108, 161
Shiraz	135
Shoman, Abdul Hamid	87
Shuaiba	148
SNAM	178
Somalia, aid to	186
Spain	104
Sri Lanka, aid to	188
Stauffer, T.	182n
Stock Exchanges	72, 75, 87
Stone & Webster	178
Sudan, aid to	184
Suez Canal	10, 20, 187
Sulphur content of oil	103
Syria, aid to	184, 187
Banking	87
Tabqa dam	140
Tabriz	128, 135, 136
Tankers*	9, 102, 111

	Page
Tanzania, aid to	184
Taxes on oil production	21
on oil products	2, 11
Tehran	125, 127, 135
Telecommunications*	120
Television & radio*	121
Tesoro	174
Tigris	139, 145
Tihama	154
Tobruk	178
Tons, defined as metric	ii
Trade*	53
Transco Energy Corporation	135
Tripoli	176
Trucial States	164
Tunisia, aid to	184
Uganda, aid to	184
Uhde	178
Umm al Nar Island	167, 170
Umm Qasr port	139, 143, 145
UNITED ARAB EMIRATES (UAE)	164 – 171
Aid	187
Banking	79
United Kingdom	4, 11, 40, 59, 203
UNCTAD	206
United States	4, 13, 18, 19, 23, 31, 59, 201
Urea	110
USSR	11, 40
Iranian gas	131
Venezuela	15, 22, 63
VLCC – very large crude carriers – see tankers	
Volkswagen	144

	Page
Water supplies*	125
Witteveen, Dr. J.	7, 188, 209
World Bank	6, 181, 190, 197
Yamani, Shaikh Ahmad Zaki	152
Yanbu	153, 159
Yemen	151
Zaire, aid to	168
Zawia	175, 178
Zayid bin Sultan al-Nahayan, Shaikh of Abu Dhabi	116, 164, 166, 188
Zirku Island	167, 170
Zuetina	178

Middle East Business MAP 1

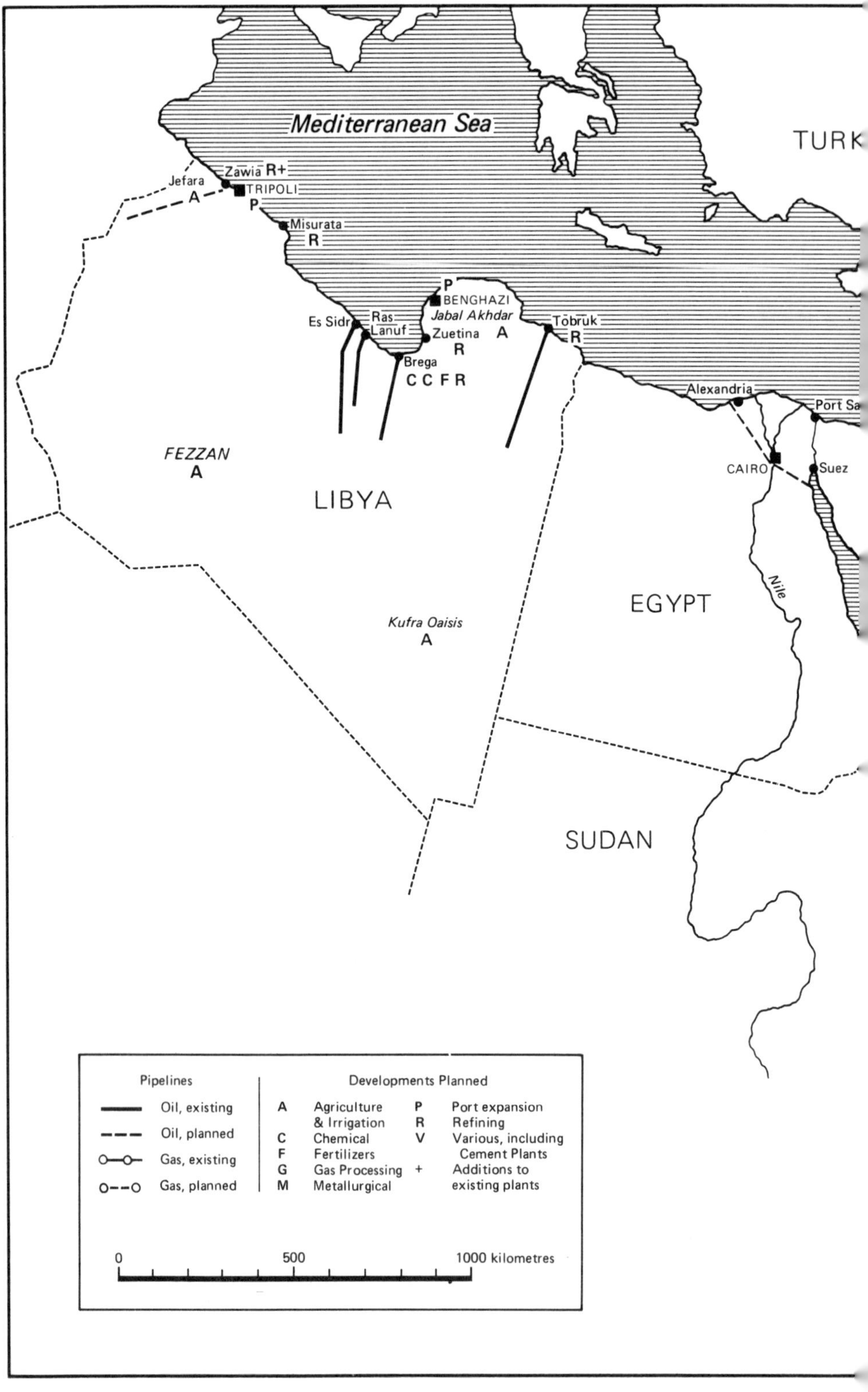

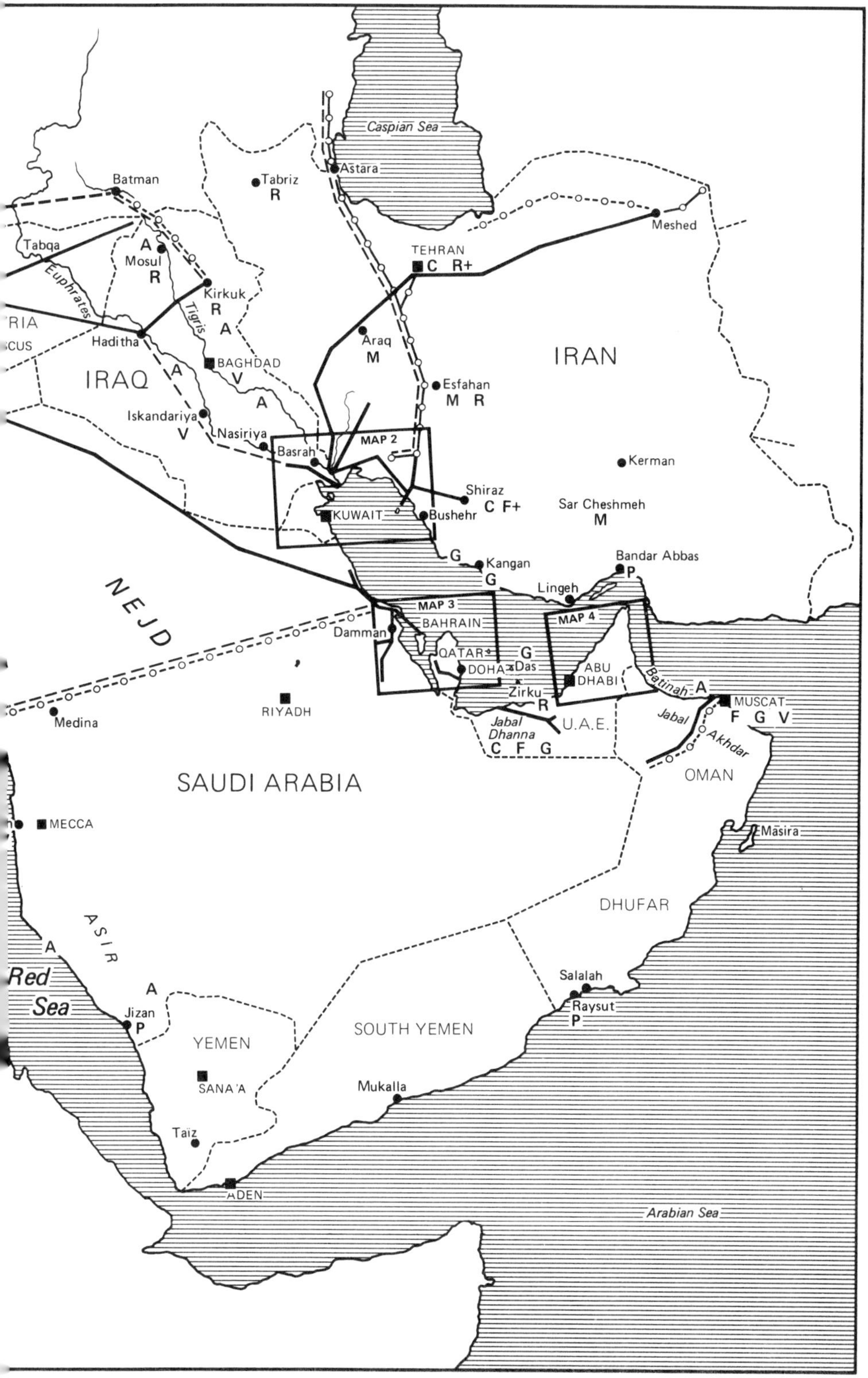
Caspian Sea
Astara
Tabriz
R
Batman
Meshed
TEHRAN
C R+
Tabqa
A
Mosul
R
Euphrates
Kirkuk
R
A
Tigris
RIA
CUS
Haditha
Araq
M
IRAN
IRAQ
A
BAGHDAD
V
Esfahan
M R
A
Iskandariya
V
Nasiriya
MAP 2
Basrah
Kerman
Shiraz
C F+
Sar Cheshmeh
M
KUWAIT
Bushehr
G
Kangan
G
Bandar Abbas
P
NEJD
Lingeh
MAP 3
BAHRAIN
MAP 4
Damman
QATAR
G
DOHA
Das
ABU DHABI
Batinah
A
MUSCAT
F G V
Zirku
R
Jabal
Akhdar
Medina
RIYADH
Jabal Dhanna
C F G
U.A.E.
OMAN
SAUDI ARABIA
MECCA
Masira
DHUFAR
ASIR
A
Red Sea
A
Salalah
Jizan
P
Raysut
P
YEMEN
SOUTH YEMEN
SANA'A
Mukalla
Taïz
ADEN
Arabian Sea

Middle East Business MAP 2

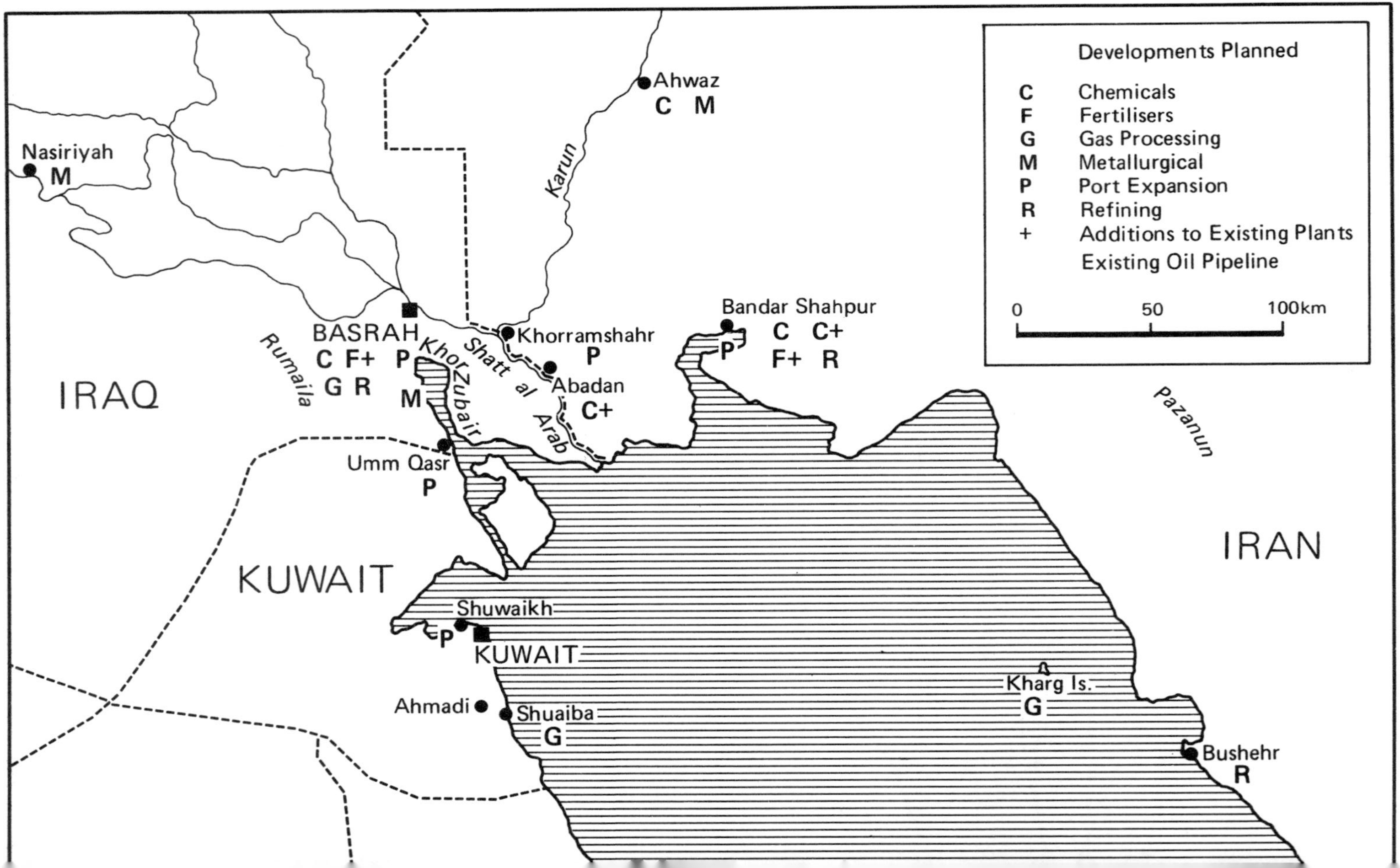

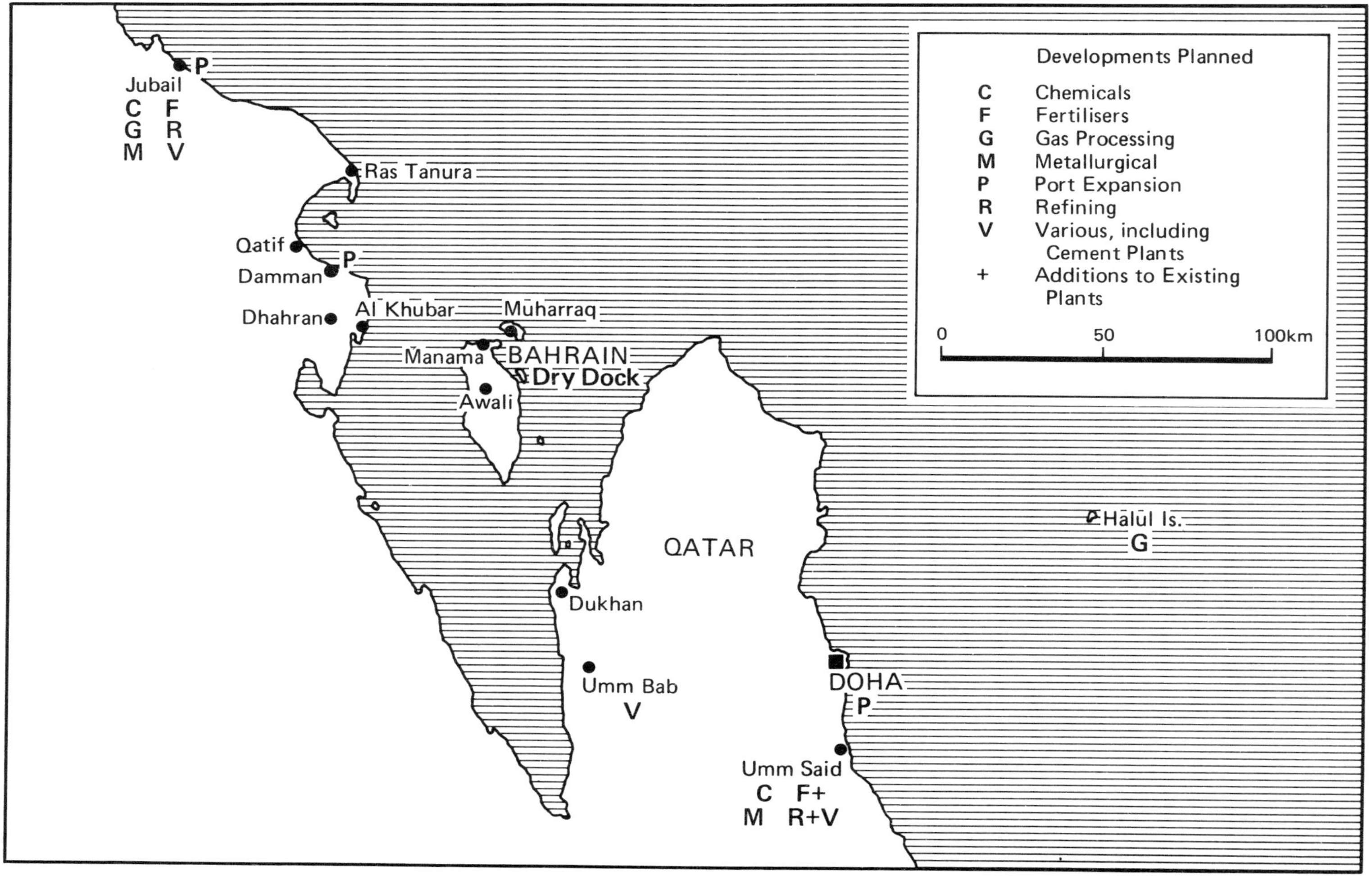
Developments Planned
C Chemicals
F Fertilisers
G Gas Processing
M Metallurgical
P Port Expansion
R Refining
V Various, including Cement Plants
+ Additions to Existing Plants
0
50
100km
Jubail
P
C F
G R
M V
Ras Tanura
Qatif
P
Damman
Dhahran
Al Khubar
Muharraq
Manama
BAHRAIN
Dry Dock
Awali
QATAR
Dukhan
Umm Bab
V
DOHA
P
Umm Said
C F+
M R+V
Halul Is.
G

Middle East Business MAP 4

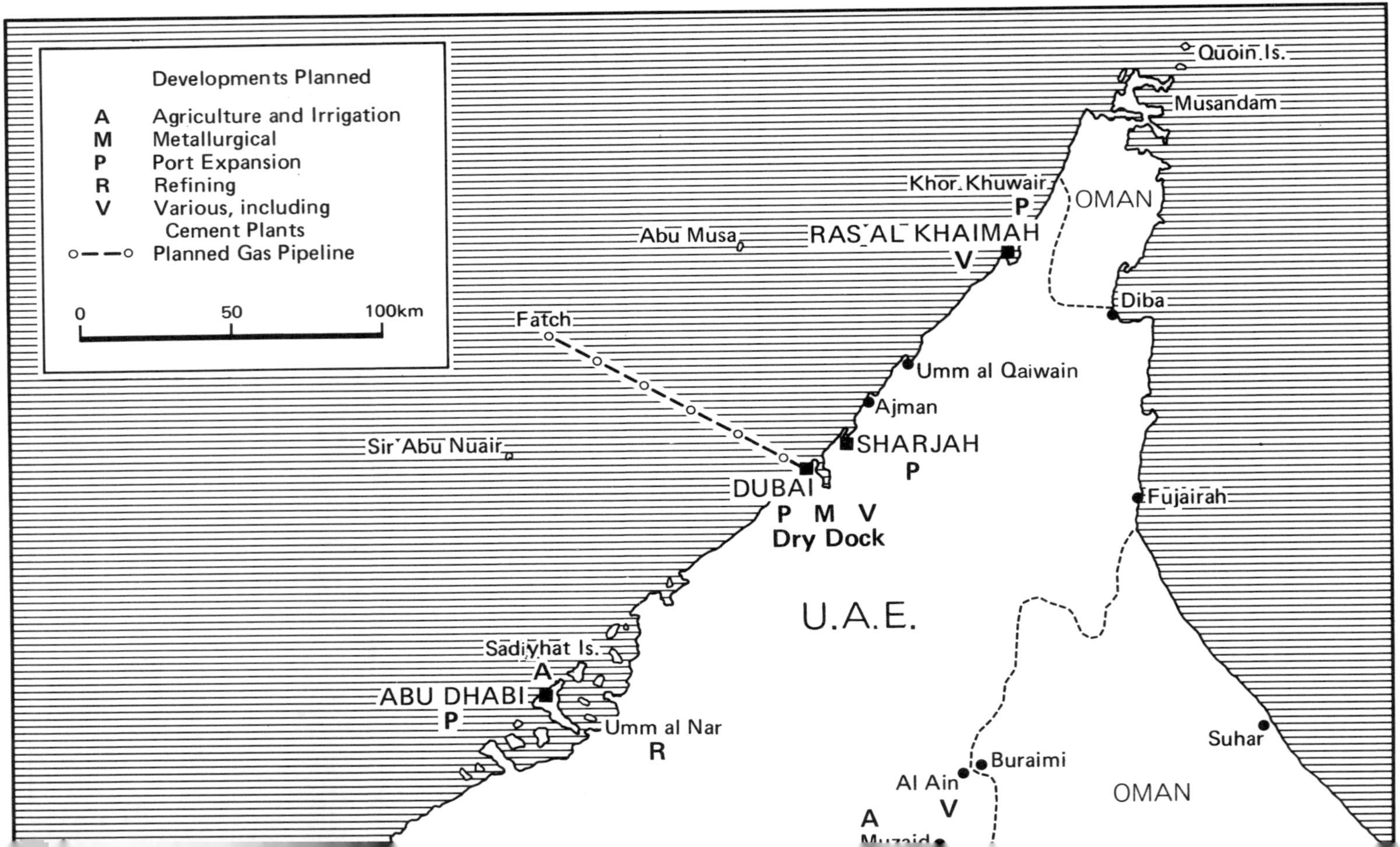